Daughter Zion's Trauma

Biblical Intersections

17

Biblical Intersections explores various topics beyond theological or exclusively historical exegetical studies, including the relationship of Hebrew and Christian scripture to philosophy, sociology, anthropology, ecenomics, cultural studies, intertextuality and literary studies.

Daughter Zion's Trauma

A Trauma Informed Reading of Lamentations

James W.S. Yansen, Jr.

Gorgias Press

2019

Gorgias Press LLC, 954 River Road, Piscataway, NJ, 08854, USA

www.gorgiaspress.com

2019

ISBN 978-1-4632-0744-1 **ISSN 1943-9377**

A Cataloging-in-Publication Record is Available from the Library of Congress.

Printed in the United States of America

To Nadiège, Jedd and Joachim, for your love, patience and support

If you want to humble an empire it makes sense to maim its cathedrals. They are symbols of its faith, and when they crumble and burn, it tells us we are not so powerful and we can't be safe."— Nancy Gibbs

TABLE OF CONTENTS

ACKNOWLEDGMENTS

I am truly grateful for the collective genius and sacrifices of countless sojourners who have graciously sown the precious gifts of faith, knowledge and wisdom into my life: from my parents, who instilled in me a love for God and challenged me to think critically, to my parishioners, past and present, who have dared me to spiritual authenticity and intellectual honesty; from my early mentors and teachers, who believed in and affirmed my gifts, to my colleagues in ministry and academia, past and present, who have inspired me to live and serve with compassion and humility; from my extraordinary professors and teachers, who instilled in me the passion for truth, to my fellow sojourners who have held my hands and lifted my spirit along the way.

I thank Professors Kathe Darr, Jonathan Klawans, and Shelly Rambo for your guidance through the early stages of this study. Your patience, insights, and guidance have been invaluable. I am indebted to Camaria Holder and Shelley Lyons for editing this work. Whatever contributions this work might make to the ongoing conversations about trauma studies and biblical scholarship are the fruits of the investments of my mentors and colleagues. Its shortcomings and limitations are mine.

Glory to God! Great is Thy Faithfulness!

LIST OF ABBREVIATIONS

AB	Anchor Bible
ABD	*Anchor Bible Dictionary*
ABRL	Anchor Bible Reference Library
ANET	*Ancient Near Eastern Texts Relating to the Old Testament*
AOTC	Abingdon Old Testament Commentaries
APA	American Psychological Association
BDB	Brown, F., S. R. Driver, and C. A. Briggs. *A Hebrew and English Lexicon of The Old Testament.* Peabody, MA: Hendrickson Publishers, 1996.
BEATAJ	Beiträge zur Erforschung des Alten Testaments und des antiken Judentum
BI	*Biblical Illustrator*
BibInt	*Biblical Interpreter*
BZNW	Beihefte zur Zeitschrift für die neutestamentliche Wissenschaft
CBQ	*Catholic Biblical Quarterly*
CBR	*Currents in Biblical Research*
Enc	*Encounter*
FOTL	Forms of the Old Testament Literature
HBT	*Horizons in Biblical Theology*
IBC	Interpretation: A Bible Commentary for Teaching and Preaching
ICC	International Critical Commentary
Int	*Interpretation*
ITC	International Theological Commentary

JANES	*Journal of Ancient Near Eastern Studies*
JAOS	*Journal of the American Oriental Society*
JBL	*Journal of Biblical Literature*
JLTS	*Journal of Literature and Trauma Studies*
JNSL	*Journal of Northwest Semitic Languages*
JQR	*Jewish Quarterly Review*
JSJSup	Supplements to the Journal for the Study of Judaism
JSOT	*Journal for the Study of the Old Testament*
JSOTSup	Journal for the Study of the Old Testament: Supplement Series
JTS	*Journal of Theological Studies*
KJV	*King James Version*
LCBI	Literary Currents in Biblical Interpretation
LHB/OTS	Library of Hebrew Bible/Old Testament Studies
LXE	*LXX English Translation*
NASB	*New American Standard Bible*
NCBC	The New Century Bible Commentary
NEB	*The New English Bible*
NIB	*The New Interpreter's Bible*
NIV	*New International Version*
NJPS	*New Jewish Publication Society Translation*
NKJV	*New King James Version*
NRSV	*New Revised Standard Version*
OBT	Overtures to Biblical Theology
OTL	Old Testament Library
RB	*Revue biblique*
RevExp	Review and Expositor
RSV	*Revised Standard Version*
SANt	Studia Aarhusiana Neotestamentica
SANT	Studien zum Alten und Neuen Testaments
SBL	Society of Biblical Literature

SBLABib	Society of Biblical Literature Academia Biblica
SBLAIL	Society of Biblical Literature Ancient Israel and Its Literature
SBLDS	Society of Biblical Literature Dissertation Series
SBLMS	Society of Biblical Literature Monograph Series
SJOT	*Scandinavian Journal of the Old Testament*
SubBi	Subsidia biblica
TynBul	*Tyndale Bulletin*
UF	*Ugarit-Forschungen*
VT	*Vetus Testamentum*
VTSup	Supplements to Vetus Testamentum
WBC	Word Biblical Commentary
ZAW	*Zeitschrift für die alttestamentliche Wissenschaft*

INTRODUCTION

The book of Lamentations shocks its readers with its unbridled and poignant expressions of pain and suffering. This book has occupied a significant place in both Jewish and Christian traditions.[1] Biblical scholars generally agree the book was written during the sixth (or early fifth) century BCE, following Neo-Babylonia's military assault on Judah in 586 BCE.[2] This watershed period in Judah's history was defined by disaster, defeat and rupture.[3] The book presupposes and reflects the impact of the traumatic realities of the times, including the collapse of the Davidic Dynasty, the demise of the Kingdom of Judah, the forced deportation of many of its inhabitants, and the razing of its capital city and central temple. Thus, reading Lamentations with a sensitivity to trauma and its potential effects is crucial for understanding the book. Specifically, reading with insights from contemporary trauma studies sheds light on the many complex features of its contents, structure and meaning(s), and, consequently, opens new interpretive possibilities.[4]

---

[1] In Jewish traditions, the book of Lamentations is recited annually on Tisha b'Av ('the ninth of Av', which is in the fifth month of the Jewish year and corresponds to July–August) to commemorate the destructions of the First and Second Temples (586 BCE and 70 CE, respectively), as well as other catastrophes in Jewish history. In Christian traditions, portions of the book are read during the Holy Week liturgies of Tenebrae and Good Friday.

[2] See F. W. Dobbs-Allsopp, 'Linguistic Evidence for the Date of Lamentations', pp. 1–36.

[3] Jill Middlemas, *The Troubles of Templeless Judah*, p. 1.

[4] By trauma studies I am referring to works that address psychic trauma in individuals and collectivities, particularly the latter, and their

The poems preserved in Lamentations bear witness to radical caesura and disruption in life experiences that are consistent with typical experiences of trauma and its aftermath.[5] A close reading of Lamentations' five poems reveals significant structural ruptures such as imperative outbursts, anticlimactic features, and seemingly erratic shifts in perspectives and voices.[6] The poems also contain evidence of theological dissonance or discord and deep psychological anguish, which signal the struggle intrinsic to testifying to experiences of trauma.[7] Biblical scholarship has made tremendous progress during the latter twentieth and early twenty-first centuries in attending to the imprints of trauma on, and the interpretive possibilities of this field of scholarship for biblical texts, including the book of Lamentations.

The Neo-Babylonian attack on Judah that began in 597 BCE and culminated in 586 BCE, as well as the collapse of Judah's major religious, social, and political structures, significantly shaped the book of Lamentations. These traumatic events affected survivors in different ways and their impacts no doubt had far reaching and

---

implications as a theoretical critical lens for reading history and literature, specifically biblical history and literature. I draw on studies that address cultural and national trauma, particularly studies that address war-related catastrophes. Some of the pioneer theorists in contemporary trauma studies include Shoshana Felman and Dorie Laub, Cathy Caruth, and Dominick LaCapra. See Shoshana Felman and Dorie Laub, *Testimony: Crisis of Witnessing in Literature, Psychoanalysis, and Theory*; Dominick LaCapra, *History, Theory, and Trauma: Representing the Holocaust*; Cathy Caruth, *Unclaimed Experience: Trauma, Narrative, and History*.

[5] I define *trauma* as a life-altering rupture that results from the experience of extreme or overwhelming violence by an individual or group. I use the expression *traumatic event* to refer to an event that results in experiences of trauma for some or all of its survivors.

[6] See D. R. Hillers, *Lamentations: A New Translation with introduction and Commentary*, 2nd ed., pp. 28–30; William F. Lanahan, 'The Speaking Voice in the Book of Lamentations', pp. 41–49.

[7] See examples of theological dissonance in Lam 2; 3:1–20, 45–47; 4: 1–5, 11–12, 18–20; and 5:19–22; psychological outbursts, Lam 1:1–2, 9, 12, 16–22; 2:8–10, 18–19, 22; 3:1–20, 52–54; 4:18–20; 5:2–6, and 8–10.

enduring implications for survivors. Lamentations preserves the imprints of the effects of trauma. There is a growing interest among biblical scholars in exploring the interpretive possibilities of the concept of trauma for biblical scholarship.[8] Specifically, several biblical scholars have intentionally applied insights from contemporary trauma studies to their reading of Lamentations.[9] This study is an additional witness to the hermeneutical prospects of this field within biblical studies.

---

[8] In 2013 the Society of Biblical Literature established the Consultation on 'Biblical Literature and the Hermeneutics of Trauma'. The stated function of this Consultation is to study 'methods for employing various definitions of trauma to interpret particular sets of biblical and extra-canonical texts, giving attention to the relationship between personal and communal dimensions of trauma, and to applying biblical interpretation in other theological disciplines'. See 'Biblical Literature and the Hermeneutics of Trauma', Society of Biblical Literature, accessed July 7, 2015, http://www.sbl-site.org/meetings/Congresses_CallForPaperDetails.aspx?MeetingId=23&VolunteerUnitId=611.

[9] For recent representative examples of some of the possibilities of using trauma studies as an interpretive lens through which to read biblical texts, see the followings articles in *Interpreting Exile*: D. L. Smith-Christopher, 'Reading War and Trauma', pp. 253–274; William Morrow, 'Deuteronomy 7 in Postcolonial Perspective: Cultural Fragmentation and Renewal', pp. 275–293; David M. Carr, 'Reading into the Gap: Refractions of Trauma in Israelite Prophecy', pp. 295–308; David G. Gaber, Jr., 'A Vocabulary of Trauma in the Exilic Writings', pp. 309–322; and Janet L. Rumfelt, 'Reversing Fortune: War, Psychic Trauma, and the Promise of Narrative Repair', pp. 323–342. For more exhaustive applications of insights from trauma studies to biblical texts, see, Katheleen M. O'Connor, *Jeremiah: Pain and Promise*; D. Janzen, *The Violent Gift: Trauma's Subversion of the Deuteronomistic History's Narrative*; D. M. Carr, *Holy Resilience: The Bible's Traumatic Origins*; L. Stulman and H. C. P. Kim, *You are My People: An Introduction to Prophetic Literature*; and R. Poser, *Das Ezechielbuch als Trauma-Literatur*.

TRAUMA STUDIES AND BIBLICAL STUDIES

The English word 'trauma' derives from Greek *trauma*, which is typically translated 'wound', 'hurt', or 'injury'. In contemporary society the term has become a cultural trope—a way to explain and express varied effects, experiences and responses to extreme violence or catastrophic events. Literary and cultural theorist Kirby Farrell argues that 'trauma is both a clinical syndrome and a trope…, a strategic fiction that a complex, stressful society is using to account for a world that seems threateningly out of control'.[10] The *APA Dictionary of Psychology* defines *trauma* as:

> … any disturbing experience that results in significant, helplessness, DISSOCIATION, confusion, or other disruptive feelings intense enough to have a long-lasting negative effect on a person's attitudes, behavior, and other aspects of functioning. Traumatic events include those caused by human behavior (e.g., rape, war, industrial accidents) as well as by nature (e.g., earthquakes) and often challenge an individual's view of the world as a just, safe, and predictable place.[11]

Trauma studies developed from advances in the fields of psychiatry and psychoanalysis, and from sub-fields in psychology, during the twentieth century.[12] The clinical diagnosis of Post-Traumatic Stress Disorder (PTSD) provides a way of categorizing specific types of symptoms evident in survivors of wars (including combatants), natural disasters, rape, physical and psychological abuse, and other experiences of extreme violence.

---

[10] Kirby Farrell, *Post Traumatic Culture: Injury and Interpretation in the Nineties*, p. 2.

[11] Gary R. VandenBos, ed., *APA Dictionary of Psychology*, 2nd ed., p. 1104, ProQuest ebrary, accessed July 9, 2015, http://site.ebrary.com.ezproxy.bu.edu/lib/bostonuniv/reader.action?docID=11033030.

[12] For useful summaries of the history and genealogy of trauma studies see, Luckhurst, *The Trauma Question*, pp. 23–76; Judith L. Herman, *Trauma and Recovery: The Aftermath of Violence—From Domestic Abuse to Political Terror*, pp. 7–32; Van der Kolk, *et al*, 'History of Trauma in Psychiatry', pp. 47–74.

The Diagnostic and Statistical Manual of Mental Disorder defines PTSD as:

> ...the development of characteristic symptoms following exposure to an extreme traumatic stressor involving direct personal experience of an event that involves actual or threatened death or serious injury, or other threat to one's physical integrity; or witnessing an event that involves death, injury, or a threat to the physical integrity of another person; or learning about unexpected or violent death, serious harm, or threat of death or injury experienced by a family member or other close associate.... The person's response to the event must involve intense fear, helplessness, or horror....[13]

Building on the official, technical definitions, I define *trauma* as a life-altering rupture resulting from individual and group experiences of extreme or overwhelming violence. My focus is more on psychological than pathological trauma (though the two are often interrelated). The former refers to the debilitating aftermath of the experience of traumatic events that often results from physical injuries or violence, while the latter refers to a physical wound or injury. The psychological effects of trauma are typically life shattering and disruptive for survivors. More specifically, I focus on the belated, enduring effects of trauma on survivors of extreme violence, which, in the field of psychiatry is generally labeled Post-Traumatic Stress Disorder (PTSD).

It can be difficult to define or circumscribe the term *trauma* as an academic or scientific category on account of the popularizing or trivializing of this term in popular culture. Nevertheless, the explanatory and signification power of the term, beyond its function in its original field of psychiatry, remains relevant for contemporary scholarship.

---

[13] *The Diagnostic and Statistical Manual of Mental Disorder: DSM-IV-TR*, 4th ed., p. 463.

Traumatic Event

I use the expression *traumatic event* to refer to an experience that results in trauma for some or all of its survivors, recognizing that such events do not affect all survivors in precisely the same ways. To distinguish traumatic events from general experiences of suffering or discomfort, however, I limit the use of this expression to events that result in significant life shattering effects. Thus, I understand traumatic events as catastrophic events that traumatize survivors by rupturing their lives or worlds. To avoid repetition of the expression 'traumatic events', I use it synonymously with 'catastrophe', 'extreme violence', 'toxic event', 'limit event', 'overwhelming suffering' and similar expressions.

Based on the foregoing definition, the June 17, 2015 massacre of nine worshipers at the Emmanuel Methodist Episcopal Church in Charleston, South Carolina, can be labeled a traumatic event. Experienced as a rupture in life, this event is no doubt traumatic for many of the survivors, including those who escaped death that night and other members of the faith community. For many survivors, observers, and aid workers, the terrorist attacks of September 11, 2001 in the United States of America, the 2004 Indian Ocean earthquake and tsunami, the January 2010 Haiti earthquake, and the April 2015 Nepal earthquake, to name just a few, were traumatic events, albeit in different ways for different individuals and groups. Similarly, for many survivors, the brutal massacres led by Boko Haram in Nigeria and the so-called 'Islamic State in Iraq and Syria (ISIS)' are painfully traumatic. On the individual level, my definition of trauma includes victims of violent assaults, rape, persons exposed to extreme violence due to warfare, people who survive horrific accidents, and those who experience these events or situations as life-altering and world-shattering ruptures.

Collective and Individual Trauma

The experience of trauma is not homogeneous. Personal history, cultural heritage, and social, cultural, political, and religious contexts of individuals and collectivities can shape the ways they experience and respond to trauma.[14] Thus, the experience of extreme violence does not, *a priori*, constitute trauma. In his discussion of the social process of cultural trauma, cultural sociologist Jeffery C. Alexander argues, 'societies can experience massive disruptions that do not become traumatic'.[15] In order for social crises or catastrophes to become traumatic, they must be interpreted as a 'fundamental threat' to that collectivity's 'sense of who they are, where they came from, and where they want to go'.[16] In individuals, a personal assault or horrific accident is traumatic when it is experienced as a life altering rupture or a threat to personal existence. Judith Herman notes that the study of psychological trauma, that is, psychic trauma,[17] entails coming 'face to face both with human vulnerability in the natural world and with the capacity for evil in human nature'.[18] The experience of trauma is therefore typically associated with feelings of fear and helplessness. The trauma of a collectivity is different from individual trauma. However, while the responses to trauma might be different for individuals and collectivities, for

---

[14] Social anthropologist Paul Connerton argues that group membership, particularly kinship, religious, and class membership, shapes *how* catastrophic events are remembers (P. Connerton, *How Societies Remember*, pp. 20, 36.

[15] Jeffery C. Alexander, *Trauma: A Social Theory*, p. 15.

[16] Ibid. Alexander makes a distinction between individual responses and group/community responses typically associated with the experience of trauma. Individuals typically react to trauma 'with repression and denial, gaining relief when these psychological defenses are overcome, bringing pain into consciousness so they are able to mourn' (Alexander, *Trauma*, p. 3). However, for collectivities the response to trauma typically involves 'symbolic construction and framing, of creating stories and characters, and moving along from there' (ibid.).

[17] The *APA Dictionary of Psychology* defines 'psychic trauma' as 'an experience that inflicts damage on the psyche, often of a lasting nature. Examples are sexual assault and child abuse' (VandenBos, ed., *APA Dictionary of Psychology*, p. 854, http://site.ebrary.com.ezproxy.bu.edu/lib/bostonuniv/reader.action?docID=11033030).

[18] Herman, *Trauma and Recovery*, p. 7.

both, the experience of trauma is associated with a breach or rupture in life, a shattering of the world as it is known, or as it has been constructed.

These understandings of trauma do not diminish the significance or reality of the life rupturing horrors of traumatic events; rather, they resist simple generalizations of the experience of trauma. As Laura S. Brown observes, 'Each experience of an encounter with a traumatic stressor is unique and is given unique meaning by the life history of the person [or collectivity] to whom it occurs'.[19] Social, political, cultural, and religious contexts are crucial for understanding how individuals and collectivities understand, respond to, and work through trauma.[20]

Furthermore, this approach recognizes the political and rhetorical nature of the 'creation' of trauma.[21] The 'trauma process' has the potential to become a watershed moment that serves as a catalyst for restructuring and re-engaging life in the aftermath of trauma.[22] According to Judith Herman, advancements in trauma studies are closely tied to alliances with powerful political movements.[23] Trauma is a process; it is created—shaped in the intersection of the extreme events, the individual/group identities, and the social contexts in which trauma arises—the *trauma matrix*. More specifically, trauma matrix includes the beliefs systems, social net-

---

[19] Laura S. Brown, *Cultural Competence in Trauma Therapy: Beyond the Flashback*, p. 4.

[20] See Boris Droždek, 'The Rebirth of Contextual Thinking in Psychotraumatology', in *Voices of Trauma: Treating Survivors Across Cultures*, p. 9.

[21] See Alexander, *Trauma*, 6–30; J. C. Alexander, 'Toward a Theory of Cultural Trauma', in *Cultural Trauma and Collective Identity*, J. C. Alexander, pp. 1–30; J. C. Alexander and Elizabeth B. Breese, 'On Social Suffering and its Cultural Construction', in *Narrating Trauma: On the Impact of Collective Suffering*, pp. xi–xxxv.

[22] Alexander, *Trauma,* pp. 30. The social process of cultural trauma, or the social construction of trauma is the central thesis in Alexander's work. See also Irene Visser, 'Trauma Theory and Postcolonial Studies', pp. 270–282; and Herman, *Trauma and Recovery*, pp. 7–32.

[23] Herman, *Trauma and Recovery*, p. 9.

works, available economic and institutional resources, and other factors that can shape perceptions and experiences of trauma.[24]

It is important to note that the academic field of trauma studies is a twentieth century, Western invention. Thus, it is anachronistic to speak of posttraumatic stress (in the technical sense) in biblical characters or biblical texts. Anthropologist Allan Young, for example, argues that Post-Traumatic Stress Disorder 'is not timeless, nor does it possess an intrinsic unity. Rather, it is glued together by the practices, technologies, and narratives with which it is diagnosed, studied, treated, and represented and by the various interests, institutions, and moral arguments that mobilized these efforts and resources'.[25] Consequently, being intentionally self-critical is crucial in applications of insights from trauma studies to biblical texts. It is important to avoid the distinctive danger of ethnocentrism in 'imposing the western trauma model' on non-Western entities and texts.[26]

Trauma as Trope: Interpretive Possibilities

Today, the impact of trauma as a concept and category extends beyond the fields of psychiatry and psychoanalysis. As Cathy Caruth explains, 'the phenomenon of trauma has seemed to become all-inclusive, but it has done so precisely because it brings us to the limits of our understanding'.[27] In her view, 'if psychoanalysis, psychiatry, sociology, and even literature are beginning to hear each other anew in the study of trauma, it is because they are listening

---

[24] See Saul, *Collective Trauma, Collective Healing*, p. 8.

[25] A. Young, *The Harmony of Illusions: Inventing Post-Traumatic Stress Disorder*, p. 5. Ruth Leys draws a similar conclusion. See R. Leys, *Trauma: A Genealogy*, pp. 5–7.

[26] Visser, 'Trauma Theory and Postcolonial Studies', p. 272.

[27] Cathy Caruth, 'Recapturing the Past', in *Trauma: Explorations in Memory*, p. 4; Dominick LaCapra, *History and Memory after Auschwitz*, p. 23. Trauma theory builds on Sigmund Freud's work on trauma (see S. Freud, *Beyond the Pleasure Principle*, Revised Edition; Freud, *Moses and Monotheism*.

through the radical disruption and gaps of traumatic experience'.[28] Providing a detailed analysis of the history of the use of the concept of trauma in a variety of fields lies beyond the scope of this study.[29] I am, however, among a growing number of biblical scholars who explore the interpretive possibilities of reading biblical texts with a sensitivity to the issues of trauma and its possible, latent aftereffects.[30] Trauma studies provide a critical interpretive lens through which to (re)read history and literature, including biblical literature, from what Caruth calls '*the site of trauma*'.[31]

Advancing the possibilities of trauma oriented, critical readings, I focus on how trauma, as a trope, might function as an interpretive lens through which to read the book of Lamentations. What are some of the potential benefits of a trauma informed, critical reading of Lamentations? Does such an approach illumine features of the book that have typically proven problematic in Lamen-

---

[28] Caruth, 'Recapturing the Past', p. 4. Caruth further develops her perspectives on using trauma as a critical lens for reading literature in *Unclaimed Experience: Trauma, Narrative, and History*.

[29] For useful summaries of the history and genealogy of trauma studies, see Luckhurst, *The Trauma Question*, pp. 23–76; Herman, *Trauma*, pp. 7–32; Van der Kolk, *et al*, 'History of Trauma in Psychiatry', p. 47–74; and Leys, *Trauma: A Genealogy*.

[30] For a recent collection of essays on the intersection of biblical studies and trauma studies, see Becker, Dochhorn, and Holt, eds., *Trauma and Traumatization in Individual and Collective Dimensions*. See also David G. Garber, 'Trauma Theory and Biblical Studies', pp. 24–44. Garber offers an historical overview of applications of trauma theory in biblical studies. He argues that trauma 'is part and parcel of the human condition that lies beneath the production of a wide variety of biblical texts' (ibid., 25). I use the term 'trauma criticism' to refer to trauma-oriented, trauma-sensitive critical readings of biblical texts. Thus, trauma criticism is not a rigorous methodology or approach; it is more of a critical orientation, or sensitivity to reading and interpreting biblical texts. See also, Daniel L Smith-Christopher, 'Reading War and Trauma: Suggestions Toward a Social-Psychological Exegesis of Exile and War in Biblical Texts', p. 256.

[31] Caruth, 'Recapturing the Past', 11; see also idem, *Unclaimed Experience*, p. 56.

tations scholarship?[32] In what ways might a trauma sensitive reading of Lamentations open up meaningful interpretive trajectories or vistas for understanding the book in its final form?[33] These are some of the critical questions that guide this study. Ultimately, reading Lamentations with a sensitivity to trauma and its potential effects continues a long-lived history of utilizing social-scientific approaches in biblical studies.[34]

My application of trauma studies to the book of Lamentations proceeds as follows. First, I explore the features of trauma studies that I find most useful for my reading of the book, including an overview of some of the current trauma oriented approaches in biblical scholarship (Chapter 1). Next I discuss the book's traumatic matrix, attending to the historical realities that likely shaped its contents (Chapter 2). In Chapter 3, I analyze elements of the book's five poems that appear to bear the imprint of trauma, particularly the intrusive experience of caesura in lives. In this chapter, I focus on analyzing the book's disruptive generic and structural features through the lens of trauma. In Chapter 4, I demonstrate how the concept of non-referential history is useful for understanding the book's use of tropic, stereotypical, and hyperbolic language. Here, I argue that, using insights from trauma studies, Lamentations can be read as a type of *history*, and not merely creative poetry void of actual historical referents. Finally, I analyze how the book functions rhetorically to ensure the survival of the group(s) whose voices it preserves (Chapters 5 and 6).

---

[32] Here I point to the ongoing challenge of identifying precise historical events and experiences in elements within the book of Lamentations. Identifying the specific genre(s) (established literary forms) of the book's five poems is another challenging conundrum in biblical scholarship.

[33] My focus here is on the book of Lamentations as it appears in the Masoretic Text (MT), rather than its complex compositional history.

[34] Social-scientific criticism approaches focus on reconstructing the social worlds, including the worldviews, social structures, and institutions, that shaped the lives of the people who lived in those worlds within ancient Israel. See Robert R. Wilson, *Sociological Approaches to the Old Testament*; David J. Chalcraft, ed., *Social-Scientific Old Testament Criticism*.

This study seeks to provide graduate students of the Hebrew Bible, as well as clergy and religious educators, with an introduction to and an application of the interdisciplinary approach of reading biblical texts, specifically the book of Lamentations, with insights from contemporary trauma studies.

CHAPTER 1. READING WITH INSIGHTS FROM TRAUMA STUDIES

INTRODUCTION

The use of insights from trauma studies to analyze biblical texts is growing within the field of biblical scholarship. Such critical readings of biblical literature have typically focused on texts purportedly dating from the exilic and post-exilic periods of ancient Israelite history. Scholars who utilize trauma sensitive readings differ in their construal and application of this inter-disciplinary approach. For example, some scholars focus, though not exclusively, on insights from psychiatry, particularly psychoanalysis, while others have focused on insights from literary trauma theories that were developed in close association with Holocaust studies. Some scholars emphasize suggestive insights from disaster, war, refugee, and post-colonial studies, while others are content loosely to apply or identify trauma motifs in their readings of biblical texts. Consequently, utilizing trauma studies as a lens to read biblical texts is not a fixed approach. It is a fluid orientation, or sensitivity in reading with different possible emphases.

PSYCHOANALYTICAL ORIENTED READINGS

One of the most extensive, thoroughgoing examples of a psychoanalytically oriented trauma reading in biblical studies is Ruth Poser's *Das Ezechielbuch als Trauma-Literatur.* Poser provides an overview of the history of psychotraumatology (the study of psychological trauma) and includes a detailed analysis of the effects of trauma on individuals and collectivities.[1] She also goes to great lengths to establish the traumatic contexts for the book of Ezekiel, including the horrors of ancient siege warfare, forced deportation,[2] and the trauma-inducing realities of the 586 BCE Babylonian destruction of Jerusalem and its accompanying catastrophes. Building on these suppositions, Poser pursues a psychoanalytical, diagnostic analysis of the prophet Ezekiel.[3]

Though psychoanalytically oriented in its thrust, Poser's work also incorporates elements from literary trauma theories. Drawing on the work of literary theorist Ronald Granofsky,[4] Poser reads the book of Ezekiel as an example of trauma literature, specifically the trauma novel. In this sense, the book is involved in the meaning-making process that is essential for survivors seeking to move beyond their trauma. Read as a trauma novel, the book's structure, which struggles to respond to trauma, reveals elements of fragmentation, regression, and reunification.[5] Thus, it bears the imprint of experiences of trauma and their effects. It mirrors and responds to trauma, allowing survivors to attempt to regain control of, explain, and work through their experiences.[6] Such a conclusion can imply a covert attempt to evade the very difficult task of attending to the book's complex compositional history. In my view, however, trauma oriented readings of biblical texts are not intended to replace traditional questions, approaches and concerns in biblical scholarship. Trauma informed readings raise different questions, thereby

---

[1] See Poser, *Das Ezechielbuch als Trauma-Literatur*, p. 57–119. Other examples include, S. E. Balentine, 'Traumatizing Job', p. 214, 219; K. Nielsen, 'Post-traumatic Stress Disorder and the Book of Job', pp. 62–70; D. G. Garber, Jr., 'Traumatizing Ezekiel, the Exilic prophet', pp. 215–235; Garber, 'Facing Traumatizing Texts: Reading Nahum's Nationalistic Rage', pp. 285–294.

[2] Poser, *Das Ezechielbuch als Trauma-Literatur*, pp. 121–248.

[3] Ibid., pp. 12–35.

[4] Ibid., pp. 116–119, 665–668; See Ronald Granofsky, *The Trauma Novel: Contemporary Symbolic Depictions of Collective Disaster.*

[5] Poser, *Das Ezechielbuch als Trauma-Literatur*, pp. 334–339, and 409–412.

[6] Poser, *Das Ezechielbuch*, pp. 341–637.

offering new possibilities for addressing old concerns. Claiming the imprint of extreme violence on the structure of a biblical text does not negate the responsibility of exploring other plausible realities that could have shaped the text in its final form.

LITERARY TRAUMA THEORIES ORIENTED READINGS

The works of biblical scholars who have utilized literary trauma theories typically reflect the influence of theorists like Cathy Caruth. While psychoanalysis has shaped and informed these theories, their focus fall on indications or evidence of the potential, latent effects of trauma in/on post-traumatic literature—literature produced by trauma survivors and/or their descendants, or shaped by experiences of trauma.[7] These theories also draw attention to the functions of this type of literature in bearing witness (explicitly or implicitly) to, and working through, experiences of extreme violence.

David Janzen's work, *The Violent Gift*, exemplifies the application of literary trauma theories to biblical texts—in this case, the Deuteronomistic History (DtrH).[8] Janzen's main argument is that despite the DtrH's passing references to traumatic events associated with the 586 BCE Neo-Babylonian assault on Judah and Jerusalem (including siege, famine, mass death, and forced migration), the experience of trauma should be viewed as central to our interpretation of the entire work.[9] First, his argument is based on the assumption that the DtrH was written during the exilic period to explain and make sense of the trauma associated with Judah's fall, which exilic audiences/readers had experienced directly and indirectly, and were continuing to endure.[10] The Deuteronomistic historians' 'master narrative' sought to establish a direct correlation between the people's rebellious actions (sins) and their traumatic

---

[7] See S. Felman and D. Laub, *Testimony, Literature and Psychoanalysis*.

[8] See Janzen, *The Violent Gift: Trauma's Subversion of the Deuteronomistic History's Narrative*. Another examples of this approach is D. Carr's *Holy Resilience*.

[9] Janzen, *The Violent Gift*, pp. 3, 45–59.

[10] Ibid.

experiences (punishment).[11] Second, the overt absence of significant attention to the traumatic events of 586 BCE in the DtrH actually bears witness to an overarching reality of trauma through the work's numerous interruptions of the master narrative—interruptions that subvert its explanatory logic and undercut its assumptions.[12]

This second premise, Janzen suggests, is borne out in trauma studies: 'Trauma can recur or intrude into the lives of those who suffer from it.... Such intrusions are not subject to conscious recall but recur in a manner dissociated from the self, unintegrated by the ego and its web of normal memories that it uses to make sense of the world'.[13] Thus, while trauma may be absent to the self, its effects are powerfully present, albeit uncontrollably, in the psyche and literary works of survivors and their descendants.[14] Again, drawing on the insights of literary trauma theories, Janzen asserts that posttraumatic literature typically reflects trauma's resistance to narrative. The survivors' experience of trauma is elusive—neither fully grasped nor fully known.[15] Since trauma is usually associated with rupture in memory, which tends to lead to the repetition compulsion in survivors, literary repetition is a feature of posttraumatic literature.[16] Furthermore, Janzen notes, traumatic experiences usually lead to a collapse in ethics and language, rendering it impossible to set trauma within ethical and explanatory frameworks.[17] One advantage of utilizing literary trauma theories is their ability to provide critical lenses through which to read and analyze certain anomalous features in biblical texts.

---

[11] Ibid., pp. 53–58. Given the complexity of the DtrH, it might be problematic to speak about *a* 'master narrative.'

[12] Ibid., pp. 4, 59–63.

[13] Ibid., pp. 4, 26–31.

[14] Ibid., pp. 4, 31–35.

[15] Ibid., pp. 35–38.

[16] Ibid., pp. 38–42. Literary repetition is also a prominent feature in most Hebrew poetry and prose. This is not a feature that I emphasize in my analysis of the book of Lamentations.

[17] Ibid., pp. 42–45.

INTEGRATIVE READINGS

In their analyses of the potential, traumatic effects of realities such as warfare, national disasters, and forced deportations in ancient Israel's history, some scholars have employed insights from modern disaster, refugee, and warfare-related trauma studies.[18] Brad E. Kelle, for example, utilizes this integrative approach to read the book of Ezekiel.[19] Such an approach helps 'to foreground the traumatic nature of the experiences of war, destruction, and deportation suffered by Ezekiel and his audience'.[20] In addition, this orientation in reading provides a plausible explanation for some of the bizarre rhetoric and imagery in the book of Ezekiel (example, Ezek 4).[21]

Building on her earlier, trauma oriented readings of portions of the book of Jeremiah, Kathleen M. O'Connor combines insights from literary trauma theories with disaster studies.[22] Specifically, she explores how the book of Jeremiah might have functioned for its earliest readers—survivors of traumatic and disastrous events associated with the sixth century BCE Babylonian destruction of Jerusalem. O'Connor uses *trauma* to refer to the effects of the experience of violence on individuals and *disaster* to describe the effects of traumatic violence on entire societies.[23] She focuses on four pos-

---

[18] See, for example, Smith-Christopher, *A Biblical Theology of Exile*; Smith-Christopher, 'Reassessing the Historical and Sociological Impact of the Babylonian Exile (597/586–539 BCE)', pp. 7–36; Smith-Christopher, 'Reading War and Trauma'; Smith-Christopher, 'Trauma and the Old Testament'; William Morrow, 'Deuteronomy 7 in Postcolonial Perspective: Cultural Fragmentation and Renewal', pp. 275–293; and Janet L. Rumfelt, 'Reversing Fortune: War, Psychic Trauma, and the Promise of Narrative Repair', pp. 323–342.

[19] See also Nancy Bowen, *Ezekiel*.

[20] Brad E. Kelle, 'Dealing with the Trauma of Defeat: The Rhetoric of the Devastation and Rejuvenation of Nature in Ezekiel', p. 470. Here I assume that Kelle is referring to the book's earliest audience/readers.

[21] Ibid.

[22] See K. M. O'Connor, 'Lamenting Back to Life', pp. 34–47; O'Connor, 'Family Comes Undone: Jeremiah 2:1 – 4:2', pp. 201–212.

[23] Ibid., p. 3.

sible effects of traumatic experiences. First, trauma ruptures experience.[24] Second, traumatic experiences are, by nature, unutterable, unspeakable, and elusive. Third, such experiences tend to shut down human feelings and responses as a consequence of the sheer shock of traumatic events.[25] Fourth, experiences of trauma or disaster can destroy or undermine both individuals' and societies' trust in God, others, and the world.[26] O'Connor argues that reading Jeremiah through the lenses of trauma and disaster studies 'pr[ies] open the book…to deep reflection'.[27] Further, such a critical orientation in reading releases the book 'from the constricting interpretations concerned only with the book's composition or the prophet's true words or from unquestioning interpretations of disaster as God's punishment for sin'.[28]

O'Connor also asserts that the chaotic or tumultuous nature of the book of Jeremiah points to trauma's disruptive effects. The book's lack of order reflects a search for meaning, expression, and interpretation that helped survivors to rebuild as a people in the aftermath of Judah's fall.[29] The search for meaning in the wake of toxic events is illustrative of trauma's effects on language—there are no words, tropes, or images adequate to express trauma fully. Consequently, Jeremiah uses symbolic, often poetic, language to express the horrors that survivors were forced to endure.[30] Such evocative and tropic language is not 'historical' or referential in the scientific sense of those words. As O'Connor asserts, 'Rather than confronting matters head on [that is, historical or factual descriptions], Jeremiah tells and retells the catastrophe indirectly, metaphorically, in unforgettable ways. In the process, the book tells the truth'.[31]

---

[24] Ibid., pp. 22–23.

[25] Ibid., pp. 23–25.

[26] Ibid., pp. 4, 25–26.

[27] Ibid., p. 27.

[28] Ibid.

[29] Ibid.

[30] Ibid., p. 33. Cf., E. K. Holt, 'Daughter Zion: Trauma, Cultural Memory and Gender in OT Poetics', pp. 162–176.

[31] Ibid.

Daniel L. Smith-Christopher's analyses of Ezekiel and Lamentations in *A Biblical Theology of Exile*[32] also utilize an integrative approach. Smith-Christopher draws insights from modern refugee studies, disaster studies, and trauma studies, applying them to various aspects of these biblical books. He contends that Ezekiel and Lamentations are early examples of responses to the trauma of exile from Babylonian and Judean perspectives, respectively.[33] In fact, Smith-Christopher argues, tragic, toxic events, specifically the horrific realities of siege warfare, are foregrounded in these works. Thus, understanding the implications of this wider context of trauma is critical for interpreting both books.[34]

TRAUMA MOTIFS ORIENTED READINGS

Utilizing trauma related motifs[35] as one facet of their eclectic methodological approaches, Louis Stulman and Hyun C. P. Kim propose innovative and creative ways of reading prophetic literature. Their approaches, as they acknowledge at the onset, are much more 'intuitive and artistic than systematic and scientific'.[36] Stulman and Kim view prophetic literature as survival literature from the exilic and postexilic periods.[37] Thus, the Babylonians' sixth century BCE destruction of Jerusalem, including the exile of many of its inhabitants to various parts of the Babylonian Empire, provides the most appropriate interpretive framework for these works. Stulman and Kim are particularly attuned to the experience of extreme violence in modern societies and to the responsibility of biblical inter-

---

[32] Smith-Christopher, *A Biblical Theology of Exile*, pp. 75–104.

[33] Ibid., p. 76.

[34] Ibid.

[35] This approach to trauma sensitive readings of biblical texts is different from the previous approaches in that it does not attempt to engage directly with or analyze trauma studies. It is closely related to the integrative approach in that it presupposes insights from different academic fields, for example, disaster studies, survival literature, and postcolonial studies.

[36] Stulman and Kim, *You are My People*, p. 1; see also L. Stulman, 'Reading the Bible through the Lens of Trauma and Art', p. 177–192.

[37] Ibid.

preters to engage their current contexts. In their view, modern interpreters of the Bible cannot, or at least should not, ignore the traumatic realities of our times.[38]

Reading prophetic literature with a sensitivity to trauma's effects on individuals and communities, Stulman and Kim assert that biblical prophecy represents attempts to find meaning in the aftermath of overwhelming suffering, especially war-related suffering, and to foster a trajectory of hope in disaster-stricken communities.[39] The often chaotic and tumultuous structures evident in prophetic books testify to the struggles to give expression to the trauma endured by the survivors and their descendants who produced these texts.[40] What is more, these texts reflect attempts to move beyond the death-dealing effects of trauma to herald hope for survivor-communities.[41] For Stulman and Kim, prophetic literature as meaning-making survival literature 'will not accept disaster as the final word and the collapse of the world as the death of community'.[42]

Evaluation of Trauma Oriented Readings

My categorizations of these critical readings—psychoanalytical, literary, integrative, and trauma motif oriented—function heuristically. Each of these emphases employs insights from trauma studies in biblical interpretation; and each includes strengths and shortcomings. Psychoanalytical trauma readings help to shed light on Jeremiah, Ezekiel, and the books bearing their names. The concept of trauma offers a lens through which to read the often bizarre, violent, disruptive, and anomalous features of the books attributed to these prophets. Literary trauma theories permit scholars to be sensitive to some of the ways extreme violence can affect survivor literature. This orientation in reading has enabled scholars to advance credible theories regarding the possible functions of these biblical texts as meaning-making texts for their earliest read-

[38] Ibid., pp. 4–6.

[39] Ibid., pp. 7–8.

[40] Ibid., pp. 11–14.

[41] Ibid., pp. 15–21.

[42] Ibid., pp. 21–22.

ers/audiences. Hence, it is possible that biblical, post-traumatic, survivor literature helped survivors and their descendants find meaning after, conceptualize, and work through their traumatic experiences. The new vistas of interpretive trajectories that trauma studies permit are particularly useful when we read biblical survivor literature with a sensitivity to the traumatic realities of our modern world.

Trauma informed readings of biblical texts have typically been utilized in efforts to re-examine problematic, disturbing, and enigmatic features of these texts. Such applications are evident in all four of the emphases in trauma sensitive readings that I have discussed. Tumultuous and anomalous aspects of texts purported to be survivor or post-traumatic literature are attributed to the effects of overwhelming suffering. Stulman's conclusion about traditional historical-critical approaches to the book of Jeremiah is insightful: although 'historical or referential queries' have yielded 'important conclusions', these approaches have 'not succeeded in solving many of the problems which they have helped to recognize'.[43] While the insights from trauma oriented readings are useful and necessary, however, there is the danger of 'abusing' the concept of *trauma* to placate the terrors of troubling texts and gloss over the complexities of composite literature.[44]

I do not contend that trauma informed readings avoid traditional historical-critical considerations; rather, I am suggesting that some trauma oriented readings of biblical texts reflect a tendency to find 'order amid chaos,' to borrow the title of Stulman's work on Jeremiah. Experiences of trauma are often messy and resist integration and structuring. Further, while the complex, compositional

---

[43] Louis Stulman, *Order Amid Chaos: Jeremiah as Symbolic Tapestry*, p. 167; Stulman, *The Prose Sermons of the Book of Jeremiah: A Redescription of the Correspondences with the Deuteronomistic Literature in the Light of Recent Text-Critical Research*, pp. 7–31.

[44] Katheryn P. Darr asserts that while 'modern disaster and trauma studies can illumine biblical texts', interpreters should guard against the interpretive slippery slope of making texts like Ezekiel 'more agreeable by blurring its harshest features…' (Katheryn P. Darr, 'The God Ezekiel Envisions', in *The God Ezekiel Creates*, p. 22).

histories of biblical texts is a cliché in some circles of biblical scholarship, the dearth of credible information on the compositional histories of these texts resists any simple or straightforward explanations of these complexities. Neither trauma oriented readings, nor traditional referential approaches, can—or have been able to—account conclusively for complexities evident in biblical texts. 'Diagnosing' an ancient prophet with PTSD does not diminish the troubling, often terrorizing, aspects of the prophet's 'words'. Similarly, reading biblical texts as survivor or post-traumatic literature does not lessen the troublesome, often bizarre, complexity of the texts so labeled. Rather, trauma oriented readings highlight the imprints of traumatic events and their effects on relevant biblical writers and literature while recognizing and affirming the relevance of ongoing critical, referential and compositional queries informed by insights from trauma studies.

While I draw on insights from all four of the emphases in trauma oriented readings described above, my application of trauma studies follows the integrative approach exemplified in the works of Smith-Christopher and O'Connor. This approach is the most nuanced and self-critical of the four emphases in trauma informed readings. I recognize that in employing trauma studies as an interpretive lens through which to read biblical texts there is a rick of totalizing and generalizing experiences of *trauma*.[45] To be fair, this same tendency is present in the works of many trauma studies experts. Several scholars presuppose that trauma is a unified concept with universally identical effects. Typically, these scholars do not reckon with the potential impact of the trauma matrix on the ways survivors experience, conceptualize, and respond to extreme violence. For example, in non-Western (and/or ancient) contexts (and even within Western contexts), conceptions of, and responses to overwhelming suffering vary.[46] As Smith-Christopher notes, uncritical applications of insights from trauma studies run the risk of leveling out 'the experiences of all peoples into a kind of generic

---

[45] See Darr's discussion in 'The God Ezekiel Envisions', pp. 5–11.

[46] See Rothberg, preface to *The Future of Trauma Theory*, p. xii; and Balaev, ed., *Contemporary Approaches in Literary Trauma Theory*; Buelens and Durrant, eds, *The Future of Trauma Theory*.

'trauma experience' that denies the unique histories and experiences of the peoples in question'.[47] Hence, nuanced and self-critical approaches to trauma oriented critical readings of biblical texts are necessary.[48]

READING LAMENTATIONS WITH INSIGHTS FROM TRAUMA STUDIES

Three characteristics of experiences of trauma make the concept useful as a critical lens through which to read certain biblical texts in general, and the book of Lamentations in particular. The first is that trauma survivors' testimonies typically convey a history that is not directly referential.[49] The use of metaphors, exaggerated speech, and highly emotive language often characterizes the testimonies of victims of trauma. Cursory evaluations of these types of expressions usually lead to the conclusion that they are void of actual historical referents. However, trauma studies indicate that survivors' testimonies bear witness to a type of history that is not based on direct referents. The second characteristic is that trauma causes caesura or rupture in life, more specifically memory. Extreme violence tends to shatter, or at least significantly disrupt, the lives, identity, social networks, and worldviews of individual and collective survivors. Many survivors experience a break with the past, present and future. Often, this experience of rupture in life challenges survivors to find creative ways of re-integrating their lives as they seek to regain a measure of control over, and a sense of normalcy in, their lives post-trauma.

The third characteristic relates to rhetorical dimensions of the trauma process—how individuals and communities use the concept of trauma to reconstitute themselves following catastrophic experiences. By 'rhetorical' I am referring to the persuasive aspects

---

[47] Smith-Christopher, 'Reading War and Trauma', p. 269.

[48] Darr advances a similar view in her essay, 'The God Ezekiel Envisions', pp. 1–23. See also Christopher G. Frechette, 'The Old Testament as Controlled Substance: How Insights from Trauma Studies Reveal Healing Capacities in Potentially Harmful Texts', p. 23.

[49] See, e.g., Caruth, *Unclaimed Experiences*, pp. 10–24.

of the trauma process. Usually collectivities that survive toxic events *use* their experiences as a catalyst for change, assigning blame, or pursuing justice. In this regard, Kirby Farrell correctly asserts that, 'People not only suffer trauma; they use it, and the idea of it, for all sorts of ends, good and ill'.[50] While it is anachronistic to speak of biblical texts *using trauma*, I believe that biblical texts that bear witness to overwhelming suffering function rhetorically to bring about change—whether for the earliest, or subsequent generations of readers of these texts. Once exposed to the graphic, brutal realities of extreme violence, secondary witnesses—readers, writers, historians, artists, and investigators—including observers or attentive audiences, are invited to identify with and share in the experiences of the sufferers, and, ultimately, to participate in the process of change.

Together, these three characteristics of post-traumatic experiences provide a useful heuristic aid to re-engaging some of the challenging aspects of Lamentations scholarship.[51] Although trauma experts, including literary trauma theorists, disagree about the specific construal and extent of these three features, there is general consensus that they are typical components of trauma and its effects. What are the contours of these three salient features of post-traumatic experiences, and in what ways are they relevant for reading Lamentations? I address these questions in the following paragraphs.

Non-Referential History

One of the potential, painful indicators, and crippling aftereffects of traumatic events is that victims often 'relive the event as though it were continually recurring in the present'.[52] This repetition com-

---

[50] Farrell, *Posttraumatic Culture*, p. 21.

[51] Erhard S. Gerstenberger asserts the following regarding Lamentations' complexities: 'More than other Hebrew writings, the enigmatic queries for origin, use, and theology of the small Book of Lamentations cannot easily be appeased. There are too many discrepancies in our literary, historical, and theological data of these five chapters of literature'. (Gerstenberger, 'Elusive Lamentations: What are They About?', p. 121.

[52] Herman, p. 37.

pulsion is typically intrusive and disruptive. In her discussion of the relationship between theory and literature in the context of trauma, Caruth argues that for survivors, the re-lived experiences are normally elusive—they are neither completely grasped nor fully known.[53] In this sense the traumatic experience is typically not readily available to 'consciousness until it imposes itself again, repeatedly, in the nightmares and repetitive actions of the survivors'.[54]

Typically, trauma is not fully grasped at the time it occurs; it is inaccessible, a 'missed'—that is, *non-referential*—experience that is not completely known.[55] It is not that the traumatic event itself is missed; rather, the psychological effects and/or impact of the traumatic events are often belated and enduring. The missed encounter with death forms the basis for the *repetition compulsion* evident in the experiences of many survivors of traumatic events. Repetition does not pertain simply to the incomprehensibility of a death not experienced. It also, and equally, relates to the enigma of survival: why did I (we) survive?[56] For many survivors of traumatic

---

[53] This assumption is contested in some recent trauma scholarship. See, for example, Bowman, *Individual Differences in Posttraumatic Response*; Michelle Balaev, ed., *Contemporary Approaches in Literary Trauma Theory*; and Gert Beulens, Sam Durrant and Robert Eaglestone, eds, *The Future of Trauma Theory: Contemporary Literary and Cultural Criticism.* Despite the recent critiques of the category of non-referential history, specifically the view that trauma dislocates history, this category in trauma theory has not been completely negated. As Rothberg insightfully posits, 'it is difficult ...to imagine trauma as not involving dislocation of subjects, histories, and cultures'. These dislocations are even evident in non-European representations of the experience of trauma in literature. See Rothberg, preface to *The Future of Trauma Theory*, pp. xii–xiii.

[54] Caruth, *Unclaimed Experiences*, p. 4.

[55] See Caruth, *Unclaimed Experience*, pp. 11, 62; Dominick LaCapra, *Writing History, Writing Trauma*, p. 1–42; Lawrence L. Langer, *Using and Abusing the Holocaust*, pp. 1–4; and LaCapra, *History and Memory after Auschwitz*, pp. 9–12.

[56] See Caruth, *Unclaimed Experience*, 64. 'Individuals with Posttraumatic Stress Disorder may describe painful guilt feelings about surviving

events, the enigma of survival is experienced as a sensation(s) of being dead while yet alive.[57] Thus, the testimonies of survivors typically bear witness not only to the real horrors of the toxic events that continue to haunt them, but also to the unsettling elusiveness of effects of those very events. Based on this understanding of trauma, survivor-testimonies—the narratives, works of art, diaries, and literature that they produce in the aftermath of trauma—preserve a history that is not 'straightforwardly referential'.[58] Such a history is based neither on simple correlations between experience and referents nor on verifiable truth claims[59] that have been so crucial to the modern western academic discipline of historiography.[60]

In his analysis of historiography and the challenges of bearing witness to trauma, historian Dominick LaCapra contends that 'conventional stereotypes of transparent representation' or notions of 'self-sufficient research paradigm' are no longer tenable in modern historiography.[61] For LaCapra, the question of experience, critically invoked, is foundational to historiography.[62] Building on this premise, he poses several critical questions:

> [W]hat is the relation between experience and nonexperiential aspects of history…? What is the relation between the differentiated experience of agents or subjects in the past and the differentiated experience of observers or secondary witnesses…? How does one relate actual and imaginary or virtual experience? How is experience related to truth claims and to critical value judgments? How do trauma or traumatic "experi-

---

when others did not survive or about the things they had to do to survive' (*The Diagnostic and Statistical Manual of Mental Disorder: DSM-IV-TR*, p. 465).

[57] See Langer, *Using and Abusing the Holocaust*, p. 2.

[58] Ibid., p. 11.

[59] Ibid.

[60] For a useful overview of the complexities of historiography that attends to traumatic experiences, especially the testimonies of survivors, see LaCapra, *Writing History, Writing Trauma*, pp. 1–85.

[61] LaCapra, *Writing History, Writing Trauma*, p. 36.

[62] Ibid.

> ence" disrupt experience and raise specific problems for representation and writing...?[63]

LaCapra acknowledges that traumatic experiences affect both the observed and observers.[64] Moreover, 'Trauma is a disruptive experience that disarticulates the self and creates holes in existence...'.[65] The type of history that gives credibility to experience, specifically traumatic experience, is not referential in the sense of a simple correlation between experience and reference; it moves beyond so-called objective reconstructions of the past. The disruptive experience of trauma, as well as the elusive testimonies of survivors and observers who bear witness to it, are credible and authoritative sources of history.[66] The accounts of survivors might not provide datable or verifiable information about the traumatic event. Nevertheless, these accounts bear witness to a reality that is beyond their full grasp and comprehension—the reality that something world-shattering and painfully disruptive has occurred with ongoing, debilitating consequences. Survivor testimonies might lack recognizable historical character and characters; nevertheless, they are *historical* is the sense that they bear witness to the ruptured realities and horrid dislocation that are ubiquitous in the aftermath of trauma. Although trauma is often related to specific events, it cannot be restricted to 'terms of a discrete, dated experience'.[67] Trauma typi-

---

[63] Ibid., p. 37.

[64] LaCapra, *Writing History, Writing Trauma*, p. 41. One of LaCapra's critiques of Caruth's approach to this issue is that in her work she approaches history through the medium of theory and literature. Such an approach excludes historiography itself and the possible 'contributions or resistances it might pose to her analysis in both intellectual and institutional terms' (LaCapra, *Writing History, Writing Trauma*, p. 183).

[65] LaCapra, p. 41.

[66] Caruth, 'Recapturing the Past', p. 151–157. Caruth argues that, 'For the survivor of trauma...the truth of the event may reside not only in its brutal facts, but also in the way that their occurrence defies simple comprehension' (p. 153). See also Bessel A. van der Kolk and Onno van der Hart, 'The Intrusive Past: The Flexibility of Memory and the Engraving of Trauma', in *Trauma: Explorations in Memory*, p. 158–182).

[67] LaCapra, *Writing History, Writing Trauma*, p. 186.

cally results in a 'shattering break or cesura in experience which has belated effects'.[68]

In clarifying his view of historiography that attends to experience, LaCapra differentiates between *writing about trauma* and *writing trauma.* The former is an aspect of historiography that focuses on 'reconstructing the past as objectively as possible without necessarily going to the self-defeating extreme of single-minded objectification….'[69] The latter, by contrast, is a metaphor in that 'writing indicates some distance from trauma….'[70] It is the result of what he calls 'traumatic and post-traumatic writing'.[71] Writing trauma involves giving voice and bearing witness to extreme suffering.[72] Thus, extreme or toxic historical events or situations that demonstrably traumatize survivors and observers can be labeled 'traumatic events'. Literature produced by these survivors (and their descendants) and observers—survivor literature—including poetry, narratives, or culturally specific histories that attempt to give voice to and bear witness to those traumatic events, can legitimately be construed as a type of history—posttraumatic history—or at least as the result of credible effects of those traumatic events on survivors and/or witnesses.

Rupture in Life

Caesura or rupture in life, more specifically, in memory, is usually associated with experiences of trauma.[73] Traumatic experiences can severely fragment and dismantle the world of survivors. Familial and community attachments can be breached in the aftermath of trauma. Constructions of the self and identity *vis à vis* relational ties and group membership are often ruptured in traumatic experiences.[74] Moreover, trauma often brutally assaults beliefs and worldviews that previously gave meaning to existence and explana-

---

[68] Ibid.

[69] Ibid.

[70] Ibid.

[71] Ibid.

[72] Ibid.

[73] LaCapra, *Writing History, Writing Trauma*, p. 186.

[74] Herman, *Trauma and Recovery*, p. 51.

tions for life in the world and in society.[75] Herman's summary, though generalizing, is insightful: 'Traumatized people feel utterly abandoned, utterly alone, cast out of the human and divine systems of care and protection that sustained life'.[76] Victims typically experience alienation from family, community, and religion.[77]

In *History and Memory After Auschwitz*, LaCapra poignantly notes that trauma often brings about 'a lapse or rupture in memory that breaks continuity with the past, thereby placing identity in question to the point of shattering it'.[78] The potentially disruptive nature of traumatic experiences can create 'holes in existence'.[79] The holes or ruptures in memory that trauma tends to create are open wounds in the past that continue to resist being completely fleshed-out, healed, or integrated into the present.[80] Caesura in life is by no means universally true of all trauma survivors. Nevertheless, in instances where survivors experience a rupture in memory or a breach in existence, this feature is significant for understanding the content, nature, and forms of their testimonies. In such cases, survivors' testimonies 'achieve articulation in different combinations of hybridized forms'.[81] Said differently, the testimonies of survivors of extreme violence who experience caesura—whether represented in their physical actions, or in the narratives, songs, poetry, plays, and histories they produce—typically bear the imprint of their experiences of rupture.[82]

---

[75] Tal, *Worlds of Hurt*, p. 15.

[76] Herman, p. 52.

[77] Ibid.

[78] LaCapra, *History and Memory After Auschwitz*, p. 9.

[79] LaCapra, *Writing History, Writing Trauma*, p. 41.

[80] LaCapra, *History and Memory after Auschwitz*, p. 109.

[81] Ibid., p. 186.

[82] See Diana Lary, 'Writing and War: Silence, Disengagement, and Ambiguity', pp. 45–62. Lary's analyzes the relevance of utilizing literature produced in the aftermath of trauma for historical reconstruction of traumatic events. See also, LaCapra, *Writing History, Writing Trauma*, p. 96.

The Rhetoric of the Trauma Process

Studies in collective and cultural trauma offer significant insights into how post-traumatic testimonies—whether in the form of oral testimonies, memorials, narratives, art, poetry, or other mediums—can function for some communities in the aftermath of toxic events.[83] Catastrophic losses, extreme damage to familial relations, networks, structures and systems are trauma-causing realities that often leave communities with feelings of betrayal and abandonment,[84] especially when the perpetrating structures, groups, or individuals were expected to be defenders or protectors.[85] Particularly for survivors who experience caesura in life in the aftermath of toxic events, the process of bearing witness to trauma can be very complex and challenging.[86] The degree of complexity and challenge is directly connected to the trauma matrix. As a consequence, different individuals and collectivities work through trauma in very different ways.[87]

Cultural trauma refers to the ways collectivities choose to represent, reconstruct, bear witness to, memorialize, and/or signify their collective experience of toxic events.[88] Cultural trauma occurs when members of a collectivity experience a limit event, which permanently scars the group's consciousness, 'marking their memories forever and changing their future in fundamental and irrevo-

---

[83] See Jack Saul, *Collective Trauma, Collective Healing: Promoting Community Resilience in the Aftermath of Disaster*; Arthur G. Neal, *National Trauma and Collective Memory: Extraordinary Events in the American Experience*, Second Edition.

[84] See Saul, *Collective Trauma, Collective Healing*, p. 4.

[85] See Jenny Edkins, *Trauma and the Memory of Politics*, p. 4.

[86] LaCapra, *Writing History, Writing Trauma*, p. 45.

[87] See Gregory K. Moffatt in, *Survivors: What We Can Learn from How They Cope with Horrific Tragedy*, pp. 1–24. Muffatt asserts, '[W]e all face various events throughout life that are difficult. How we handle them varies by person and event' (Ibid, 23). See also Saul, *Collective Trauma, Collective Healing*, pp. 1–18.

[88] See Moffatt, *Survivors*; Richard F. Mollica, *Healing Invisible Wounds: Paths to Hope and Recovery in a Violent World*; and Saul, *Collective Trauma, Collective Healing*.

cable ways'.[89] Such traumatic events shatter social and relational bonds within those communities, resulting in significant damage to the structures, systems, and worldviews on which communal identity was built.[90] Collective trauma usually involves two or more of the following experiences: extensive destruction or damage to property, widespread or enormous loss of lives and livelihood, significant loss of resources, and human agencies are directly or indirectly responsible for the overwhelming suffering.[91]

The process of constructing and representing trauma often entails rhetorical dimensions. Thus, representations or significations of the elusive experience of trauma are typically persuasive in nature—they seek to inspire change. These 'trauma dramas', as Alexander and Breese call them, are the works of culture creators,[92] including the communities' 'novelists, painters, poets…and intellectuals',[93] who signify or represent the catastrophic events that the community has experienced as traumatic. The representations they produce typically respond to four questions: 'What happened? Who were its victims? Who were its perpetrators? What can be done?'[94] These significations are not intended to be descriptions or precise historical representations of the events signified as traumatic. Rather, they function as '*arguments* for what must have been and, at least implicitly, of what should be'.[95] The significance of these witnesses to extreme violence lies not in the historical accuracy of their descriptions, but in what they accomplish or, at the very least, intend to accomplish for trauma survivors.[96] While representations of traumatic events can be either consensual or polarizing, success-

---

[89] Alexander, *Trauma*, p. 6. See also, Alexander, 'Toward a Theory of Cultural Trauma', in *Cultural Trauma and Collective Identity*, p. 1.

[90] Kai T. Erickson, *Everything in Its Path: Destruction of Community in the Buffalo Creek Flood*, p. 154.

[91] Saul, *Collective Trauma, Collective Healing*, pp. 1–4.

[92] Alexander and Breese, introduction to *Narrating Trauma*, p. xxvii.

[93] Ibid., p. xxii.

[94] Ibid., p. xxvii. See also Alexander, *Trauma*, pp. 17–25; Alexander, 'Toward a Theory of Cultural Trauma', pp. 12–21.

[95] Ibid.; emphasis added.

[96] Ibid.

fully enacted, they have the potential to exert extraordinary, positive influence on the re-organizing and re-structuring of social worlds in the aftermath of catastrophe.

Another feature of the rhetorical function of post-traumatic representations of the experiences of extreme violence is their capacity to protest against and subvert the status quo. Jenny Edkins succinctly asserts, '[t]he testimony of survivors can challenge structures of power and authority'.[97] Similarly, Kalí Tal affirms that survivors' testimonies tend to be 'highly politicized.'[98] In a very real way, 'telling it like it was' challenges established power structures, whether political, social, or religious, that control the status quo.[99] Especially in instances when human beings are the perpetrators of extreme suffering, giving voice to trauma, speaking the unspeakable, and naming that which remains elusive involves assuming a posture of resistance against the perpetrator(s) of those horrors. In such situations, bearing witness to toxic events typically can be construed as an act of aggression.[100] Its ultimate goal is to bring about changes in traumatizing social and political structures.[101] Such changes are possible only when survivors retain control of the process of trauma creation, thereby giving meaning to their overwhelming suffering.[102] Through the process of giving voice to trauma, these survivors reassert their humanity and reclaim their identity, albeit through ruptured mediums. The works of culture creators provide the collectivities for which they speak with avenues for trauma signification, and, by extension, the trauma signification process can ultimately furnish traumatized communities with a framework 'to define new forms of moral responsibility and to redirect the course of political action'.[103]

---

[97] Edkins, *Trauma and the Memory of Politics*, p. 5.

[98] Tal, *Worlds of Hurt: Reading the Literatures of Trauma*, p. 7.

[99] Ibid.

[100] Ibid.

[101] Ibid.

[102] Ibid.

[103] Alexander, *Trauma*, p. 30.

Relevance of Trauma Studies for Reading Lamentations

Questions of history and historicity regarding the book of Lamentation abound in biblical scholarship. Does credible evidence exist for datable historical events in Lamentations? Does its ubiquitously tropic, stereotypical, and often hyperbolic expressions point to actual historical referents? In what ways is this book related to the 586 BCE Neo-Babylonian assaults against Judah and Jerusalem and their catastrophic aftereffects? While it might be impossible to provide conclusive answers to these and other intriguing critical questions related to the history and historicity of Lamentations, the non-referential history that often characterizes testimonies of survivors of extreme violence offers an alternative interpretive framework for engaging them. Such a reading of Lamentations does not silence or evade the very challenging questions of history, including temporal history. Nevertheless, reading the book with insights from trauma studies offers a different vantage point from which to analyze these questions. If Lamentations is read as post-traumatic, survivor literature created by a culture creator (a poet) in the wake of a toxic, ancient event, then we should not expect the book's poetic descriptions always to correspond to actual referents. Thus, reading the book with a critical orientation toward trauma and its potential aftereffects offers the possibility of moving beyond the impasse *vis à vis* history and historicity.[104]

Another debated issue in Lamentations scholarship concerns the precise genre(s) of the book's five poems. Studies of comparable lament, dirge, and/or elegy traditions in ancient Near Eastern literature, as well as in the Hebrew Bible, are insightful, but they are not conclusive. The issue of literary genre(s) in the book remains a topic of debate. At points, the structures of the poems seem fractured or ruptured, they appear to depart from the recognizable generic forms they utilize. Read with a sensitivity to the experience of trauma and its potential impact, these structural anomalies can be interpreted as imprints of the experiences of rupture in life that

---

[104] K. M. O'Connor comes to a similar conclusion (O'Connor, 'How Trauma Studies Can Contribute to Old Testament Studies', pp. 213, 219–220).

haunt many trauma survivors. Thus, the ruptured forms (literary genres) in Lamentations' poems can serve as (nearly) perfect media for their contents. Of course there are other, valid explanations for the structural and generic anomalies in the book's poems, including its complex compositional history. However, critical readings of Lamentations oriented toward the potential effects of extreme violence can provide equally valuable interpretive possibilities. As LaCapra notes, 'any attentive secondary witness to, or acceptable account of, traumatic experiences must in some significant way be marked by trauma or allow trauma to register in its own procedures'.[105] Read as an ancient testimony of survivors of a series of traumatic events, Lamentations' uses of literary genre provide glimpses into the ruptured lives of those survivors.

Strategic, rhetorical features of the book of Lamentations remain matters of debate among biblical scholars. What is the book's overall rhetorical thrust? What are its strategic rhetorical features and functions? What does the book seek to accomplish by means of its rhetoric? These questions, raised in conjunction with insights from trauma studies, can provide important insights for interpreting and constructing the book's meaning. The element of protest, for instance, is prominent in Lamentations: the poet subverts and contests several traditional facets of ancient Israelite worldviews as best we are able to identify them. Among other things, it undercuts and undermines the view that Zion's extreme suffering was/is just punishment for her extreme rebelliousness. Often in Lamentations, acknowledgement of culpability leads not to penitence or repentance, but to protest. These aspects of the book's strategic rhetorical functions come into sharper focus when viewed with a sensitivity to the ways collectivities process trauma. According to Alexander, if the trauma process is worked through within a religious context, then its concerns will typically be linked to trauma and theodicy: Why would God permit such evil to befall us?[106] Lamentations' unsettling, destabilizing, and disruptive features can be understood as powerful protests from a collectivity, or from individuals within that collectivity, who feel either abandoned, or violated, by their

---

[105] LaCapra, *History and Memory after Auschwitz*, p. 110.

[106] Alexander, *Trauma*, p. 20.

deity. They resist being silenced, at times to the point of blasphemy, attempting to put into words—however inadequately—their experience(s) of trauma.

In my reading of Lamentations, I presuppose some general, basic features of traumatic experiences. The most significant feature is that extreme violence tends to disrupt or rupture the lives of survivors (albeit in potentially different ways). Further, I presuppose that traumatizing experiences tend to register their imprints on the modalities that survivors use to bear witness to, and attempt to move beyond, their painful experiences. However, the individuals and groups that constituted the earliest readers/audiences of Lamentations might have conceptualized and responded to the traumatic events depicted most prominently in the book in different, even conflicting, ways. Read as post-traumatic, survivor literature, the book of Lamentations opens new possibilities for exploring the conceptualizations of, and responses to, experiences of extreme violence in its poems.

Lamentations offered survivors a medium and context for bearing witness to experiences of toxic events. Its poems intentionally and creatively provide language, including tropes, to repeat and re-tell experiences of overwhelming suffering associated with siege warfare, famine, defeat, displacement, rupture of certain worldviews, and the shattering of particular social networks, institutions, and structures. Lamentations incorporates complex, competing, and, often conflicting conceptions of and responses to these traumatic experiences. Pursuing an integrative emphasis in my reading of Lamentations provides plausible ways of understanding some of its inconsistencies, anomalies, and apparently disruptive structural features. Nevertheless, I hold this view in tension with the view that some of these challenging textual features might also be due, in part, to the book's compositional history.

Survival, rather than the theological categories of guilt and hope, forms the fulcrum of the book of Lamentations.[107] Kelle argues that the priest/prophet Ezekiel takes the traumatic experienc-

---

[107] See Linafelt, *Surviving Lamentations: Catastrophe, Lament, and Protest in the Afterlife of a Biblical Book*, p. 18. See also Claus Westermann, *Lamentations: Issues and Interpretation*, pp. 81, 86.

es of the Judeans and 're-narrates them into a plot line based on Yahweh's own sovereignty and purity'.[108] The book of Lamentations, by contrast, expresses ongoing refusal to integrate the survivors' trauma into their collective life; it does not re-narrate the trauma into a unified plot line.

SUMMARY

Biblical scholars, with varying degrees of precision and selectivity, have demonstrated the viability and interpretive possibilities of trauma informed readings of biblical texts. Their works highlight the sorts of insights that the interdisciplinary venture of trauma sensitive readings can generate. Though still emerging, ongoing discourses among trauma informed readings, more traditional approaches, and biblical texts are necessary and fruitful. The features of trauma studies that I find most useful for my reading of the book of Lamentations are non-referential history, rupture in memory, and the rhetorical dimensions of the trauma process.

In my reading of Lamentations, I affirm that identities (individual and/or collective), social contexts, worldviews, and other factors shape conceptions of and responses to traumatic realities. Different individuals or groups can register various effects of extreme violence in very different ways. Hence, it is possible that the tumultuous and chaotic nature of the book of Lamentations points to some of these competing responses to overwhelming suffering. Beyond meaning-making, the book engages in the task of survival, giving voice to trauma. Reading Lamentations as post-traumatic literature that engages in a meaning-making process allows this ancient Judean text to become more accessible to modern interpreters and readers. Trauma studies invites these readers and interpreters to re-read biblical texts with a sensitivity to experiences of trauma and its potential effects. Nevertheless, it also—and equally—challenges us to recognize that post-traumatic literature might also be traumatic literature—it can rupture our conceptions of literature, history, scripture, and even God.

---

[108] Brad E. Kelle, 'Dealing with the Trauma of Defeat', p. 484.

CHAPTER 2.
LAMENTATIONS: LITERARY AND HISTORICAL CONSIDERATIONS

INTRODUCTION

In this chapter, following brief remarks regarding Lamentations' authorship and date, I will discuss various literary features of the book, including the poet, the narrator, and personification. The main thrust of this chapter is to explore the nature and extent of the sixth century BCE Neo-Babylonian attacks on Judah and Jerusalem. These attacks and their aftermaths have significant implications for reading the book of Lamentations as post-traumatic literature. Historical, archaeological, and biblical data provide the evidence for the traumatic events that likely informed the book's contents.

AUTHORSHIP AND DATE

Attempts to identify the author(s) of Lamentations with any certainty are perplexing pursuits.[1] The history of scholarship on this aspect of the book demonstrates the validity of this statement—it is impossible to establish Lamentations' authorship definitively.[2]

---

[1] Some scholars have bracketed such questions and have chosen to read Lamentations without references to historical critical questions. See Paul Joyce, 'Sitting Loose to History: Reading the Book of Lamentations Without Primary Reference to its Original Historical Setting', in *In Search of True Wisdom* (Sheffield: Sheffield Academic Press, 1999), pp. 246–262.

[2] For a useful overview of the difficulties associated with determining the authorship of Lamentations see, e.g., Paul R. House, *Lamentations*, pp. 283–303.

Determining the precise date of the composition of the book of Lamentations is just as precarious as establishing the book's author(s). There is a general consensus among biblical scholars that the most plausible date for its composition is between 586 BCE, its *terminus a quo*, and 520 BCE, its *terminus ad quem*.[3] Historically, most scholars have dated the poems sometime shortly after Jerusalem's destruction.[4] However, some recent scholars have argued that the poems were most likely written several decades after Jerusalem's fall.[5] Others have questioned the possibility of identifying specific historical referents in Lamentations and, by extension, establishing its precise date of composition.[6] Whether immediately following, or several decades after, the 586 BCE Babylonian assault on Judah and Jerusalem, I accept the sixth century BCE as the most plausible period for the book's composition, and Judah as its likely provenance.[7]

THE POET

I follow the lead of scholars like Dobbs-Allsopp in affirming the essential unity of the book, presupposing that it is the work of a single author or editor.[8] The book's likely author was knowledgeable about ancient Israel's worship practices and traditions regarding the temple.[9] It also seems plausible, as Rainer Albertz has argued, that the poet responsible for Lamentations represents a group(s)

---

[3] See Westermann, *Lamentations*, pp. 24–55; House, *Lamentations*, pp. 283–303. Some scholars have rejected this consensus. See, for example, S. T. Lachs, 'The Date of Lamentations V', pp. 46–56.

[4] See Westermann's summary of scholarship on this issue in *Lamentations*, pp. 54–55, 61–63.

[5] See Berlin, *Lamentations*, pp. 33–36.

[6] See Iain W. Provan, *Lamentations*, pp. 7–19.

[7] See Berlin, *Lamentations*, pp. 33–36; and Dobbs-Allsopp, 'Linguistic Evidence for the Date of Lamentations', pp. 1–36. For a useful discussion of the Judean provenance of Lamentations, see J. Middlemas, *The Troubles of Templeless Judah*, pp. 177–184.

[8] See Dobbs-Allsopp, *Lamentations*, p. 5.

[9] House, *Lamentations*, p. 300.

with a 'nationalistic religious orientation'[10] prior to Jerusalem's fall. If the poet is a representative of this group, then he is genuinely shocked by Jerusalem's/Zion's (and Judah's) destruction, the capture and exile of the Davidic king, and the notion that YHWH (Zion's covenant partner) would actually inflict such gruesome wounds on his beloved people.[11] In addition, Lamentations' poet is likely very familiar with painful events associated with Jerusalem's demise and their aftermath. It is plausible to assume that the book's poet was a survivor of those events, or at least had access to survivors (secondary witness).[12]

It seems evident from a close reading of Lamentations that its poet was familiar with the tenor of some prophetic judgment traditions that asserted that YHWH would destroy Jerusalem, unless the people returned to covenant obedience. According to these traditions, Jerusalem's destruction would be a direct consequence of the people's unfaithfulness to YHWH. In addition, Lamentations' likely poet seems to have mastered the dirge and lament traditions and conventions of his time,[13] and was adept at mixing genres to create new forms.[14] Beyond these informed speculations, however, little more can be said about the poet of Lamentations.

The Narrator

While the precise identity of the author or poet of Lamentations remains a matter of speculation, the 'narrator(s)' of the book's poems is(are) ubiquitous.[15] J. L. Ska defines 'the narrator' as 'a func-

---

[10] Albertz, *A History of Israelite Religion in the Old Testament Period*, p. 376.

[11] Ibid.

[12] House, *Lamentations*, p. 300.

[13] Nancy C. Lee has identified a female poet as one of the dominant voices (singers) in Lamentations (See Lee, *The Singers of Lamentations: Cities Under Siege, From Ur to Jerusalem to Sarajevo*, pp. 53–73).

[14] House, *Lamentations*, p. 300.

[15] It is possible that there are multiple narrators in the poems. By 'narrator' I am referring to the dominant poetic voice in the poems that readers often conflate with the voice of the poet.

tion, a rôle, or a "voice"'.[16] The narrator is the *voice* that tells the story.[17] In the book of Lamentations, the narrator provides the descriptions or depictions of the plight of the sufferers, whether Zion, an individual or group, or a survivor-community. In Lamentations 1 and 4, the narrator's descriptions of the sufferers' predicament are cast exclusively in the third person.[18] In Lamentations 2, the narrator uses both third person and first person forms to describe and respond to the sufferers' plight. Lamentations 3 includes the voices of an individual sufferer who narrates his personal tragedies (Lam 3:1–24, 52–66), a sufferer who narrates his personal anguish over the fate of his city (Lam 3:48–51), and a community stand-in who speaks on behalf of a suffering community (Lam 3:40–47). The narrative voice of Lamentations 5 is communal—a representative speaks on behalf of the suffering community. For simplicity, I use the singular term 'narrator', rather than the plural narrators in my discussion of this role or function in the poems.

PERSONIFICATION

Lamentations teems with noteworthy poetic features; more specifically, it is ancient religious poetry. Therefore, any meaningful interpretation of this book must reckon with its poetic features. While a

---

[16] J. L. Ska, *'Our Fathers Have Told Us': Introduction to the Analysis of Hebrew Narratives*, p. 44. See also G. Genette, *Figures III*, pp. 259–265. For a detailed discussion of the role of the 'narrator' in narratives, see P. C. Hogan, *Narrative Discourse: Authors and Narrators in Literature, Film, and Art*, pp. 24–30, 37–46. For an analysis of this role in poetry, see T. R. Austin, *Poetic Voices: Discourse Linguistics and the Poetic Text*, pp. 96–135. In this study I define narrator as the 'voice' or 'speaker' in the poems who tells the story. The narrator exists in the world of the poem.

[17] Ska, *"Our Fathers Have Told Us,"* pp. 44.

[18] Ska notes that it is a little more difficult to discover the narrator in stories told in the third person (Ibid). In such instances, distinctions between the author and the narrator can be blurred. I use the term 'poet' to refer to the author(s)/editor(s) who wrote and or compiled the poems, and the term 'narrator' to refer to speaking voices in each poem that are distinct from the voices of personified Zion (see discussion below) and other entities, persons or groups that are clearly identified in the poems.

thorough analysis of the book's poetry lies beyond the scope of this study, certain prominent poetic features are crucial for my reading of Lamentations in this study.

Personification is one prominent poetic trope in Lamentations that functions within a trauma-informed reading of the book.[19] As a rhetorical device, personification attributes human characteristics or qualities, including thoughts and emotions, to inanimate/non-human objects. Thus, personification is a type of metaphor and/or simile.

Personification, Metaphor, and Other Tropes

The study of metaphors, similes, and other tropes is a complex field within the disciplines of literary studies.[20] However, Janet M. Soskice's 'interanimation' theory of metaphor suffices for the purposes of this study.[21] Soskice defines metaphor as 'that figure of speech whereby we speak about one thing in terms which are seen to be suggestive of another'.[22] Based on this definition, speaking about inanimate things in terms that are seen to be suggestive of humans and their qualities is often metaphorical. For example, metaphors like 'Lonely sits the city' (Lam 1:1aα) and 'Zion's roads

---

[19] For a summary of other poetic features of the book of Lamentations see Hillers, *Lamentations* (1992), pp. 15–31. For detail analysis of the contours of Hebrew verse in Lamentations, see F. W. Dobbs-Allsopp, 'The Enjambing Line in Lamentations: A Taxonomy (Part 1)', pp. 219–239; and Dobbs-Allsopp, 'The Effects of Enjambment in Lamentations (Part 2)', pp. 370–385. For an excellent discussion of the use of personification in biblical literature, see Joseph R. Dodson, *The 'Power' of Personification: Rhetorical Purpose in the Book of Wisdom and the Letter to the Romans*.

[20] See, e.g., K. P. Darr, *Isaiah's Vision and the Family of God*, pp. 13–35. For an extensive discussion of the use of metaphors in the Hebrew Bible, see P. van Hecke, ed., *Metaphors in the Hebrew Bible*. This collection contains several essays on the use of metaphors in the book of Lamentations, e.g., A. Labahn, 'Wild Animals and Chasing Shadows: Animal Metaphors in Lamentations as Indicators for Individual Threat', pp. 67–97; and G. Eidevall, 'Spatial Metaphors in Lamentations 3:1–9', pp. 133–137.

[21] See J. M. Soskice, *Metaphor and Religious Language*, p. 15.

[22] Ibid.

mourn' (Lam 1:4aα) are personifications, as a city does not literally sit lonely, and roads do not mourn. Note, however, that while personifications are always tropic, not all metaphors and similes are personifications.[23] For example, the sufferer in Lamentations 3 describes YHWH as 'a bear lying in wait' and 'a lion in hiding' (Lam 3:10). The sense of these metaphors is that the sufferer has experienced YHWH as a predator, and not a protector (cf. Psalm 23). These metaphors are not personifications. Rather, the references to 'bear' and 'lion' are consistent with their typical animalistic qualities.

Personification and Allegory

Another trope that is related to, but distinct from, personification is allegory. An allegory is an extended metaphor.[24] Joseph R. Dodson notes that an allegory may consist of 'multiple personifications [or metaphors] sustained for a paragraph and beyond'.[25] Thus, personifications can appear in allegories, but not all allegories contain personifications.[26] 'Daughter Zion' (that is, Jerusalem, Judah's capital city) is the most prominent personification in the book of Lamentations. Personifications of Jerusalem extend through several verses, particularly in Lamentations 1, 2 and 4. Based on Dodson's definition of allegory, the multiple, sustained personifications of Zion in these chapters are allegorical.

The Purposes of Personifications

In his analysis of the use of personification, Dodson highlights six primary purposes of this rhetorical device: decorate or amplify; educate or clarify; motivate or manipulate; expose the cause of something; provide new insight; and deflect attention from difficult topics.[27] The central rhetorical thrust of the dominant personifications of Zion in Lamentations is to motivate or manipulate. Through various personifications of Zion, the poet seeks to per-

---

[23] Dodson, *The 'Powers' of Personification*, p. 34.

[24] Ibid., pp. 34–35.

[25] Ibid., p. 35.

[26] See ibid.

[27] Ibid., pp. 41, 42–50.

suade YHWH and other observers—including ancient and modern readers and hearers of this text—to pay attention to, and join in solidarity with, the sufferers whom Zion represents, speaks for, and with whom *she* identifies. The graphic depictions of personified Zion's anguish heightens the persuasive power of the book of Lamentations.[28] As Delbert R. Hillers rightly argues, the book is not simply concerned with the plight of a fallen nation, a survivor, or an entire group of survivors; rather 'a greater person…is in anguish: Zion, the city of God, the community of the elect, who in her historical being is not identical with those alive at any one time'.[29]

Personifications of Zion in Lamentations

Personifications of Zion in Lamentations are not unified or consistent; rather, the poet develops varied representations of the destroyed city and its inhabitants. In Lam 1:1, for example, the poet personifies the city as a lonely woman who is 'like a widow' (כְּאַלְמָנָה [*kĕʾalmānâ*]). The personified city is depicted as abandoned by her 'friends', conquered by her 'foes', and bereft of 'comforters' (Lam 1:2–5). The text also portrays this lonely woman-city as a mother whose children have been captured (Lam 1:5). Zion as mother also appears in Lam 1:11, 16; 2:19; and 4:2. Personified Zion refers to her children as 'my first-born sons' (Lam 1:15) and 'my maidens and my youth' (Lam 1:18; cf. 2:21). In addition to woman, widow, and bereaved mother, Zion is also depicted as a blameworthy woman (Lam 1:5, 8, 14, 20, 22; 2:14).

Furthermore, personified Zion is a 'female' city, a geographical entity, with political and cultic functionaries—'leaders', 'priests', and 'elders' (Lam 1:6, 19; 2:6, 9)—and cultic appurtenances—'sanctuary' and 'altar' (Lam 1:10; 2:6–7). As a city, Zion has 'gates', 'walls', 'streets', and other physical structures (Lam 1:4; 2:5, 7–9, 18; 4:11–12). Thus, personified Zion (as trope) is also a city (literally, the city of Jerusalem)—a geographical and structural entity with

[28] See D. A. Bosworth, 'Daughter Zion and Weeping in Lamentations 1–2', pp. 217–237; and C. R. Mandolfo, *Daughter Zion Talks Back to the Prophets: A Dialogic Theology of the Book of Lamentations*, pp. 79–102.

[29] Hillers, *Lamentations* (1992), pp. 79–80.

inhabitants, political functionaries, and cultic fixtures. Zion is also a woman (likened to a widow), a mother bereaved of at least some of her children, a friend, and a culpable woman.

Additional human characteristics are also ascribed to Zion in Lamentations. Zion weeps and mourns (Lam 1:2, 16; 2:19),[30] and she has body parts—cheeks, bones, hands, and feet (Lam 1:2; 2:13–14, 17; 2:19). Zion can feel lonely (Lam 1:1), she is sensitive to derision from her enemies (Lam 1:9), she feels anguish (Lam 1:12), and she acknowledges personal culpability (Lam 1:20). In Lamentations, Zion is not simply spoken *about* or *to*; Zion speaks in her own voice (Lam 1:9c, 11c–16, 18–22; 2:20–22).[31]

While the foregoing discussion is not an exhaustive analysis of the various personifications of Zion in Lamentations, it allows us to draw a few preliminary conclusions. First, personifications of Jerusalem/Zion in Lamentations are not consistent or unified. The poet depicts several different portraits of Zion: she is woman-city, like a widow, a bereaved mother, a mother in deep anguish, and a destroyed city. Personified Zion represents, depicts, voices, and embodies the painful fate of a city and its inhabitants. Second, the use of female tropes to personify Zion heightens the book's emotional impact. As woman and mother, Zion is both vulnerable and resilient. Her person, body, and children are sites of trauma in the book of Lamentations. What she says and does bears the imprint of the traumatic experiences of her children (inhabitants).

The Meanings of bat X/bĕtûlat bat X *in Lamentations*

Within the context of the foregoing discussion of personifications in Lamentations, we must examine the meanings of phrases like בַּת־צִיּוֹן [*bat ṣîyōn*] ('daughter of Zion'), בַּת־יְהוּדָה [*bat yĕhûdāh*]

[30] For an analysis of the rhetorical function of the personification of Zion as a weeping woman in Lamentations see Bosworth, 'Daughter Zion and Weeping in Lamentations 1–2'. For an analysis of the motif of weeping goddess in ancient Near Easter city laments see F. W. Dobbs-Allsopp, *Weep, O Daughter Zion: A Study of the City-Lament Genre in the Hebrew Bible*, pp. 75–90. In Lamentations the city is personified as a weeping woman.

[31] See Mandolfo, *Daughter Zion*, pp. 79–102. See also M. J. Boda, C. J. Dempsey, and L. S. Flesher, eds, *Daughter Zion: Her Portrait, Her Response.*

('daughter of Judah'), בַּת יְרוּשָׁלָם [*bat yĕrûšālaīm*] ('daughter of Jerusalem'), בְּתוּלַת בַּת־צִיּוֹן [*bĕtûlat bat ṣîyōn*] ('maiden daughter of Zion'), בְּתוּלַת בַּת־יְהוּדָה [*bĕtûlat bat yĕhûdāh*] ('maiden daughter of Judah'), and בַּת־עַמִּי [*bat ʿammî*] ('daughter of my people') in the book. All of these phrases function metaphorically to refer either to Zion, the geographic entity (the city of Jerusalem)[32] or to personified Zion, the mother-city and her children.[33] The distinction between these two usages of the *bat* X/*bĕtûlat bat* X phrases is sometimes blurred (see Lam 2:13–16). Ultimately, the *bat* X/*bĕtûlat bat* X phrases are best understood as a personified, geographical location. Since the *bat* X/*bĕtûlat bat* X epithets are used synonymously of personified Zion—they function metaphorically—they are best construed as expressions of the complex, composite personifications of Zion in Lamentations. These phrases continue the uses of female imagery that describe the fate of Judah, particularly Jerusalem, and its people.

Scholars disagree about the most suitable rendering of the *bat* X/*bĕtûlat bat* X epithets.[34] The forms of the *bat* X/*bĕtûlat bat* X phrases in Lamentations are grammatically in construct. However, the meanings of these epithets should not be determined strictly from their grammatical forms or syntactical relationships; rather, attention must be given to how these expressions function in their

---

[32] See Lamentations 2:1–10. For example, בַּת־צִיּוֹן [*bat ṣîyōn*] (2:1a, 4c, 8a, 10a) and בַּת־יְהוּדָה [*bat yĕhûdāh*] (2:2b, 5c) are used synonymously with 'Zion', the city (2:6b). Further 'Jacob' (2:2a, 3c) and 'Israel' (2:3a, 5a) are also used synonymously with 'Zion'. בַּת־עַמִּי [*bat ʿammî*] (2:11b) refers to inhabitants of בַּת־צִיּוֹן [*bat ṣîyōn*] (2:10a), that is, Jerusalem (2:10c).

[33] See Lamentations 2:13, 18. In addition, בַּת־צִיּוֹן [*bat ṣîyōn*] (1:6a) as personified city, is used synonymously with personified 'Jerusalem' (1:7–9b, 10–11b).

[34] For an overview of this debate see Michael H. Floyd, 'The Daughter of Zion Goes Fishing in Heaven', in *Daughter Zion: Her Portrait, Her Response*, pp. 177–200. See also, Floyd, 'Welcome Back, Daughter of Zion', pp. 484–504; and J. A. Dearman, 'Daughter Zion and Her Place in God's Household', pp. 144–159. See W. F. Stinespring, 'No Daughter of Zion: A Study of the Appositional Genitive in Hebrew Grammar', pp. 133–141; Hillers, *Lamentations* (1992), p. 31; Provan, *Lamentations*, p. 41.

literary contexts within the book of Lamentations. Since the phrases are typically used synonymously with personifications of 'the city' as a geographical entity, as well as a daughter, and a mother-city and her children, their meanings cannot be limited to one particular group or institution within Zion. Hence, I support the view that the nouns in *bat* X/*bĕtûlat bat* X epithets are best rendered appositionally. Furthermore, epithets highlight one of the important rhetorical functions of the personifications of Zion in Lamentations—the plight of Jerusalem's most vulnerable inhabitants.

The varied personifications of Zion in Lamentations allow her to identify with and give utterance to the tragic perils of children, mothers, wives, and other survivors in general, including male survivors—*all* of her children. She plays multiple roles. Her utterances are best characterized as polyphonic rather than monophonic. She speaks as a distressed and destitute woman (Lam 1:9c, 11c–13, 20–21), a distraught bereaved mother (Lam 1:16), a repentant yet defiant woman-city (Lam 1:18–22), and an intercessor (2:20–22). These female personifications of Zion serve to heighten the emotional impact, and highlight the sheer enormity, of the catastrophes that Zion and her children suffered during, and in the wake of Jerusalem's destruction. Daughter Zion, especially in Lamentations 1–2, gives voices to, defends, weeps for, intercedes for, and succors all of her children. She embodies their predicament; her children's trauma is her trauma.

THE SIX CENTURY BCE NEO-BABYLONIAN ASSAULTS ON JUDAH AND JERUSALEM

In 597 BCE the Neo-Babylonian empire, under the leadership of Nebuchadnezzar II (634–562 BCE), laid siege to Jerusalem. The Babylonians captured Jehoiachin, the Judean king, raided treasures from the temple, and exiled many of the city's elite citizens, including the king (see 2 Kings 24:16). Nebuchadnezzar then appointed Jehoiachin's uncle, Mattaniah, whom he renamed Zedekiah, as a puppet-king over the colony of Judah. Subsequently, Nebuchadnezzar responded to Zedekiah's ill-fated revolt by attacking Judah and laying siege to Jerusalem (2 Kings 25:1–2; Jer 39:1–3; 52:4–5; cf. Lam 2:20–22; 4:1–18). Ultimately, the Babylonians breached the city's wall (2 Kings 25:3–4; Ezek 4:1–2) and razed the city, burning its palatial buildings and temple complex. 2 Kings 25 describes with surprising brevity the traumatic events associated with Jerusalem's demise,[35] including the severe famine (v. 3; see Jer 52:6; see also Lam 1:11, 19; 2:11–12, 19–20; 4:4–5, 9–10; 5:9–10), breaching of its walls (v.4), capture of the Davidic king, execution of his sons (vs 5–7; cf. Jer 52:7–11; cf. Lam 1:3, 6; 2:2; 4:19–20), razing and torching of palatial buildings (v. 9; cf. Jer 52:13; cf. Lam 2:3–5, 7; 4:11), destruction of the city's walls (v. 10; cf. Jer 52:7; cf. Lam 2:7–9), forced deportation of the remaining elite (vs 11; Jer 39:9–0; cf. Lam 1:1, 3, 5, 18; 2:9, 14; 4:22), massacre of religious and political leaders (vs 18–21; Jer 39:6; cf. Lam 1:15; 2:20; 5:12), and plunder and destruction of the temple complex (vs 13–17; Jer 51:51; cf. Lam 1:10; 2:6–7).[36]

Regarding Jerusalem's destruction, Paul R. House posits that from a historical-political perspective, the city was not completely innocent. In the years leading up to the 586 BCE debacle, Judah's political leaders were politically fickle, vacillating between allegiances to super powers like Assyria, Babylon, and Egypt to further their own interests. Furthermore, House avers, 'The fact of the city's destruction indicates that Jerusalem played a dangerous political game and lost that game, having angered allies and deadly foes in

---

[35] See discussion by Janzen, *The Violent Gift*, p. 1–7.

[36] Following the 586 BCE destruction of Jerusalem, the Babylonians appointed Gedaliah, son of Ahikam, as governor over the now destroyed colony (2 Kings 25:22; Jer 39:14; 40:7). In about 580 B.C.E., Gedaliah was assassinated at Mizpah (2 Kings 25:25; Jer 41:2–3), an apparent political and worship center after Jerusalem's fall (Jer 40:8–12; 41:5). In response to Gedaliah's assassination, the Babylonians may have again attacked Judah and inflicted additional wounds on the region. See Betlyon, 'Neo-Babylonian Military Operations Other than War', p. 267; Ephraim Stern, *Archaeology of the Land of the Bible, Vol. II: The Assyrian, Babylonian, and Persian Periods (732–332 BCE)*, pp. 306–307, 321–322; and Oded Lipschits, *The Fall and Rise of Jerusalem: Judah under Babylonian Rule*, pp. 109–118. Lipschits discusses the status of Mizpah and Jerusalem after the sixth century Neo-Babylonian assaults.

the process'.[37] Consequently, many of Jerusalem's innocent citizens suffered as a result of the poor political policies of its leaders.[38] While I agree with House's historical-political analysis of events surrounding the 586 BCE fall of Judah, Lamentations is best read through a religeo-psychological lens. It is fair to assume that the ancient Judeans who survived those traumatic events perceived them through religious and psychological lenses, rather than strictly historical-political lenses. The destruction of Jerusalem was YHWH's doing; and it resulted in extreme anguish.

Drawing from archaeology of the Levant, modern disaster studies and other disciplines, biblical scholars have sought to reconstruct the impact and extent of events associated with Jerusalem's downfall.[39] Albertz refers to these events as a 'national catastrophe'.[40] Elsewhere, he uses 'incalculable catastrophe' to describe the tragedies Judeans suffered during this period. [41] Examining the archaeological data for certain important Judean cities, towns, and villages from the post-586 BCE period, B. Oded notes that they 'suffered violent destruction'.[42] J. W. Betlyon refers to those as-

---

[37] P. R. House, 'Outrageous Demonstrations of Grace: The Theology of Lamentations', in *Great is Thy Faithfulness: Reading Lamentations as Sacred Scripture*, ed. R. Parry and H. A. Thomas, p. 38.

[38] Ibid., p. 39.

[39] See G. N. Knoppers, *et al*, eds., *Exile and Restoration Revisited: Essays on the Babylonian and Persian Periods in Memory of Peter R. Ackroyd*; H. M. Barstad, *The Myth of the Empty Land: A Study in the History and Archaeology of Judah during the "Exilic" Period*; Avraham Faust, *Judah in the Neo-Babylonian Period: The Archaeology of Desolation.*

[40] Albertz, *A History of Israelite Religion in the Old Testament Period*, p. 370.

[41] Albertz, *Israel in Exile*, p. 139.

[42] B. Oded, 'Where is the "Myth of the Empty Land" to be Found: History versus Myth', in *Judah and the Judeans in the Neo-Babylonian Period*, p. 66. See also David S. Vanderhooft, *The Neo-Babylonian Empire and Babylon in the Latter Prophets*, pp. 106–110; and Vanderhooft, 'Babylonian Strategies of Imperial Control in the West: Royal Practice and Rhetoric', p. 251.

saults as causing 'massive destruction'.[43] In similar fashion, O. Lipschits discusses the 'severity of the collapse' evident in the archaeological data for several Judean settlements, especially Jerusalem, from the end of the Iron Age (early sixth century BCE).[44] These descriptions of Judah's and Jerusalem's woes during the Neo-Babylonian period represent a general consensus among biblical scholars that events of this nature were likely traumatic for many of the Judeans who survived them.[45]

The Nature and Extent of Judah's and Jerusalem's Sixth Century BCE Destruction

While there is general consensus that some survivors of the 586 BCE assaults on Judah and Jerusalem remained in their land (see 2 Kings 25:12, 22–24; Jer 40:5–12), disagreements persist regarding the precise nature and extent of the catastrophes. Some scholars have argued that while the Babylonian assaults resulted in extensive damage to Jerusalem and a few of its outlying towns and villages, life in other regions continued 'as usual'.[46] Other scholars have argued on the basis of archaeological evidence that a major collapse occurred in Judean society as a whole during the post-586 BCE period, though not all areas were affected equally.[47] Scholars on both sides of this issue affirm that Jerusalem suffered enormous

---

[43] J. W. Betlyon, 'Neo-Babylonian Military Operations Other Than War in Judah and Jerusalem', in *Judah and the Judeans*, p. 266.

[44] O. Lipschits, 'Demographic Changes in Judah between the Seventh and the Fifth Centuries BCE', in *Judah and the Judeans in the Neo-Babylonian Period*, p. 340. See also A. Faust, *Judah in the Neo-Babylonian Period*, pp. 167–207.

[45] See Poser, *Das Ezechielbuch als Trauma-Literatur*, pp. 121–162.

[46] See, Barstad, *The Myth of the Empty Land*, p. 42; Barstad, *History and the Hebrew Bible: Studies in Ancient Israelite and Ancient Near Eastern Historiography*, p. 132; Lipsichits, 'Demographic Changes in Judah between the Seventh and the Fifth Centuries BCE', pp. 360–366; C. E. Carter, 'Ideology and Archaeology in the Neo-Babylonian Period: Excavating Text and Tell', pp. 301–222; and J. Middlemas, *The Troubles of Templeless Judah*, pp. 24–71.

[47] See Ephraim Stern, *Archaeology of the Land of the Bible*, pp. 308–309.

damage during these Babylonian attacks on Judah. The significance and extent of Jerusalem's destruction feature prominently in 2 Kings 25, Jeremiah 39 and 52.[48] These accounts indicate that the Babylonians mercilessly ravaged Judah's holy city, home to YHWH's sacred shrine, as well as the royal palace and administrative buildings of the Davidic kings. Thus, even if there were no substantial material evidence for widespread destruction, significant depopulation, or massive loss of life during the sixth century BCE in regions beyond Jerusalem, the city's collapse likely caused significant consternation and anguish among some survivors. Bewilderment over Jerusalem's fall and its religious implications seem to overwhelm Lamentations' poet and the community for which he speaks (see Lam 1:4–5, 10; 2:1–9; 5:19–22). In addition to the anguish over Jerusalem's fall, Lamentations' poet depicts post-catastrophe existence as particularly traumatic (Lam 1:11; 2:11–12; 4:4–5, 9–10; 5:1–5, 11–16). While it is impossible to definitely reconstruct daily life for survivors in post-586 BCE Judah and Jerusalem, archaeology continues to contribute to our knowledge of the period.

The Nature and Extent of Judah's Destruction

Based on his survey of relevant archaeological evidence, Ephraim Stern asserts that in the wake of Babylonian domination of Palestine during the sixth century BCE, there was '*total* destruction and devastation of *all* the main cities that had flourished during the Assyrian period'.[49] He further notes that with the exceptions of Phoenicia, Benjamin, and Transjordan, *all* of Palestine's cities lay in ruins by the end of the Babylonian period.[50] Massive destruction layers in the archaeological records mark this era.[51] While Stern might have overstated the implications of the actual archaeological evidence, his conclusions highlight the significant devastation that

---

[48] See also Pss 74, 79, 102; Isa 63:7–64:11. Like Lamentations, these biblical laments seem reminiscent of the realities of post-586 BCE Judah.

[49] E. Stern, *Archaeology and the Land of the Bible*, p. 309 (emphasis added).

[50] Ibid.

[51] Ibid.

befell many Judean cities, towns, and villages during the sixth century BCE.[52]

The Babylonian attacks seem to have disrupted trade, economic, and prosperity patterns in Judah.[53] Several sites reveal significant social and cultural breaks from institutions of the preceding period (Iron Age).[54] In fact, as Vanderhooft argues, the archaeological record of post-586 BCE Palestine reflects a sharp, if not total, break from the prior period.[55] The Babylonians caused extensive destruction in Judah, and they made no attempts to rebuild what they had destroyed.[56] The Neo-Babylonian assaults seem also to have resulted in significant population decline and dramatic demographic shifts.[57]

Based on his evaluation of the archaeological evidence, Faust argues that about two-thirds of the population of Judah disappeared between the Iron Age (*ca.* 1200–586 BCE) and the Persian Period (*ca.* 539–332 B.C.E.).[58] This demographic collapse, Faust

---

[52] See Vanderhooft, 'Babylonian Strategies of Imperial Control in the West', p. 253.

[53] Vanderhooft, 'Babylonian Strategies', p. 255.

[54] Faust, *Judah in the Neo-Babylonian Period*, p. 233.

[55] Vanderhooft, 'Babylonian Strategies of Imperial Control in the West', p. 256.

[56] Betlyon, 'Neo-Babylonian Military Operation Other Than War in Judah and Jerusalem', p. 266; See also Stern, *Archaeology of the Land of the Bible*, pp. 324–350.

[57] See Lipschits, *The Fall and Rise of Jerusalem*, pp. 185–271; Lipschits, 'Demographic Changes in Judah between the Seventh and the Fifth Centuries B.C.E.,' pp. 323–376.

[58] Faust, *Judah in the Neo-Babylonian Period*, p. 131. Both Barstad and Lipschits have argued for less drastic population decline in Judah as a whole. They have also advanced the view that life in Judah continued uninterrupted and that the Babylonian assaults primarily affected life in Jerusalem. See Barstad, *The Myth of the Empty Land*; and Libsichts, *The Fall and Rise of Jerusalem*. While I agree with scholars like Faust, Valkama, Oded, and Vanderhooft, who have argued that Barstad and Lipschits have overstated their claims of widespread continuity of life in Judah after the Baby-

avers, probably resulted from mass deportations to Mesopotamia, death from the wars, epidemics and famine during and after the wars, slaughters after the sieges, and the absence of those who were either deported or became refugees in other geographical regions.[59] The resulting collapse, Stern asserts, 'persisted despite the efforts of those who remained behind and those who slowly drifted back'.[60] He further opines that the existence of the survivors must have been so rudimentary that 'it has proved extremely difficult to find its traces in the material remains'.[61] While it is possible that both Faust and Stern overstate the implications of the evidence in order to conform with certain biblical descriptions of this period,[62] their analyses of the evidence, at the very least, support the view that the Babylonian assaults on Judah and Jerusalem resulted in significant experiences of rupture for some survivors. Lamentations' poet depicts and envisions precisely such a community—one that has experienced a sharp rupture between pre- and post-catastrophe conditions.

In addition to significant population decline, the Neo-Babylonian assaults on Judah and Jerusalem likely resulted in the collapse of their economic, social, and cultural structures.[63] Stern notes that the assaults and related factors resulted in 'total economic collapse'.[64] A survey of affected towns and cities shows that many were entirely destroyed, while others were inhabited by only

---

lonian sixth century BCE assaults, establishing the validity of either position (if this is even possible) is not critical for my argument in this study.

[59] Faust, *Judah in the Neo-Babylonian Period*, p. 141. Faust analyzes these features of population decline in the context of ancient warfare (Ibid., pp. 141–143); see also Stern, *Archaeology of the Land of the Bible*, p. 323.

[60] Stern, *Archaeology of the Land of the Bible*, p. 323.

[61] Ibid.

[62] See discussions in Carter, 'Ideology and Archaeology in the Neo-Babylonian Period: Excavating Text and Tell', in *Judah and Judeans in the Neo-Babylonian Period*, p. 301–322.

[63] Stern, *Archaeology of the Land of the Bible*, p. 323; see also Lipschits, *The Fall and Rise of Jerusalem*, p. 69.

[64] Stern, *Archaeology of the Land of the Bible*, p. 323.

the poorer survivors. There are also indications of several new settlements during this period.[65] Many survivors likely lost their pre-catastrophe livelihoods due to the massive destruction and disruption of economic infrastructures. Faust argues that no archaeological evidence for continuity of international trade during the Neo-Babylonian period exists.[66] In addition, there is no evidence of a centralized economy during this time.[67] Survivors probably subsisted on basic agriculture.[68] With the exile of a significant number of Judah's nobility (2 Kings 25:11–12; Jer 39:10; 52:15–16), some survivors gained access to better land (with possible attending economic advantages).[69] Significant social and cultural changes likely accompanied these economic changes.[70] Faust argues that the noteworthy decline and ultimate cessation of building new Judahite tombs and four-room (pillared) houses during the Persian period was probably the result of the significant population decline.[71] Such drastic population decline likely resulted in 'a social and cultural disintegration'.[72]

The Nature and Extent of Jerusalem's Destruction

Excavations of sites in Jerusalem and its environs indicate that the city was almost completely destroyed during the sixth century BCE. In fact, Lipschits and other scholars have argued that Jerusalem was totally destroyed and remained completely desolate during the Neo-Babylonian period until the early Persian period.[73] Evidence

---

[65] Ibid.

[66] Faust, *Judah in the Neo-Babylonian Period*, pp. 73–92; see also Vanderhooft, 'Babylonian Strategies of Imperial Control in the West', p. 255.

[67] Faust, *Judah in the Neo-Babylonian Period*, p. 237.

[68] Ibid.

[69] Ibid.

[70] Ibid., pp. 93–117; see also Valkama, 'What do Archaeological Remains Reveal', pp. 56–59.

[71] Faust, *Judah in the Neo-Babylonian Period*, p. 106.

[72] Ibid.

[73] Lipschits, *The Fall and Rise of Jerusalem*, pp. 210–218; Lipschits, 'Demographic Changes in Judah', pp. 326–334.

for continuity of life in the city after its demise is extremely sparse[74] and seems to indicate that Jerusalem (and its environs) suffered near complete destruction. The discovery of destroyed buildings and remains of sections of the city's walls, a layer of ash (destruction layer), along with Babylonian arrowheads are reminiscent of some aspects of the biblical representations of the city's destruction (2 Kings 25:8–10; Jer 39:1–2, 8; 52:12–14).[75] Citing the conclusions of earlier archaeologists, Lipschits asserts, 'Jerusalem was wretchedly poor, not just in the period after the destruction, but also at the height of the time of the return to Zion'.[76]

Drastic depopulation due to mass deportations, the ravaging effects of famine and pestilence, casualties and collateral damage from barbaric wars, mass executions, and the self-imposed exodus of numerous refugees are all factors that likely led to the significant decline in Jerusalem's population. Survivors seem to have formed a quasi-government in Mizpah (Tell en-Naşbeh) after the city fell. The heart of the Southern Kingdom of Judah, Jerusalem, was completely razed to the ground, a reality that no doubt challenged the core of the nation's religious and political identities for many survivors. In addition, after the city's destruction, the Babylonians appointed Gedaliah son of Ahikam as governor over those remaining in Judah (see 2 Kings 25:22–26; Jeremiah 40–41).

Although the Babylonians appointed Gedaliah son of Ahikam, a pro-Babylonian, non-Davidic ruler, as governor of Judah after they destroyed the city, this political arrangement was short lived. Ishmael, a member of the Judean royal household, assassinated Gedaliah early in his governorship (2 Kings 25:25; Jer 41:2). Ishmael also killed and captured many of the Judeans who were with Gedaliah at Mizpah (Jer 41:3; 41:14, 16). Beyond these references to the chaos and anarchy that prevailed in the aftermath of Jerusa-

---

[74] See Faust, *Judah in the Neo-Babylonian Period*, pp. 24, 45–48; see also G. Barkay, 'The Redefinition of Archaeological Periods: Does the Date 588/586 BCE Indeed Mark the End of the Iron Age', in *Biblical Archaeology Today: Proceedings of the Second International Congress on Biblical Archaeology, Jerusalem, June-July 1990*, pp. 106–109.

[75] See Stern, *Archaeology of the Land of the Bible*, p. 309.

[76] Lipschits, *The Fall and Rise of Jerusalem*, p. 329.

lem's demise, there is no evidence that the Babylonians proscribed or encouraged activities (religious or otherwise) in or around Jerusalem.[77] Ultimately, in the wake of the Neo-Babylonian assaults, Judah's religious and political center was decimated, and Davidic kingship ended in Judah,[78] though a Davidic king (Jehoiachin) remained alive in Babylon for a time (2 Kings 24:12). Lamentations presupposes and alludes to these traumatic realities of post-586 BCE Jerusalem.

Intrinsic Evidence and *Historical* Allusions

Certain intrinsic features and allusions in the book of Lamentations bolster the view that the post-586 BCE period is the most plausible background for its composition in its final form. Though often couched in stereotypical, tropic, and hyperbolic language, these features and allusions signal certain realities that are consistent with what is generally known about conditions in Judah, particularly Jerusalem, during the sixth century BCE. The book's poems seem particularly reminiscent of the aftermath of the Babylonian assaults on Jerusalem. The poet appears to have intimate knowledge of the experiences associated with the siege of the city (Lam 2:20–22; 4:1–18), its destruction (Lam 2:7–9), the demise of the temple along with its institutions and services (Lam 1:10; 2:6–7), the exile of significant numbers of the nation's inhabitants, especially those in and near Jerusalem (Lam 1:1, 3, 5, 18; 2:9, 14; 4:22), the capture of the Davidic king (Lam 1:3, 6; 2:2; 4:19–20), Judah's experience of vassalage (Lam 5:3–9), and the perils of living during and in the aftermath of the city's destruction (Lam 1:11, 19; 2:11–12, 19–20; 4:4–5, 9–10; 5:9–10). While the Hebrew Bible records other instances in which ancient Israel or Judah suffered military defeat and/or experienced the debilitating realities of siege warfare (see 2 Kings 6:24–33), the elements of extreme violence that Lamentations' poems

---

[77] See Vanderhooft, *The Neo-Babylonian Empire and Babylon in the Latter Prophets*; Vanderhooft, 'Babylonian Strategies of Imperial Control in the West'.

[78] See Lipschits, *The Fall and Rise of Jerusalem*, p. 82. The accounts of Nehemiah, who surveyed the extent of the damage to Jerusalem some 130 years later, also affirm the extent of the city's collapse (Neh 2:13–15, 17).

allude to seem particularly redolent of events associated with Jerusalem's fall. This conclusion does not necessarily mean that the poems were composed from 'whole cloth' specifically in response to those events; rather, it suggests that those events served as the major traumatic impetus for the creation, redaction, collation, and ultimate shaping of these poems in (more or less) their final form. In addition, passages like Neh 2:13–17 indicate that more than a century after Jerusalem's demise, the city's walls and other structures still lay in ruins; and the traumatic effects of these realities were still felt by some descendants of individuals who survived the catastrophe.

Destruction and Desolation of the City

Readers of Lamentations cannot escape the conclusion that 'the city' (הָעִיר [*hāʿîr*]) has experienced a major catastrophe or tragedy (see Lam 1:3a, 19b, 2:11c, 15c). Its painful reversal of fortunes is evident in tropic depictions of the lamentable plight of 'Daughter Zion' (see Lam 1:6a; 2:13a, 18a), or 'Daughter Jerusalem' (see Lam 2:13b, 15b), or 'Daughter Judah' (Lam 2:2b) and 'her children' עולל Lam 1:5c; 2:11c, 19c; 4:4b; יונק Lam 2:11c; 4:4a; בן Lam 1:16c; 4:2). Zion is variously described as having 'collapsed' or being 'ruined' (Lam 2:11b, 13c; 3:47, 48; 4:10b). The city's fortifications have been 'demolished' (Lam 2:2b) and 'ruined' (Lam 2:5b), and its 'citadels' or 'palaces' have been 'devastated' (Lam 2:5b; cf. 2:7b; see 2 Kings 25:4, 9–10//Jer 52:7, 13–14; 39:2, 8). Even Zion's 'foundations' have been 'consumed' (Lam 4:11b). In addition, the city's gates have been 'deserted' (Lam 1:4b) and 'destroyed' (Lam 2:9a; cf. Neh 1:3; 2:3, 13–15). Ultimately, 'Mount Zion' itself is depicted as 'deserted' or left 'desolate' (Lam 5:18; cf. 1:4a; cf. Isa 64:9). Admittedly, the preceding depictions of Jerusalem's destruction are often metaphorical, stereotypical, and hyperbolic. As a result, it can be difficult to identify precise historical referents behind these depictions, including specific dates and events. At the very least, however, these depictions indicate that the texts presuppose that Jerusalem has suffered a significant tragedy.

Destruction by Conflagration

Numerous passages in Lamentations depict Zion's destruction using tropic language involving fire, or fire-related imagery.[79] For example, Lam 4:11 states:

> YHWH has expressed his (fiery) rage;
> He has poured out his burning חֲרוֹן [*ḥărôn*]) anger;
> He has kindled a fire in Zion,
> Which has consumed its foundations.

Zion's demise is depicted as the result of 'fire' אֵשׁ [*ʾēš*]) sent from above (Lam 1:13a). YHWH has acted like an enemy and destroyed Zion in a fit of fiery fury (see Lam 2:3a, c, 4b, and 6c). Similarly, other laments that scholars typically date to the post-586 BCE (pre-520 BCE) period[80] depict various aspects of Jerusalem's destruction as the result of conflagration (see Ps 74:7a, 8b; Isa 64:10b). Tropic depictions of Zion's demise utilizing fire-related imagery are consistent with certain historical details in descriptions of the 586 BCE Babylonian attacks on Jerusalem elsewhere in the Hebrew Bible (see 2 Kings 25:9//Jer 52:13; 39:8; cf. Neh 1:3; 2:3, 13). Thus, despite the use of metaphorical and stereotypical language in Lamentations' descriptions of Zion's demise, these poetic depictions certainly evoke certain historical features of the 586 BCE destruction of Jerusalem.

Exile/Captivity

Closely associated with Zion's misfortunes are references in Lamentations to exile or forced deportation (captivity) as one of the tragedies that befell the city's inhabitants. 'Exile' (גלה [*gālāh*]) or 'captivity' (שְׁבִי [*šĕbî*]) is also one reason for Jerusalem's depopulation. Using hyperbolic language, the poet asserts that 'Judah has

---

[79] For a discussion of the use of fire related metaphors and images in Lamentations, see A. Labahn, 'Fire from Above: Metaphors and Images of God's Actions in Lamentations 2:1–9', pp. 239–256.

[80] Scholars typically date the following laments to the post-586 BCE period: Psalms 74, 79, 89, 102, 106, 137, Isa 63:1—64:11. See J. Middlemas, *The Templeless Age*, pp. 35–45.

been deported' (Lam 1:3a) and 'her children have become captives' (Lam 1:5c). Similarly, Lam 1:18c asserts that Zion's maidens (בְּתוּלֹת [*bĕtûlōt*]) and first-born sons (בַּחוּר [*baḥûr*]) 'have gone into captivity' (שֶׁבִי [*šĕbî*]), 'Her king and her princes are among the nations' ('in exile;' Lam 2:9b). Provan observes that, based on available evidence, these depictions do not correspond to reality at any point in Judah's history.[81] That is, 'Judah as an entity' never went into exile, not even in 586 BCE.[82]

These depictions of the exile or captivity of Judah as an entity—the entire population—including *all* its maidens, young men, and leaders, stand in tension with other assertions in the text. For example, Lam 1:4bc, 11ab; 2:10, 12 suggest that people remained in Jerusalem, including maidens and officials, survivors who were not exiled (see 2 Kings 25:12; Jer 39: 10; 52:15).[83] Provan points to these tensions to draw attention to the 'demonstrably hyperbolic' language or the 'exaggeration [that] is apparent in the text'.[84] He concludes that the use of hyperbolic language renders historical reconstruction based solely on these texts problematic. Moreover, it is impossible to tie allusions in these texts to specific dates or particular events.[85] While I concede that Provan's conclusion and implied caution are valid (and necessary), demonstrably hyperbolic language does not necessarily equal demonstrably ahistorical language, or prove that the text is void of historical value.[86] I cite references to exile or captivity in Lamentations simply to indicate that exile of some Judeans was likely one of the traumatic realities that informed the composer of the book of Lamentations. Furthermore, exiles and other survivors had no way of knowing precisely how many were exiled. Survivors of such catastrophes, especially in ancient times, typically would not have had access to the bigger picture—the full extent of the tragedy.

---

[81] Provan, *Lamentations*, p. 6.

[82] Ibid.

[83] Ibid.

[84] Ibid.

[85] Ibid., p. 13.

[86] See Smith-Christopher, *A Biblical Theology of Exile*, pp. 96–104.

End of Religious Festivals and Other Temple Related Rituals

Another important reality that Lamentations presumes is the end of religious festivals and other rituals related to the temple. According to Lam 1:4a, pilgrims no longer attend religious festivals in Zion. YHWH has caused 'festival' (מוֹעֵד [*môʿēd*]) and 'Sabbath' (שַׁבָּת [*šabbāt*]) 'to be forgotten' in Zion (Lam 2:6b). These descriptions indicate that the poet presupposes a time when certain religious rituals have been discontinued or, as least, undergone severe disruption. Within the context of Lamentations, such a caesura is directly related to tragedies that the city has suffered. This rupture is consistent with the biblical, archaeological, and historical evidence for conditions in Jerusalem during the post-586 BCE period. Some cultic activities may have taken place at the site of the ruined temple after 586 BCE (see Jer 41:4–5): a day after the assassination of Gedaliah son of Ahikam, eighty men arrived from Shechem, Shiloh, and Samaria intending to perform some type of cultic mourning ritual.[87]

Destruction and/or Desecration of the Temple

Closely related to the interruption of religious festivals and rituals that Lamentations describes is the categorical assertion that the temple has been completely destroyed and its sanctity desecrated by foreigners (see Lam 1:10; 2:6a, 7; 2 Kings 25:9, 13–17//Jer 52:13, 17–22; see also Pss 74:7; 79:1a-b; Isa 63:18; 64:10). Thus, the book presupposes or remembers a time when Jerusalem's sacred shrine was ruined and despoiled. Admittedly, these circumstances are applicable to multiple historical referents, including the 167 BCE attack on Jerusalem and the desecration of its temple by Antiochus IV (2 Macc 5:11–17; 6:1–6). Nevertheless, it is unlikely that the book of Lamentations was composed in response to this later destruction of the temple.[88]

---

[87] See A. J. Nevins, 'When Was Solomon's Temple Burned Down? Reassessing the Evidence', pp. 8–9, and 6–7. Nevins posits an alternative interpretation of this episode.

[88] See Provan, *Lamentations*, p. 13.

Vassalage/Colony

Although Judah was a vassal (first under the Assyrians, and later under the Babylonians) for a long time prior to its fall, the book of Lamentations describes vassalage as one indication of Jerusalem's negative reversal of fortunes. The book highlights a period when David's descendants no longer ruled Judah (Lam 2:9b; 4:20), which is consistent with a post-586 BCE date. Zion's adversaries have become her masters (ראשׁ [*ro'š*]; Lam 1:5a). In fact, 'slaves' (עֲבָדִים [*ʿăbādîm*] now rule over her;[89] her people's 'heritage' (נַחֲלָה [*naḥălāh*]) has been passed to 'foreigners', and their dwellings to 'aliens' (Lam 5:2). Survivors of the tragedies that befell Zion must pay for basic necessities (Lam 5:4) and risk their lives to obtain food (Lam 5:9).

Conditions Consistent with Siege Warfare and its Aftermath

Lamentations preserves graphic depictions of horrific realities reminiscent of siege warfare and its traumatic aftermath. The book depicts the scarcity of food (Lam 1:11; 4:4; 5:9–10), survivors' ongoing struggles to sustain themselves (Lam 1: 20c; 4:9), the plight of women/mothers and children/infants, including references to cannibalism (Lam 2:11–12; 20b; 4:4, 10; 5:11), clinging to hope for assistance from ally nations (Lam 4:17), and ubiquitous, gruesome scenes of death (Lam 1:19b, 20c; 2:21; 3:43; 4:13b).

SUMMARY

Taken individually, the preceding 'evidence' and allusions from the book of Lamentations can reasonably be construed as indicative of a verity of potential historical referents. In fact, the book's survival

---

[89] Hillers asserts that the reference to 'slaves' is a derogative reference to the Babylonian officials, particularly the lower officials with whom the people came in contact (Hillers, *Lamentations* [1992], p. 164). Westermann suggest that the phrase refers to the suffering that survivors endured at the hand of occupying forces (Westermann, *Lamentations*, p. 214). It is also possible that the poet has Gedaliah in mind since he, his father, Ahikam, and his grandfather, Shaphan, were previously in the service of Davidic Kings (see, 2 Kings 22:3, 12).

is due, in part, to its malleability—it can be and has been read against the background of multiple historical catastrophes in both Jewish and Christian history.[90] Taken together, however, these textual details are consistent with what we can reasonably posit about life in sixth century BCE Judah, and especially Jerusalem, when the Babylonians dealt a lethal blow to Judah, razing its royal city and temple complex. Adding to the forced migration of a decade earlier (597 BCE), the Babylonians deported even more of Jerusalem's inhabitants. The long siege that preceded the breaching of the city's walls undoubtedly resulted in significant losses of life and livelihood.[91] The subsequent military assault brought additional loss of lives and indiscriminate destruction of property, decimating the city, and further endangering its surviving population.[92] Both during and after the siege, starvation and pestilence further ravaged survivors, especially in Jerusalem and its environs. The central economic, political, and religious structures and institutions that had supported the city collapsed in the wake of the Babylonian debacle, and Jerusalem's populace diminished significantly.

While not all towns and cities in Judah suffered the same (or similar) fate, events related to the destruction of Jerusalem and its effects were not simply tragic—they were painfully traumatic for many survivors. Although the book's language is demonstrably stereotypical, hyperbolic, and tropic, it likely presupposes historical conditions consistent with events and conditions in post-586 BCE Judah, particularly Jerusalem. Different groups of survivors would have interpreted and responded to these events and conditions in different ways. Nevertheless, Lamentations contains a graphic snapshot of the reactions and responses of at least some survivors, and it highlights the debilitating effects often associate with trauma and its aftermath.

---

[90] See Linafelt, *Surviving Lamentations*.

[91] For a brief overview of siege warfare in the Hebrew Bible see, T. R. Hobbs, *A Time for War: A Study of Warfare in the Old Testament*, pp. 177–181.

[92] See Boyd Seevers, *Warfare in the Old Testament: The Organization, Weapons, and Tactics of Ancient Near Eastern Armies*, pp. 255–257.

CHAPTER 3. RUPTURE IN THE BOOK OF LAMENTATIONS

INTRODUCTION

In the aftermath of trauma, survivors typically experience caesura or rupture in life, more specifically, in memory. This chapter explores interpretive implications of this aspect of traumatic experiences for reading the book of Lamentations. The book contains numerous structural complexities and anomalies, which push the limits of, and at certain points even fracture, the disciplining structures that the poet uses to convey some of the responses and reactions to traumatic events that inform the book. A close analysis of these poetic structures reveal several significant dramatic breaks, including seemingly erratic shifts in voice and breaks in logical sequence. The *ruptures* in the poems mirror and testify to trauma survivors' experiences of *rupture in life.*

RUPTURED FORMS: STRUCTURAL ANALYSIS OF THE BOOK OF LAMENTATIONS

As I have already argued, the devastating events associated with the sixth century BCE destruction of Jerusalem were world-shattering for many survivors. For those who remained in Judah, and especially Jerusalem's inhabitants, the city's physical destruction and the extensive loss of human life and livelihood were traumatic. In addition, the brutal effects of severe famine and pestilence and the forced deportation of many of the city's inhabitants and consequent disruption of familial and community ties created significant ruptures in the lives of many survivors. The reality of these ruptures intrudes in and registers its effects upon the literary structures and forms of the poems comprising the book of Lamentations.

Generic Considerations

The precise genres[1] of the five poems within the book of Lamentations remains a much debated topic in biblical scholarship, especially among form critics. Adele Berlin notes that the book resists 'neat genre categorizations'.[2] Claus Westermann argues that though some unanimity exists among scholars regarding the classifications of certain sections of Lamentations, these classifications rest on tenuous evidence.[3] Some of the poems, Westermann posits, deviate from expected patterns at critical points.[4] The challenge of determining a precise taxonomy(ies) for Lamentations reflects, more broadly, some of the inherent limitations of traditional form criticism (*Formgeschichte* or *Gattungsgeschichte*).[5]

---

[1] Claus Westermann defines genre as 'a structured literary form characterized by a fixed sequence of motifs' (Westermann, *Lamentations*, p. 7). Peter Seitel provides an excellent analysis of how genre functions as a 'form-shaping ideology' that allows creators and critics to engage in 'dialogue with the collective wisdom of a tradition', and provides 'orienting frameworks' for 'both creation and interpretation' (Peter Seitel, *Powers of Genre*, pp. 3, 4).

[2] Adele Berlin, *Lamentations*, p. 24; see also Westermann, *Lamentations*, pp. 58–61; Provan, *Lamentations*, pp. 5–6. Hillers, reflecting on the challenges of genre classifications in Lamentations, suggests that form critical analysis provides 'relatively little help' for interpreting this book. Further, Hillers points to the resemblances between the book of Lamentations and Mesopotamian laments. He also notes that Lamentations may draw from what he calls the 'city-lament' traditions within ancient Israel's prophetic writings (Hillers, *Lamentations* [1992], pp. 32–39). F. W. Dobbs-Allsopp develops this idea of the city-lament genre in relation to the book of Lamentations in *Weep, O Daughter Zion.*

[3] Traditionally, some biblical scholars have argued that Lamentations 1, 2, and 4 reflect the *qînāh* or dirge genre. See Westermann, *Lamentations*, pp. 1–23.

[4] Westermann, *Lamentations*, p. 59.

[5] See John Barton, 'Form Criticism', pp. 838–841; M. A. Sweeney and E. Ben-Zvi, eds., *The Changing Face of Form Criticism for the Twenty-First Century.*

Hermann Gunkel (1862–1932), a seminal pioneer of form criticism, assumed that 'each piece of literature belonged to only one genre' (*Gattung*) stemming from a fixed setting in life (*Sitz im Leben*).[6] Thus, for Gunkel, an altered or modified genre was corrupt.[7] Contra Gunkel, many modern form critics, building on the insights of genre theorists like Mikhail M. Bakhtin and others, affirm the fluidity, adaptability, and flexibility of genres.[8] F. W. Dobbs-Allsopp argues that the boundaries between genres can be blurred or fuzzy.[9] Carleen R. Mandolfo posits, 'the intermixing and evolution of genres is a form of artistic expression, not corruption'.[10]

In recent decades, form critics advancing the work of Gunkel have also affirmed the close connections between genre (form) and context (life).[11] Nevertheless, insufficient attention has been given to the possible connections between the context (*generic matrix*) of Lamentations and the forms (*intrinsic genres*) of its five poems. The poems that comprise the book of Lamentations do not simply reflect new genres, mixed-genres, or even evolutions or modification

---

[6] Kenton L. Sparks, *Ancient Texts for the Study of The Hebrew Bible*, p. 6; see Hermann Gunkel, *The Psalms*, p. 10. For a detailed analysis of Gunkel's perspective on genre, see Buss, *Biblical Form Criticism in its Context*, pp. 207–262.

[7] See Buss, *Biblical Form Criticism*, pp. 255–256; Gunkel, *Water for a Thirsty Land*, pp. 32–37. Gunkel recognized the existence of mixed-genres.

[8] See Roland Boer, *Baktin and Genre Theory in Biblical Studies.*

[9] Dobbs-Allsopp, *Weep, O Daughter Zion*, pp. 18–19.

[10] Carleen R. Mandolfo, 'Dialogic Form Criticism: An Intertextual Reading of Lamentations and Psalms of Lament', p. 70. See also Dobbs-Allsopp, *Weep, O Daughter Zion*, pp. 17–22.

[11] See Buss, *Biblical Form Criticism*, p. 415. Gunkel emphasized the close relationship between the 'various types of cult songs' and the 'various situations in which the songs were sung' (Gunkel, *The Psalms*, pp. 10, 11–28. According to Kenton Sparks *generic matrix* is 'the sum total of all determinants and contingencies that result in the production of a verbal utterance or a written text; it is context in the widest possible sense' (Sparks, *Ancient Texts for the Study of the Hebrew Bible*, p. 10).

of older genres; [12] rather, these poems reflect the painful effects of caesura in life. The recognizable generic features in Lamentations bear the imprint of extreme suffering and its fracturing effects.[13] Biblical scholars have typically identified two dominant genres in the book: *qînāh* or dirge (funeral song); and communal lament.[14] Prominent features of Mesopotamian city-laments are also evident the book.[15] Before analyzing Lamentations' specific generic features, we turn to the relationships between generic forms and contents.

Form, Function, and Context

A genre both shapes (provides form for) and is shaped by context and function.[16] Peter Seitel's work on the powers of genre in his analysis of Haya oral literature informs how I understand the functions of genres in the book of Lamentations.[17] Seitel posits that, as orienting frameworks, genre not only orients texts to other texts,

---

[12] Berlin argues that Lamentation represents a 'new' genre, which she calls the 'Jerusalem Lament'. Other examples of this genre are Psalms 44, 68, 74, 79, 102, and 137 (Berlin, *Lamentations*, p. 25). See also Bergant, *Lamentations*, pp. 16–17; O'Connor, *Lamentations*, p. 1019. O'Connor states that 'the poems in Lamentations also draw on lament forms and funeral dirges and, in particular, on the lament over the fallen city'. Dobbs-Allsopp defends the view that Lamentations must be classified 'generically as a city lament' (Dobbs-Allsopp, *Weep, O Daughter Zion*, p. 30). See also Hillers, *Lamentations* (1992), p. 32–39.

[13] Westermann, for example, deduces from the work of Norman Gottwald on Lamentations that the uniqueness of the situation that is fore-grounded in this book provided the impetus for its mixing of genres (see Westermann, *Lamentations*, pp. 60–61).

[14] The *qînāh*, an ancient funeral song or dirge, follows a particular lyrical meter. The meter contains an uneven line in poetry that consists of a longer first colon followed by a shorter second (3 + 2; 4 + 3, or 4 + 2).

[15] See Dobbs-Allsopp, *Weep*, p. 1; Paul Wayne Ferris, Jr., *The Genre of Communal Lament in the Bible and the Ancient Near East*, pp. 17–61.

[16] Peter Seitel, *Powers of Genre: Interpreting Haya Oral Literature*, pp. 3, 4.

[17] The Haya live in northwestern Tanzania (east Africa) in the Kagera Region.

but also orients the 'performance practices that produce those texts to other social practices'.[18] Genre signals a particular web of socio-cultural assumptions and presuppositions that evoke certain culturally-determined expectations and responses from audiences (readers/hearers). Drawing on insights from R. Bauman and C. Briggs, [19] Seitel observes, 'genre casts light on not only whether a particular performance follows generic forms artfully but also whether it stretches them, or ironically overturns them or mixes them with those of another genre to create various degrees of formal and semantic distance from its own generic origin'.[20] Said differently, audiences are able to discern the collective knowledge from which a culture-specific genre draws, to determine whether it agrees with or opposes conventional features and usage, and whether this example of genre also uses other traditions to create a polyphony of voices.[21]

In addition to typological—identifying forms—and dialogic—recognizing relationships among genres in a particular piece of literature—features, genres are typically used in particular social fields. That is, genres chart or create distinct worlds. Generic worlds differ, even within a single society. Thus, Seitel observes, the world of Haya folktales differs from the world of Haya epic ballads.[22] To use an example from biblical literature, the world that an individual lament evokes typically differs from the world evoked by a thanksgiving hymn (see Psalm 88 [individual lament], and Psalm 66 [thanksgiving hymn]).

Lamentations utilizes features from traditional communal dirges, communal laments, city-laments, and other literary genres to create very distinct worlds—worlds marked by the anguish of trauma caused by siege warfare and its concomitant effects, the collapse of a capital city and its central temple, and the demise of its social, political, economic, and religious institutions. Lamenta-

---

[18] Seitel, *Powers of Genre*, p. 4.

[19] Seitel, *Power of Genre*, pp. 4–6. See R. Bauman and C. Briggs, 'Genre, Intertextuality, and Social Power', pp. 131–172.

[20] Seitel, *Powers of Genre*, p. 6.

[21] Ibid., p. 10.

[22] Ibid., p. 15.

tions' poet adapts and utilizes these genres to convey the magnitude of the catastrophe and the anguish that some survivors of Jerusalem's destruction endured. As Lee rightly observes, 'the enormity of this "freight" puts structural strains on the vehicles'.[23] The fluidity of genre boundaries evident in the book appears to reflect not only the nature of genre *qua* genre, but also the struggle of survivors to find words and forms adequate for expressing their ineffable suffering. In short, Lamentations' traumatic matrix affects its form. Certain typical features and themes of communal laments, dirges, and city-laments are either entirely missing from, or significantly modified in, the poems. Other features and themes are magnified by the inordinate attention they receive compared to other examples of these genres.

Qînāh *or Funeral Song*

In his classic 1882 essay, 'Das hebräische Klagelied', Karl Budde identified the *qînāh* meter as the primary form of the poems that comprise Lamentations.[24] The *qînāh* meter consists of a longer first colon followed by a shorter, second colon (3 + 2; 4 + 3, or 4 + 2).[25] This unevenness produces a limping rhythm (see Lam 1:6aαβ, 11bαβ, 22aαβ).[26] More recently, scholars have shown that while the *qînāh* meter is certainly a prominent poetic feature in Lamentations, it does not appear consistently throughout the book.[27] Moreover, this metrical pattern appears in other biblical books in literary contexts unrelated to bereavement (see Isa 1:10–12, a judgment oracle; Isa 40:9–11, an oracle of hope). Further, some dirges do not follow the *qînāh* meter (see 2 Sam 1:17–27).[28] *Qînāh* features in the book of Lamentations are best understood as just one among many other traditional literary features. The book's poet draws from these fea-

---

[23] Lee, *Singers*, pp. 36–37.

[24] *Qînāh* (pl. *qînôt*), 'elegy', or 'dirge' (see 2 Sam 1:17; 3:33; Ezek 19:14; 32:16; 2 Chr 35:25). The *qînāh* is a funeral song or lament over the passing of a loved one. See Berlin, *Lamentations*, p. 22–24.

[25] K. Budde, 'Das hebräische Klagelied', pp. 1–52.

[26] See Hillers, *Lamentations* (1992), p. 18.

[27] Ibid.

[28] Ibid., pp. 18–19.

tures, adapting them in order to bear witness to the catastrophic events associated with Jerusalem's demise. Westermann identifies key features of the *qînāh*/dirge meter:

> An opening cry of ah!, alas!, or the equivalent; a mournful cry as such (something with the direct address of the deceased); a summons to mourn (sometimes even addressed to inanimate objects); a proclamation that a death has occurred (sometimes with reference to the mode of death); a comparing of the former with the present state of affairs (the contrast motif), including a eulogizing of the deceased; a description of the mourner's pain or of the general state of misery; reference to the effect all this is having on the bystanders; questions expressing bewilderment at what has happened.[29]

These features are especially prominent in Lamentations 1, 2, and 4—passages that also contain significant features of the communal lament.

Communal Lament

Communal laments express a community's complaint and/or anguish over an impending or actual catastrophe that is expected to befall, or has already befallen, that community (or a community for which the lamenters feel a sense of deep connection). The lament is a desperate appeal to God for intervention or deliverance.[30] Typical features of the communal lament include: an invocation; a hymn of praise; an affirmation of trust and confidence; a lament proper; an appeal and motivation for response (which can involve a plea for deliverance or for imprecations on enemies); a protestation of innocence; an affirmation of confidence and hope; and a vow of praise.[31] Ferris' study shows that some features of communal la-

---

[29] Westermann, *Lamentations*, p. 7. See also Ferris, *The Genre of Communal Lament*, pp. 69–87.

[30] Ferris, *Genre*, p. 10. Ferris analyzes communal lament features in following Psalms: Psalms 31, 35, 42, 43, 44, 56, 59, 60, 69, 74, 77, 79, 80, 83, 85, 89, 94, 102, 109, 137, and 142. He also analyzes these features in the book of Lamentations.

[31] Ferris, *Genre*, pp. 91–92.

ments are either absent from or significantly modified in Lamentations. For example, unlike some other communal laments (cf. Psalms 44, 74, 79), Lamentations does not devote much attention to the enemy's role, whether political, moral, or ethical.[32] Rather, it depicts YHWH as Jerusalem's archenemy (see Lam 2:1–9).[33] Moreover, Lamentations does not devote much attention to affirmations of confidence in God or expressions of hope.[34] The most notable exceptions to this observation appear in Lam 3:21–24, 57–62, which voices the hope of an individual, rather than a community.[35] Even the expression of hope in Lam 3:21–24 is flickering at best and fleeting at worse, because it is overshadowed by haunting, graphic depictions of extreme suffering (see Lam 3:1–20, 49–56).

As noted above, in Lamentations, features of the communal lament are intertwined with other genres and motifs, especially in its first four poems (Lamentations 1–4). Lamentations 5 comes closest to a 'pure' communal lament form. Lamentations 3, by contrast, is the most structurally and generically complex of the five poems.[36] It includes elements of individual laments (Lam 3:1–20, 49–66), sapiential reflections with didactic intent (Lam 3:25–39), and communal laments (Lam 3:40–48). In Lamentations 1, 2, and 4, communal dirge and communal lament features are prominent.

---

[32] Ibid., p. 139.

[33] Ibid., p. 140–141.

[34] Ibid., p. 145.

[35] An individual lament expresses the plight and anguish of an individual over a perceived or actual tragedy that threatens or has already befallen, her or him. In the individual lament, the sufferer typically cries out to God for deliverance or intervention. Psalm 88 is a notable example of an individual lament. See Ferris, *The Genre of Communal Lament*, p. 10.

[36] Following the lead of H. Gunkel, H. Jahnow, and other form critics, N. Lee argues that the communal dirge is the primary genre of Lamentations. Nevertheless, it has been intentionally supplemented with elements of the communal lament. See Lee, *Singers*, pp. 36–37. Westermann, by contrast, argues that the plaintive lament is the dominant genre of Lamentations, though it in-cooperates dirge motifs. Like Lee, Westermann asserts that the juxtaposition of these two features seems deliberate. See Westermann, *Lamentations*, pp. 10–11.

City-Laments

In his discussion of ancient Mesopotamian city-laments, Ferris points to significant generic differences and variations.[37] These city-laments also exhibit notable, recurring features and thematic elements.[38] For instance, references to the wrath of a particular deity or deities, linking the destruction of the city or cities in question to divine decrees, and references to divine abandonment.[39] Ultimately, responsibility for the destruction is typically assigned to the city's patron deity (deities), who is (are) displeased for one reason or another. These laments also typically contain a detailed description of the city's destruction, including references to razed structures such as walls, temples, and public buildings.[40] The catastrophe's enormous death toll, including references to unburied corpses lying in the streets, also plays a prominent role in many Mesopotamian city-laments.[41] Still other recurring themes include references to political enemies (not always identified specifically), protestations of innocence, and appeals for divine intervention on behalf of the city, or for an end to the calamity and restoration of the city to its former state.[42] Many Mesopotamian city-laments advance the view that as a result of a city's demise, its traditional social, religious, and political structures and institutions have collapsed.[43] Another important feature is the portrayal of the destroyed city's goddess mourning the demise of her city, its temple,

---

[37] See Ferris, *Genre*, pp. 17–61. See also Dobbs-Allsopp, *Weep*, pp. 30–96. Biblical scholars have not been able to determine conclusively the precise relationships between Lamentations and Mesopotamian city-laments. Suffice it to say that Lamentations shares some common motifs and themes with Mesopotamian lament literature, including graphic descriptions of the destruction of city and temple, and depictions of calamities (such as famine) associated with the demise of a city. See Berlin, *Lamentations*, pp. 26–30).

[38] Ferris, *Genre*, pp. 17–61.

[39] Ferris, *Genre*, pp. 54–57; Dobbs-Allsopp, *Weep*, pp. 45–65.

[40] Dobbs-Allsopp, *Weep*, pp. 66–70.

[41] Ferris, *Genre*, p. 60; Dobbs-Allsopp, *Weep*, pp. 70–71.

[42] Ferris, *Genre*, pp. 58–59; Dobbs-Allsopp, *Weep*, pp. 92–94.

[43] Ferris, *Genre*, p. 60; Dobbs-Allsopp, *Weep*, pp. 73–75.

and the fate of its inhabitants.[44] Recurring references to mourning, weeping, and expressions of emotional anguish or pain also appear in sundry city-laments.[45]

Many of the foregoing features appear prominently in the book of Lamentations as well. The striking similarities between Lamentations and Mesopotamian city-lament literature have led some scholars to conclude that the book is a biblical example of this genre.[46] Other scholars, however, have noted the lack of evidence for the use of city-lament generic features *vis à vis* destroyed Israelite or Judean cities prior to Jerusalem's destruction in 586 BCE.[47] For many Judeans, Jerusalem's demise had especially far reaching historical and religious implications.[48] Whether or not ancient Mesopotamian city-lament traditions directly influenced Lamentations' poet cannot be established with certainty.[49] Nevertheless, I agree with Berlin that the poet utilized conventional motifs and themes common in the ancient Near East 'for speaking of war and destruction'.[50] Much like the poet's use of the dirge and communal lament genres, the appearance of prominent city-lament motifs in Lamentations reflects significant adaptations and modifications. The traumatic circumstances that likely gave rise to Lamentations have left their imprints on the book's adaptations and use of genres. In a sense, no one genre or literary structure can adequately express the enormity of the world-shattering, life rupturing tragedy of Jerusalem's fall for survivors whose experiences, reactions, and responses are preserved in Lamentations.

---

[44] Dobbs-Allsopp, *Weep*, pp. 75–90.

[45] Ibid., pp. 90–92.

[46] Ibid., pp. 30–96.

[47] See Berlin, *Lamentations*, p. 25.

[48] Ibid.

[49] See Ferris, *Genre*, pp. 174–175; Berlin, *Lamentations*, p. 27.

[50] Berlin, *Lamentations*, p. 28. For an insightful analysis of ancient Near Eastern laments read through the lens of trauma studies, see Jan Dietrich, 'Cultural Traumata in the Ancient Near East', in *Trauma and Traumatization*, pp. 145–161.

Structural Analysis

Alphabetical Acrostic

In Chester Himes 1965 detective novel, *Cotton Comes to Harlem*, two black detectives in Harlem, Grave Digger Jones and Coffin Ed Johnson, engage in the following conversation while listening to jazz:

> 'Somewhere in that jungle is the solution to the world', Coffin Ed said. 'If we could only find it'.
>
> 'Yeah, it's like the sidewalks trying to speak in a language never heard. But they can't spell it either'.
>
> 'Naw [No]', Coffin Ed said. *'Unless there's an alphabet for emotion'.*
>
> *'The emotion that comes out of experience. If we could read that language, man, we would solve all the crimes in the world'.*
>
> 'Let's split', Coffin Ed said. 'Jazz talks too much to me'.
>
> 'It ain't [It's not] so much what it says', Grave Digger agreed. 'It's what you can't do about it'.[51]

This dialogue between Coffin Ed and Grave Digger reveals the complexity of emotive language. Grave Digger's recognition of the difficulties inherent in emotional language as it relates to jazz is also true of the language of trauma, that is, post-trauma, survivor literature. This difficulty pertains both to giving voice and understanding the language of trauma. Trauma typically lies beyond the mastery of language. One struggles to find an alphabet, or appropriate structure and language, to bear witness to overwhelming suffering. Indeed, the struggle is not so much what this type of language says, but what we cannot do about it—we cannot fully master it. The poet of Lamentations struggles with this issue, and despite the best efforts to contain the poems' contents within the disciplining structures of Hebrew alphabetic acrostics, ruptures intrude into these structures and renders them inadequate.

---

[51] C. Himes, *Cotton Comes to Harlem*, p. 47, emphasis added.

The poems in Lamentations 1–4 follow various patterns associated with the Hebrew alphabetical acrostic.[52] In poems 1, 2, and 4, each stanza begins with successive letters of the Hebrew alphabet (twenty-two stanzas). The third poem consists of twenty-two extended stanzas comprised of three lines each,[53] and each stanza begins with successive letters of the Hebrew alphabet (thus each of the three lines [verses] in the first stanza begins with א [*'ālep*], each of the three lines in the second stanza begins with ב [*bêt*], etc.). Although Lamentations 5 does not follow the pattern of an alphabetical acrostic, it is comprised of twenty-two verses, coinciding with the twenty-two letters of the Hebrew alphabet.[54] In the final analysis, the specific function and significance of the alphabetic acrostic form remains uncertain.[55]

Westermann and Salters assert that the alphabetic acrostic was most likely utilized for artistic or aesthetic reasons.[56] Westermann further avers that, '[s]uch a mechanical type of arrangement has no intrinsic connection with content'.[57] I am sympathetic to the artistic/aesthetic rationale for the use of the alphabetic acrostic in Lamentations and other biblical poems (see Psalm 119); I disagree, however, with the view that no intrinsic connection exists between structure, form, and content. Other laments over Jerusalem's fall

---

[52] Usually in alphabetic acrostic in the Hebrew Bible, the consonants שׂ (*śîn*) and שׁ (*šîn*) are used interchangeably. For a discussion of the alphabetic acrostic in Lamentations, see Elie Assis, 'The Alphabetic Acrostic in the Book of Lamentations', pp. 710–724; Assis, 'The Unity of the Book of Lamentations', pp. 306–329; J. F. Brug, 'Biblical Acrostics and Their Relationship to Other Ancient Near Eastern Acrostics', 283–304; B. Johnson, 'Form and Message in Lamentations', pp. 58–73; and H. Heater, Jr., 'Structure and Meaning in Lamentations', pp. 304–315.

[53] In this study, I count the lines of the poems based on the Masoretic Text as reproduced in *Biblia Hebraica Quinta* (BHQ).

[54] An additional verse appears in MT due to a repetition of the content of verse 21 following verse 22.

[55] See Assis, 'The Alphabetic Acrostic in the Book of Lamentations', pp. 712–715.

[56] See Salters, *Lamentations*, p. 21; Westermann, *Lamentations*, p. 99.

[57] Westermann, *Lamentations*, p. 99.

(see Psalms 74, 79, and 137) do not utilize the alphabetic acrostic; it is not an essential framework for that content. Nevertheless, arguing that the poet utilized the alphabetic acrostic arrangement solely for artistic or aesthetic reasons ignores the book's traumatic matrix and content. The poet may have used acrostics for other than artistic, aesthetic, didactic, or mnemonic reasons, including a desire to demonstrate the completeness of suffering in order to achieve emotional catharsis.[58]

Some scholars have argued that the use of the alphabetical acrostic structure in Lamentations suggests completeness or psychological control over suffering (from 'A' to 'Z').[59] O'Connor's view that acrostic devices were employed by struggling survivors 'to contain and control the chaos of unstructured pain' and/or to voice 'their deadening reality', has merit.[60] Similarly, Paul M. Joyce opines that the acrostic form may reflect an attempt to establish a semblance of order in the immediate aftermath of radical loss of meaning.[61] If the poet's aim was to bring order from chaos or to provide structure for unstructured pain, however, then that goal was never fully realized in the text. In the end, uncertainty persists; and the excesses of anguish ruptures the imposed, disciplining structures.

Following the lead of Max Löhr and others, Westermann argues that many of the disruptions and anomalies in Lamentations result from the imposition of an acrostic structure.[62] While his point is possible, disruptions in the text could also reflect the struggle endemic to expressing overwhelming suffering. Trauma tends to impose its effects on survivors. Consequently, some of the anomalies in the book's alphabetic structures can be understood to register the trauma of survivors.

---

[58] See Salters, *Lamentations*, pp. 17–21; Gottwald, *Studies*, p. 30; Westermann, *Lamentations*, pp. 98–100.

[59] See O'Connor, *The Book of Lamentations*, pp. 1018–1019.

[60] See K. O'Connor, *Lamentations and the Tears of the World.*

[61] P. M. Joyce, 'Lamentations and the Grief Process: A Psychological Reading', p. 319.

[62] Westermann, *Lamentations*, p. 100.

Elie Assis argues that the acrostic forms in the book of Lamentations were adopted in order to create a tension between deep emotional expressions on one hand, and rational reflections on suffering on the other.[63] The disciplined structure of the acrostic forms reflects organized, well-planned thoughts.[64] Assis further opines that the acrostics express an atmosphere of contemplation meant to 'lead the reader to uncover a message and meaning beyond the deep expression of pain'.[65] The poet uses the acrostic forms to convey the view that the only appropriate response to the tragedies lamented in the book is to 'turn to God, to lay their misfortunes before God and to pray to God'.[66] I find this conclusion problematic and unconvincing due to the actual evidence in the text. The structural complexity of Lamentations does not reflect rational contemplation on suffering. Indeed, readers are hard pressed to find well-ordered thoughts and consistent ideological perspectives within the poems. The 'vehicle' that bears witness to Zion's trauma is only superficially disciplined. Competing perspectives and discordant voices[67] are juxtaposed to create a sense of confusion, ambivalence and disorientation. These jolting features do not indicate that the poet has completely grappled with the emotional and theological implications of the calamities that have befallen Zion and her children. Neither has the poet arrived at a specific understanding of, and appropriate response to, these realities. Rather, the fractured structures and shaky acrostic scaffolds in the book resist Assis' conclusions.[68]

A close reading of these five poems reveals significant structural ruptures, including imperative interruptions—for example,

---

[63] Assis, 'The Alphabetic Acrostic in Lamentations', p. 717.

[64] Ibid.

[65] Ibid., pp. 717–718.

[66] Ibid., pp. 723–724.

[67] See C. W. Miller, 'Reading Voices: Personification, Dialogism, and the Reader of Lamentations 1', pp. 393–404.

[68] Assis' study seeks to affirm the theological centrality of Lamentations 3, a perspective that has dominated Lamentations scholarship for much of the twentieth century. For a useful overview and critique of this perspective see, e.g., Linafelt, *Surviving*, pp. 5–18.

רְאֵה [*rĕʾēh*] "See!" in Lam 1:9cα, 11bα and 2:20aα—anticlimactic features—the poems do not build to a crescendo—and seemingly erratic shifts in perspectives and voices—Zion, narrator/didactic voice, community, or individual.[69] Salters correctly recognizes that 'the poet appears to snatch at diverse subject matter and produce non-sequiturs, even within individual verses'.[70] Such interruptions point to the inaccessibility and tenuous grasp of the traumatic experiences that inform the book. *ʾĀlep* (א) to *tāw* (ת) can only provide, at best, a fractured framing of the elusive experience of trauma. Anticlimactic elements in the poems dash expectations, as well as provide space for the ongoing experience of bearing witness to the disruptive and debilitating realities of trauma.[71] *ʾĀlep* (א) leads to *tāw* (ת), only to return to *ʾālep* (א) again, in the first three poems. The final *tāw* (ת) in the fourth poem leads to the fifth poem, which retains only the semblance of an alphabetical structure.

These ruptures and incomplete elements within the structure of Lamentations can be understood as mirroring the caesura in life that often persists in the aftermath of trauma. The dramatic interruptions in the poems are typically associated with the excesses of suffering (see Lam 2:20–22). These interruptions often draw attention to Zion's systems and institutions that have been shattered (see Lam 1:9c–11). The incomplete elements in the poems often highlight the enormity and elusiveness of the freight that these poems seek to carry.

---

[69] See Hillers, *Lamentations* (1992), pp. 28–30. See also William F. Lanahan, 'The Speaking Voice in the Book of Lamentations', pp. 41–49.

[70] R. B. Salters, 'Structure and Implication in Lamentations 1', p. 293. While Salters discussion pertain specifically to Lamentations 1, I believe that non-sequiturs and disjointedness are features of the entire book.

[71] The foregoing and following reflections on the generic, structural, literary, ideological, and psychological features of Lamentations presuppose the trauma process. Other acrostic poems in the Hebrew Bible (notably, Psalm 119) and other poetic texts can reflect, more-or-less similar dramatic breaks. My choice and interpretation of the dramatic breaks or shifts in Lamentations are based on the socio-historical contexts that I presuppose (and argue for) in my critical analysis of the book.

Let us take a closer look at the ruptured structure of Lamentations' five poems. My discussion will proceed canonically, that is, as the poems appear in the book's final form.

Lamentations 1

Outline of Chapter:

A. Description of sufferer's (Zion's) predicament, and *plea for YHWH to pay attention to the sufferer's plight* (vs 1–9);
B. Description of sufferer's (Zion's) predicament, and *plea for YHWH to pay attention to the sufferer's plight* (vs 10–11);
C. Description of sufferer's (Zion's) predicament—Zion (vs 12–16);
D. Description of sufferer's (Zion's) predicament—poet (v. 17);
E. Sufferer's *plea for YHWH to pay attention to sufferer's plight* (vs 18–20);
F. Sufferer's last words (vs 21–22).

The alphabetical acrostic in Lamentations 1 largely consists of twenty-two stanzas comprised of three lines each; the only exception is verse 7, which contains four lines.[72] The poem begins with an exclamation of anguish and agony, 'Alas!' (אֵיכָה [*ʾêkâ*]). This expression typically appears in funeral dirges and laments. Its appearance signals a drastic, negative change in fortunes.[73] Following this initial outburst of pain, the poem's acrostic structure is thrice interrupted by the imperative רְאֵה (*rĕʾēh*), 'see!' (vs 9cα, 11bα and 20aα). The imperative form of the verb ראה (*rāʾāh*) in v. 9cα interrupts 3rd person singular descriptions of Daughter Zion's traumata in verses 1–9b and implores YHWH to take notice. In verse 10, 3rd person

---

[72] There is no scholarly consensus about possible reasons for, and resolutions of, this anomaly. See Hillers, *Lamentations* (1992), pp. 68–69, n. 7.

[73] See Robin A. Parry, *Lamentations*, p. 43; see also Isa 1:21; Jer 48:17; Ezek 26:17.

singular depictions of the extent of Zion's tragic situation return. Another shift occurs in verse 11bα, where singular imperatives beseech YHWH to pay attention. Unlike the prior interruption, however, this one precedes 1st person singular descriptions of Zion's plight (vs 12–16). Verse 17 returns to 3rd person singular depictions of Zion's pain, while verses 18 and 19 shift to 1st person singular speech forms. In the imperative address in verse 20aα, Zion again entreats YHWH to attend to her situation. The remaining verses (Lam. 1: 21–22) are cast as 1st person singular speech.

I distinguish 'paying attention to/attending to' suffering from 'describing' or 'depicting' suffering. I understand the former as reflections on suffering that involve identifying with, sympathizing with, and providing emotional support for, the sufferer. Thus, to 'pay attention' to suffering is to be present for the sufferer, to enter into the experience of the sufferer (see Lam 2:11–12; 3:49–50). In Lamentations the sufferers plead with YHWH to pay attention to their suffering. In this they seem to hope that YHWH will not only identify with them, but also be moved to change his heart concerning what he has done to them. 'Describing' or 'depicting' suffering involves recounting the tragic experiences of the sufferer. Often in Lamentations, this activity also involves justifying the suffering as equitable punishment for sins (see Lam 1:5, 8). 'Describing' traumatic experiences often entails using *history like* language.

Ultimately, the structural breaks occasioned by the imperative רְאֵה (*rĕʾēh*) can be construed as Zion's passionate, desperate attempts to draw YHWH's attention. While the alphabetical acrostic provides a structure for witnessing to Zion's destabilizing traumatic experiences, her own interjections in the text rupture this form, creating a subverting effect. Zion's interjections appear to intrude, imposing themselves on the narrator's descriptions of her predicament. Lamentations 1 begins with the narrator's description of Daughter Zion's devastating reversal of fortunes. In the midst of these descriptions, personified Zion interrupts the narrator briefly to plead with YHWH to attend to her situation. The narrator continues, only to be interrupted again by Zion's passionate appeal for YHWH's attention. Zion then dominates the rest of the poem, permitting the poet only one brief moment to speak again on her behalf (v. 17). Finally, Zion interrupts her own narration of her troubles to offer an impassioned plea for YHWH to notice her distress.

Lamentations 2

Outline of Chapter:

A. Description of sufferer's (Zion's) predicament (vs 1–10);
B. *Attention to sufferer's plight (vs 11–12);*
C. Description of sufferer's (Zion's) predicament (vs 13–17);
D. *Attention to sufferer's plight (vs 18–19);*
E. Sufferer's last words (vs 20–22).

Structuring Trauma

Like chapter 1, Lamentations 2 follows the form of an alphabetic acrostic with twenty-two verses consisting of three lines each. Each verse begins with successive letters of the Hebrew alphabet. Like Lamentations 1, the chapter begins with the interrogative cry of anguish אֵיכָה (*ʾêkâ*), 'Alas!', 'how!' The acrostic form in Lamentations 1, follows the generally recognized sequencing of letters in the Hebrew alphabet; in chapter 2, however, ע [*ʿayin*] follows פ [*pê*].[74]

Lamentations 2:1–8 depicts YHWH's merciless razing of Zion and its religious institutions.[75] YHWH acts as Zion's archenemy, the active agent in her demise.[76] A subtle shift occurs in verses 9–10; unlike the previous verses, which paint a graphic picture of YHWH's destructive fury, verse 9 depicts the state of Zion and her people in the aftermath of YHWH's wrathful judgment. Zion is gateless, signaling the people's and the city's vulnerability. Her leaders are 'among the nations', and YHWH no longer speaks through her prophets. Zion's elders and maidens have adopted a posture of mourning and grief (v.10). Much as the interjections of the imperative רְאֵה (*rĕʾēh*) to draw attention to Zion's perils in

[74] The alphabetic acrostics in Lamentations 3 and 4 also follow the inverted sequence in Lamentations 2. The significance of this inversion remains unclear. The sequence of letters in the Hebrew alphabet may not have been fixed at the time these poems were composed. See Parry, *Lamentations*, pp. 16, 34.

[75] See Dobbs-Allsopp, 'R(az/ais)ing Zion in Lamentations 2', p. 21–68.

[76] I discuss this feature is greater detail in my theological analysis of Lamentations 2.

Lamentations 1, this shift indirectly calls on YHWH to attend to Zion's situation (Lam 2:9–10).

In the alphabetic acrostic sections of כ (*kāp*) – פ (*pê*), another notable shift occurs (vs 11–16). The narrator interrupts the poem with 1st person singular descriptions of how Zion's dilemma has affected him and then recounts what appear to be some of the horrors that he has witnessed (vs 11–12). The narrator refers to Zion affectionately as בַּת-עַמִּי (*bat-ʿammî*), 'My Dear People'. Here, the narrator is not an objective observer; he shares in his people's trauma. The narrator is a sympathetic and an implicated witness—a reporter of, eyewitness to, and co-sufferer in Zion's trauma. The shift in verse 11 from 3rd person narration to 1st person witness adds a jarring effect to the poem's structure. The narrator appears to lose control for a moment, perhaps bearing witness to the experience of being moved by Zion's precarious circumstances. Linafelt rightly observes that the plight of suffering children (Lam 2:11c-12) leads to the narrator's breakdown:[77] Zion's ruin is epitomized in the imagery of languishing and dying infants. In verses 13–16, the narrator/witness adopts a didactic voice in a desperate attempt to instruct and console Dear Daughter Jerusalem.

Verse 17 reverts to the tone and tenor of verses 1–8, focusing on YHWH as the active agent in Jerusalem's demise. A passionate exhortation for Zion to plead her own cause before YHWH follows in verses 18–19. Like earlier interruptions in the poem's plot, this disruption calls attention to Zion's painful situation. Zion accepts the narrator's invitation; and in the remainder of the poem, she confronts YHWH. Verse 20 begins with the imperative רְאֵה (*rĕʾēh*), 'See!' Zion then makes an impassioned plea for YHWH to pay attention to what has befallen her at his hands. As in Lamentations 1, Zion is given the last word.

Suffering From A to Z

The foregoing insights bring into question the purpose of the alphabetic acrostic form in Lamentations. Daniel Grossberg argues that the acrostic might have functioned to express a sense of 'totali-

---

[77] Linafelt, *Surviving*, p. 57.

ty…from A to Z'.[78] However, the acrostics in Lamentations 1 and 2 do not actually impose unity on the poem's different voices and perspectives. Moreover, it is not evident that the acrostic structure conveys the 'completeness' of the suffering.[79] To the contrary, shifts and interruptions in the acrostic structure might signal that Zion's suffering is open-ended or boundless. Zion's anguish cannot be contained or controlled within any neatly-organized framework; her trauma cannot be quantified, marked off, or controlled. The extent of her suffering is both ineffable and unimaginable. א (*ʾālep*) to ת (*tāw*) offer only flickering, transitory glimpses of the traumata poignantly summarized in Lam 2:22: 'On the day of YHWH's anger, no one survived, none escaped'. Zion has not simply experienced complete suffering; she feels utterly annihilated, and her suffering persists in excess in the aftermath of trauma. Finally, it is not evident that the alphabetic acrostic structures chaos.[80] Competing voices, seemingly erratic shifts in speakers, emotional outbursts, and graphic depictions of suffering convey the poem's sense of chaos. The disorder engendered by trauma ruptures life; hence, chaos persists in these poems. They echo the tumultuous, messy and destabilizing realities which survivors of the trauma associated with Jerusalem's demise were likely forced to endure.

Lamentations 3

Chapter Outline:

A. Description of sufferer's (individual) predicament (vs 1–20);
B. *Hope for YHWH to pay attention to sufferer and end his suffering (vs 21–39);*
C. Description of sufferer's (community's) predicament (vs 40–47);

---

[78] Daniel Grossberg, *Centripetal and Centrifugal Structures in Biblical Poetry*, pp. 84–85. See discussion in O'Connor, *Lamentations*, p. 1019; Gottwald, *Studies*, pp. 30–31.

[79] See Gottwald, *Studies in the Book of Lamentation*, p. 30.

[80] See Kathleen M. O'Connor, *Lamentations and the Tears of the World*, p. 12; Parry, *Lamentations*, pp. 14–15.

B. *Attention to plight of sufferer—poet with hope for YHWH to pay attention (vs 48–51);*
C. Sufferer's (poet's) last words—poet (vs 52–66).

Individual Loss

The form of alphabetic acrostic in Lamentations 3 differs from the forms in Lamentations 1 and 2. Each unit consists of three verses, and each of these three verses begins with successive letters of the Hebrew alphabet. While the acrostics in Lamentations 1 and 2 consist of twenty-two verses (sixty-six lines), the acrostic in Lamentations 3 consists of sixty-six verses. Acrostic units א (*ʾālep*) – ו (*wāw*) in verses 1–16 constitute an individual lament. The tone and tenor of this section bears some similarity to Lam 2:1–8: in both passages, YHWH appears as the active agent in the sufferers' plight. While YHWH's fury is directed against Zion in Lamentations 2, an individual experiences God's wrath in Lamentations 3. In verses 17–20, the narrator/sufferer shifts from YHWH's wrathful actions to reflections on his predicament as a consequence of those actions.[81] As noted in the structural analyses of Lamentations 1 and 2, this interruption in the flow of the poem calls attention to the sufferer's situation. In Lamentations 1 and 2, interruptions shifted the audience's/reader's focus to Zion's painful condition. Thus, although Lam 3:1–20 contains no obvious references or allusions to Jerusalem and its destruction, depictions of the sufferer's dilemma in these verses are reminiscent of references to Zion's experiences in Lamentations 1 and 2. It is unclear whether the predicament of the individual sufferer in Lamentations 3 is related to the

---

[81] Third person masculine singular verbs feature prominently in Lam 3:2–16. For example, נָהַג [*nāhag*], 'he drove' (v. 2), בִּלָּה [*billāh*], 'he wore out' and שִׁבַּר [*šibbar*] 'he shattered' (v. 4), and בָּנָה [*bānāh*], 'he built' (v. 5). These 3rd person masculine singular verbs appear in both the Hebrew perfect and the imperfect, emphasizing that the sufferer is convinced that YHWH is directly responsible for his past and his ongoing suffering. In vs 17–20, 1st person masculine singular verbs and pronouns feature more prominently than in the previous section.

fall of Jerusalem.[82] In its present literary context, however, Lam 3:1–20 can be read as the testimony of an individual who has survived the city's demise. The use of tropic and stereotypical language in these verses, as in the rest of the book, allows the poem to bear witness to the anguish of multiple survivors of different traumatic events and experiences. Like personified Zion, the narrator/sufferer in Lam 3:1–20 identifies with, speaks for, and expresses the anguish of different individuals or groups of survivors.

Structuring Hope

In verses 21–24, the poet's tone shifts abruptly. Suddenly, we read affirmations of hope and declarations of confidence in YHWH.[83] Although this interruption in the poem's flow is unexpected, such features are not uncommon in the lament traditions in the Hebrew Bible and the ancient Near East.[84] The sufferer dares to affirm confidence and hope in YHWH—an affirmation that appears only here in the entire book. Following this affirmation, the poet turns to a series of wisdom sayings (vs 25–30) and instructions (vs 31–39) that echo the view of retribution prominent in ancient Israel's sapiential traditions (vs 25–39, acrostic units ט [*ṭêt*] – מ [*mêm*]).[85]

---

[82] See Magne Saebo, 'Who Is "The Man" in Lamentations 3:1?', pp. 131–142; and Saebo, 'Who is "the Man" in Lamentations 3?: A Fresh Approach to the Interpretation of the Book of Lamentations', pp. 294–306.

[83] See E. S. Gerstenberger, *Psalms,* pp. 11–14. Affirmation of confidence in YHWH is a prominent feature in many individual and communal complaints/laments in the Psalter. See also Ferris, *Genre*, pp. 91–103.

[84] See Ps 44:5–9 [ET, 4–8], Jer 20:11–13; and Ferris, *Genre*, pp. 91–100.

[85] The belief that God acts to reward virtue and punish wickedness appears prominently within Israel's wisdom traditions (see Ps 1; 119; Prov 10:2–11, 27–32), Deuteronomistic traditions (see Deuteronomy 28; 1 Kings 14:7–16; 2 Kings 17:7–23; 21:10–16; and 23:26–27). It also is prominent in prophetic literature (see Hosea 8–10; Isa 1:2–9; 3; Jer 11:1–17; 15:1–9; and Ezek 6, 9, 11). Job's friends also espouse the view that a direct correspondence exists between sin and punishment/suffering, and virtue and reward/blessings (see Job 4, 8, and 11). However, Job contests

These sayings continue the motif of hope introduced in the preceding verses.

Communal Loss and Plea

The next significant interruption in the poem's structure occurs in the נ (*nûn*) – ע (*ʿayin*) acrostic units (vs 40–51). Here, the disruption consists of a dramatic shift from the dilemma of an individual sufferer to the plight of a community. A community representative invites the community to return to YHWH. The narrator/leader laments on the community's behalf (vs 40–47). The 1st person plural references in these verses shift to 1st person singular references in verses 48–51, where the narrator/leader laments on behalf of his beloved people and city. He shares in the suffering of his fellow survivors. Within the structure of this communal lament, the poet interrupts the flow by shifting from 2nd person singular addresses depicting YHWH's wrathful actions against the narrator's community (vs 43–47) to 1st person singular descriptions of the narrator's/leader's anguish over his community's predicament (vs 48–51). Much like Lamentations 1 and 2, these ruptures in the poem's structure call attention to the extent of the community's suffering. The narrator's/leader's interest in, and sympathy for, his city in this unit of Lamentations 3 is comparable to what appears in preceding portions of Lamentations, especially chapter 2 (see Lam 2:11–14).

Individual Plea

In verses 55–66, the poem reverts to an individual lament. This lament includes a desperate plea to YHWH to attend to the sufferer's predicament and to vindicate his cause. The sufferer beseeches YHWH to take note of the injustices he has endured at enemy hands (v. 63). Like Daughter Zion, who has the last word in Lamentations 1 and 2, this unnamed survivor gets the last word in Lamentations 3. The apparent preference for giving a 'survivor' the last word, whether that survivor is personified Zion on behalf of her people (Lamentations 1 and 2), or the narrator/leader who la-

---

this view of retribution (see Job 9). See also Jer 12:1–4; 20:7–18; Ps 73:1–14; Eccl 7:15–18; 9:11–12; and Hab 1:2–4.

ments both his own perils and the suffering of his 'Dear People' in Lamentations 3, is significant. Yet YHWH does not respond to the sufferers' pleas. O'Connor rightly notes that ancient Israel's writers 'had resources to help them bring God to speech if they wanted to do so'.[86] In many Mesopotamian city-laments, the deities of destroyed cities speak and return to restore the city.[87] In some biblical laments, God speaks and responds to lamenter's pleas.[88] Through the literary strategy of giving the survivor the last word, readers and hearers of this poem are confronted with a heightened sense of the survivor's loneliness and abandonment. The poem concludes with neither an adequate dénouement nor resolution of the survivor's dilemma. YHWH, the deity to whom the survivor addresses his cries, does not respond or intervene. Thus, the poem's focus remains on the sufferer's anguish; and its ending signals that the survivor's suffering is open-ended and ongoing. The victim's world remains shattered, and an ominous sense of God-forsakenness persists.

Lamentations 4

Chapter Outline:

A. Description of sufferer's (Zion's) predicament (vs 1–16);
B. Sufferer's last words (vs 17–20);
C. "Oracle-like" declaration—YHWH pays attention to Zion's plight (vs 21–22).

The Plight of Zion and Her Children

The alphabetic acrostic in Lamentations 4 consists of twenty-two verses, each containing two lines. As in Lamentations 1 and 2, every verse begins with successive letters of the Hebrew alphabet. Also, like Lamentations 1 and 2, the interrogative exclamation of anguish, אֵיכָה (*ʾêkâ*; 'alas!'; or 'how!') introduces Lamentations 4. This initial expression of anguish reappears in Lam 4:2bα. In verses 1–10, the narrator provides a graphic, chilling description of the hor-

---

[86] O'Connor, *Tears of the World*, p. 85.

[87] Dobbs-Allsopp, *Weep*, pp. 92–94.

[88] See Ps 60:7–8; 108:7–8; Jer 12:5–6; 15:19–21; Job 38:1–41:34.

rors attending Zion's reversal of fortune. The repetition of certain motifs links this section to Lamentations 2: in both poems the poet affectionately refers to Zion as בַּת־עַמִּי (*bat-ʿammî*), 'My Dear People' (see Lam 2:11bβ; 4:3bα, 6aα; cf. 3:48); both poems contain disturbing depictions of the predicaments of women and children as a consequence of severe famine—conditions that are often associated with siege warfare and its effects. Mothers are unable to provide their children's basic necessities (see Lam 2:11cα, 19d; 4:4aα). Essential food, like bread, is scarce at best and completely unavailable at worst (Lam 2:12aβ; 4:4b). Survival for many 'compassionate' women (Lam 4:10a) has deteriorated into grisly cannibalism (Lam 2:20b; 4:10).[89] Linafelt observes, this concern for the plight of Zion and her children figures prominently in the book's afterlife.[90]

The graphic depictions of Zion's reversal of fortunes in Lamentations 4 bear witness to the rupture in life that survivors of Jerusalem's fall endured. It seems evident that family structures, as well as economic and political institutions have been destroyed. These traumatic realities impose themselves on the poem's structure. Unless one is utterly desensitized to the suffering others endure, it is difficult to read or hear about the extreme perils of women and their children and then simply move on to the next alphabetical unit. Rather, such shocking realities implore readers and

---

[89] Linafelt argues that the reference to cannibalism in Lam 2:20 is best understood as a literary trope (Linafelt, *Surviving Lamentations*, p. 92). See also Berlin, *Lamentations*, p. 76. Cannibalism is mentioned as a curse for disobedience to YHWH in many judgment threats (see Lev 26:29; Deut 28:53–57; Jer 19:9; and Ezek 5:10). It is typically associated with conditions of extreme famine. While there is merit to Linafelt's view that references to cannibalism in Lamentations (2:20; 4:10) are most likely literary tropes, there are references elsewhere in Biblical literature that indicate that during times of severe famine the likelihood of such a gruesome practice might be heightened (see 2 Kings 6:28–29). Severe famine is one of the effects of siege warfare highlighted in Lamentations. I agree with Berlin that while the use of this motif in Lamentations might be exaggerated, and might not correspond to actual reality, 'the image that it conjures up is extremely effective' (Berlin, *Lamentations*, p. 76).

[90] See Linafelt, *Surviving*, pp. 89–97, 104–16, and 120–22.

hearers to pause, suspend judgment, re-read, and hear again these testimonies of trauma. Ultimately, these testimonies of extreme suffering beseech readers/hearers to identify with, and join in bearing witness to, the victims' plight.

The Last Word

Verses 11–16 insist that Zion's own patron deity, YHWH, is the author of her demise. These units draw attention to the moral failures of Zion's leaders: prophets, priests, and elders. Next, the text shifts from describing YHWH's fiery wrath against Zion and its leaders to 1st person plural depictions of the perilous lives of those who have survived YHWH's fury (vs 17–20). In their final, anguished words, the community of survivors describes the political, emotional, and religious dissonance they must endure in the aftermath of Jerusalem's destruction. An address to Daughter Edom, one of ancient Israel's paradigmatic enemies, follows in verses 21–22 (cf. Ps 137:7). The two imperatives at the beginning of verse 21, 'exult!' (שִׂישִׂי [*śîśî*]) and 'rejoice!' (שִׂמְחִי [*śimḥî*]), employ sarcasm and introduce a dramatic shift. Daughter Edom should join her neighbor in solidarity and mourning,[91] because her own fate will be similar to Zion's (vs 21b, 22b).[92] The community that expresses its suffering in verses 17–20 ends on a note of hopelessness and uncertainty. At that point, the poem shifts to a judgment oracle against Edom and a proclamation of the end of Zion's exile. As Parry observes, '[t]he shift from no-hope to confident-hope is so dramatic and so unexpected that one is left disoriented'.[93] Here, someone dares to speak after the last word.[94] The audacity of this speaker

---

[91] Anderson, *A Time to Mourn, A Time to Dance*, pp. 93–94.

[92] For other oracles against Edom in the Hebrew Bible see, e.g., Isa 63 (vengeance on Edom followed by Communal Lament); Isa 11:14; 34:5–17; Jer 49:7–22; Ezek 25:12–14; 35; Amos 1:6, 9, 11; 2:1; Obadiah; Joel 3:19 Mal 1:2–5.

[93] Parry, *Lamentations*, p. 142. See Westermann, *Lamentations*, p. 205.

[94] Westermann argues that due to the connections between vs 21–22 and 1–16, Lam 4:17–20 is an insertion into the poem that displaces an earlier section of the poem (Westermann, *Lamentations*, p. 205). He does not identify the specific connections to which he alludes. Lamentations

adds to the text's complexity.[95] Unlike the previous poems, in which the sufferer has the last word, the sufferer's word is pushed to the penultimate position in Lamentations 4. However, the drastic differences between the sufferers' own last words and the poem's last words diminish the latter's force. Though the poem's last words are meant to be good news for Zion, they hang structurally and metaphorically detached and disconnected from the sufferers' own final words. Here ת (*tāw*) does not actually signal closure; rather it introduces rupture and ambivalence.

4:21–22 focuses on judgment against personified Edom. Lamentations 4:11 affirms that YHWH is responsible for Zion's fate. Zion and her religious leaders are culpable (vs 6, 13). Verses 1–16 contain no obvious indication that a political foe contributed to Zion's fate, though a passing reference to the 'nations' (גוֹיִם [*gôyim*]) appears in 4:15b. However, this reference does not justify the claim that vs 21–22 share thematic or literary links with vs 1–16. The structural anomalies in Lamentations 4, as in preceding chapters, highlight the struggle inherent in bearing witness to extreme suffering.

[95] For a discussion of some of the complexities related to Lam 4:21–22, see Westermann, *Lamentations*, pp. 205–206; and Salters, *Lamentations*, pp. 333–338. The historical provenance of Lamentations 4 is uncertain. Does it reflect those who remained in the land or those who were forced into exile? Depictions of Zion's fate in Lam 4:1–10 appear to affirm the former position—the text presupposes conditions consistent with what life might have been like for survivors of the Babylonian destruction Jerusalem who were left in the city. However, vs 17–20 seem to point to conditions consistent with the exilic period. The community is 'still waiting' for deliverance (v. 17). Reference to their 'pursuers' appear (v. 19), as does a veiled reference to the capture of their king, 'in whose shade they had expected to live among the nations' (v. 20). While it is impossible to deduce with certainty the concrete historical referents in these verses, their allusions appear to reflect the point of view of Judeans living in exile. In fact, the proclamation of the end of Zion's exile in the judgment oracle against Edom coheres with a reading of vs 17–20 as an account of the experiences of an exiled community.

Lamentations 5

Chapter Outline:

A. Plead for YHWH to pay attention to, and Description of, sufferer's (community's) predicament (vs1–18);

B. *Desperate plea for YHWH to pay attention to sufferer's predicament (vs 19–22).*

Pay Attention!: The Plea of a Community

Unlike the book's preceding poems, Lamentations 5 is not an alphabetic acrostic. Nevertheless, it consists of twenty-two verses—the number of consonants in the Hebrew alphabet. This poem opens with three imperatives: 'remember!' (זְכֹר [*zĕkōr*]); 'look!' (הַבִּיטָה [*habbîṭā*]); and 'see!' (רְאֵה [*rĕʾēh*]). The community of survivors beseeches YHWH to attend to the disgrace it has endured, and the tragedies it has suffered. Verses 2–18 depict the sufferers' anguish. Their fortunes have been reversed for the worse (vs 2–4, 12–16). Their enemies pursue them (v. 5). Their living conditions are precarious, at best (vs 4, 9, and 10). They must risk their lives to obtain basic necessities (v. 9). Zion has suffered a horrible fate, and the community of disheartened survivors has not been vindicated or restored (vs 17–18).

In verse 19, the community shifts from despair to affirmation of confidence in YHWH. Utilizing royal YHWH ideology, the sufferers assert their belief in the perpetuity and indestructibility of YHWH's reign.[96] Despite Zion's current circumstance, its deity still reigns. This confident affirmation of YHWH's reign serves as the springboard for the critical question raised in verse 20: 'why has YHWH completely forgotten and abandoned his people?' Following this question, a plea for YHWH to restore God's relationship with his people appears (v. 21). The poem ends on a melancholic note of hopelessness, suggesting that YHWH might completely reject the suffering community (v. 22). As in Lamentations 1, 2,

---

[96] Cf. Ps 102:13. While Lam 5:19 focuses exclusively on the 'throne' of YHWH, Ps 102:13 focuses on YHWH's throne and renown. Both passages present the view that YHWH's throne is indestructible. See Berlin, *Lamentations*, p. 125.

and 3, the sufferer is given the last word in Lamentations 5. Unlike Lamentations 4, no audacious speaker proclaims judgment on Zion's paradigmatic enemies, or hope for Zion herself. The community affirms its confidence with significant reservations. Hope remains fractured and tenuous.

A few motifs link Lamentations 5 with the preceding poem, particularly Lam 4:16–20. Both poems contain features of communal laments.[97] Each contains reference to the undependability of foreign nations (see Lam 4:17; 5:6). Each contains reference to invading nations disrespecting or dishonoring Zion's elders (4:16; 5:12). Both poems allude to the survivors' relentless pursuers (4:9; 5:5). Finally, both poems allude to a major attack on Davidic kingship (see 4:20; 5:16).

SUMMARY

Lamentations witnesses to the collapse of the social, political, economic, and religious structures that traditionally provided foundations for Zion's identity and security—for example, the Davidic Monarchy and YHWH's central temple in Jerusalem. The book testifies to world-shattering realities. Rupture prominently appears in the book's contents and structures. The structural functions of many of Lamentations' dramatic breaks are neither apparent nor predictable. To the readers or hearers of the book, the presence of these breaches in the poems seem unplanned and *ad hoc*. Despite the use of Hebrew alphabetic acrostic structures to frame the five poems that comprise the book of Lamentations, rupture and chaos persist in the poems. Personified Zion and the traumatic experiences she has endured resist being forced into neat forms and orderly structures. The jolting effect created by use of the dramatic breaks might well be examples of the poet's strategic use of a literary device. However, these textual ruptures both mirror and testify to the rupture of trauma. The poems fractured structures, genre adaptations, content, and shifts in voices and persons attest to lives that have been devastated and radically altered during and in the aftermath of trauma. Read through the lens of trauma studies,

[97] See Gerstenberger, *Psalm Part 1*, pp. 11–14.

these features provide a heuristic context for reading and interpreting these poems as post-trauma, survivor literature.

Each poem includes extensive descriptions of the victims' predicaments, which function strategically to motivate readers and hearers to identify and empathize with the victims. The worlds, foundational institutions, and lives of these victims—whether as an individual (Lam 3:1–20, 52–66), an entire community, or a subgroup within the community (Lam 3:41–46; 4:17–20; 5:1–10)—have been significantly ruptured in the wake of Jerusalem's fall. The survivors' suffering is excessive and open-ended. Their trauma imposes itself on, and intrudes into, the poems' disciplining structures. Ambivalence, uncertainty, helplessness and dissonance persist in surplus in the poems. Witnesses to trauma overpower fleeting affirmations of hope (Lamentations 3). In the end, the survivors' anguish remains pervasive.

The poems in the book of Lamentations convey the traumatic experiences of certain victims who survived Jerusalem's destruction. Personified Zion identifies with, intercedes and speaks for, and sympathizes with the plight of these survivors. The male sufferer/narrator in Lamentations 3 represents, speaks for, and identifies with the predicaments of many of those victims. Similarly, the narrator in Lamentations 1, 2, and sections of Lamentations 3, is implicated in, and sympathizes with, the plight of his 'Dear People'. The community stand-in/leader in Lamentations 3 and 4, and the communal voice in Lamentations 5, bear witness to the anguish of entire survivor-communities, or subgroups within those communities.

The book's five poems also offer survivors a medium, language, and space to vent their anguish. This process is crucial for the survival of trauma victims. While there is no appropriate alphabet for extreme suffering, the creative blend of metaphorical, hyperbolic, and stereotypical language, along with adaptations of relevant genres and the alphabetic acrostic façade, offer a useful vehicle to express and work through trauma. Depictions of the sufferers' predicament are often connected with pleas for YHWH to attend to their anguish (Lam 1:9c, 11c, 20a; 2:20a; 3:56; 5:1). In some instances, the narrator himself pays attention to the sufferer's plight (see Lam 2:11, 18–19; 3:49–50). Ultimately, the victims in Lamentations hold out tentative hope that YHWH might attend to their plight. The motif of 'paying attention' to trauma serves as the hinge on which the book turns. The strategic thrust of the entire book is to motivate YHWH to intervene on Zion's behalf. The poems seek to motivate readers and hearers (secondary witnesses) to join in solidarity with Zion's cause. They implore audiences to join in bearing witness to Daughter Zion's trauma.

The plea for readers and hearers to bear witness to Daughter Zion's trauma is neither simple nor straightforward. In the poems' alphabetic acrostics structures, for example, each א (*'ālep*)-unit grabs readers' and hearers' attentions and invites them to pay attention to the survivors' agony.[98] However, each ת (*tāw*)-unit leaves readers and hearers unsettled—'certainly this can't be the last word!'[99] Furthermore, each ת (*tāw*)-unit leaves unanswered the nagging questions: 'Will YHWH respond?' 'Will YHWH speak?' 'If YHWH does respond or speak, what will YHWH say?' These questions leave secondary witnesses disoriented and disconcerted. Ultimately, Zion, the representative and embodiment of the survivors and sufferers, has the final word: YHWH remains silent in Lamentations.[100] This divine silence gives preeminence and priority to the poems' voices of pain and anguish.

The process of hearing and reading Zion's trauma is traumatic. In Lamentations 1–3, each ת (*tāw*)-unit leads back to an א (*'ālep*)-unit, only to begin the process all over again. Moments of hope in the poems are fleeting and ultimately overshadowed by the horrible realities of trauma.[101] The flicker of hope in the final verses of Lamentations 4 precedes the urgent, desperate invitation to attend to the plight of the suffering community that introduces Lamentations 5. Zion's last words in Lamentations 5 leave readers and hearers to wrestle with the possibility of YHWH's absolute abandonment of Zion. The possibility of a dénouement in Zion's predicament is deferred indefinitely (Lam 5:22). Lamentations leaves Daughter Zion and her secondary witnesses grasping for hope and meaning, its structure provides a platform for the *possibility* of radi-

---

[98] The beginnings of the poems in Lamentations 1–4.

[99] The ends of the poems in Lamentations 1–4.

[100] For a discussion on divine silence in Lamentations, see Mandolfo, *Daughter Zion Talks Back to the Prophets*, pp. 79–119.

[101] Lamentations 3.

cally new beginnings. As O'Connor observes: 'Lamentations marks out the place of ruptured life, when the old story fails and a new one has yet to appear'.[102]

[102] O'Connor, *Tears of the World*, p. 85.

CHAPTER 4.
NON-REFERENTIAL HISTORY AND THE BOOK OF LAMENTATIONS

INTRODUCTION

In this chapter, I show how the notion of non-referential history—an important concept in the works of early trauma theorists—can shed light on certain aspects of the book of Lamentations, particularly the book's use of stereotypical, tropic, hyperbolic, and emotive language. In addition, I analyze the strategic functions of the fluctuations in mood or emotional volatility evident in the poems.

Non-Referential History

In her analysis of the intersections of history, literature, theory and trauma, Cathy Caruth proposes the possibility of a history not directly referential, that is, a history that is not based on simple, direct correlations between experience and referents.[1] The notion of trauma, with its often delayed, debilitating effects, permits 'history' to arise 'where *immediate understanding*' is lacking.[2] According to Caruth, 'a history of trauma' is referential only to the extent that 'it is not fully perceived as it occurs'.[3] Referents in trauma informed history is therefore indirect since trauma is a rupture in 'the mind's experience of time'.[4] This breach in the mind relates to conscious recognition of the threat to life, that is, the threat of death. As Caruth observes, this 'threat is recognized as such by the mind *one*

---

[1] Caruth, *Unclaimed Experience*, p. 11.

[2] Ibid., emphasis original.

[3] Ibid., p. 18.

[4] Ibid., p. 61.

moment too late'.[5] Thus, the threat of death is a 'missed' (belated) experience that is not yet fully known.[6] While Caruth's notion of trauma theory is much more complexed and nuanced, I am particularly interested in the possibilities that this theory hold for reading literature, specifically biblical poetic literature, as a type of 'history'.

Dominick LaCapra also explores the intersections of history, theory and literature with reference to trauma.[7] However, while Caruth's study approaches history through theory and literature, LaCapra's analysis pays greater attention to historiography itself.[8] He contends that 'conventional stereotypes of transparent representation' or notions of 'self-sufficient research paradigm' are no longer tenable in modern historiography.[9] For LaCapra, the question of experience, critically invoked, is foundational to historiography.[10] He acknowledges that traumatic experiences affect both the observed and observers.[11] The type of history that gives credibility to experience, specifically traumatic experience, moves beyond so-called objective reconstructions of the past. While there are notable differences between Caruth and LaCapra in their construal of the concept of non-referential history, both agree that post-traumatic literature/history conveys a type of 'history' that does not rest on direct correlations between experience and verifiable truth claims.

---

[5] Ibid., p. 62; emphasis original.

[6] Ibid.

[7] See LaCapra, *Representing the Holocaust: History, Theory, Trauma*; La-Capaa, *History and Memory after Auschwitz*; idem, *Writing History, Writing Trauma*.

[8] See LaCapra, *Writing History, Writing Trauma*, pp. 181–191.

[9] LaCapra, *Writing History, Writing Trauma*, p. 36.

[10] Ibid.

[11] LaCapra, *Writing History, Writing Trauma*, p. 41. One of LaCapra's critiques of Caruth's approach to this issue is that she approaches history through the medium of theory and literature. Such an approach excludes historiography itself and the possible 'contributions or resistances it might pose to her analysis in both intellectual and institutional terms' (LaCapra, *Writing History, Writing Trauma*, p. 183).

Disruptive experiences of trauma and elusive testimonies of survivors and observers who bear witness to it are credible and authoritative sources of this type of *history*.[12] The accounts of survivors might not provide datable or verifiable information about the traumatic events they survived. Nevertheless, these accounts bear witness to a reality that is beyond their full grasp and comprehension—the reality that something world shattering and painfully disruptive has occurred with ongoing consequences. Although trauma is often related to specific events, it cannot be restricted to 'terms of a discrete, dated experience'.[13] This understanding of non-referential history, which prominently appears in the works of early trauma theorists like Caruth and LaCapra, informs my analysis of issues of history and historicity within the book of Lamentations.

Daniel Smith-Christopher, drawing on the works of Caruth and V. Volkan, asserts that non-referential history holds potential, interpretive challenges and possibilities for biblical scholarship.[14] According to Smith-Christopher, 'many experiences of trauma are not often explicitly or even rationally discussed—they can only be analyzed by decoding/exegeting latent effects—and these traumatized responses can sometimes only be seen in artistic expressions, poetry, or images'.[15] The notion that trauma can be expressed through 'artistic or non-rational' mediums raises important questions for interpreting non-historical biblical literature.[16] Despite the inherent challenges of this theory, Smith-Christopher correctly recognizes the interpretive possibilities of the concept of indirect 'his-

---

[12] See Caruth, 'Recapturing the Past', pp. 151–157. Caruth argues that, 'For the survivor of trauma…the truth of the event may reside not only in its brutal facts, but also in the way that their occurrence defies simple comprehension' (p. 153; see also Bessel A. van der Kolk and Onno van der Hart, 'The Intrusive Past: The Flexibility of Memory and the Engraving of Trauma', pp. 158–182).

[13] LaCapra, *Writing History, Writing Trauma*, p. 186.

[14] Smith-Christopher, 'Trauma and the Old Testament: Some Problems and Prospects', pp. 223–243.

[15] Smith-Christopher, 'Trauma and the Old Testament', p. 238.

[16] Ibid.

tory' for certain biblical texts.[17] This insight is consistent with the view that the book of Lamentations can be read as an ancient example of writing trauma.

While Lamentations' language is demonstrably tropic, stereotypical and hyperbolic, it is neither fraudulent nor fictional. Smith-Christopher correctly observes, such language 'may be the culturally acceptable way to express precisely the emotional reactions to an actual catastrophic event'.[18] Further, 'while some critical scholars seem intent on blaming a "Sunday school" bias (cf. Barstad) for the view that an actual crisis took place in 587', it is equally objectionable to replace this view with a 'culturally insensitive Western bias that seems disappointed that Mediterranean peoples do not mourn 'as we do' or refer to events 'as we do'.[19] Thus, while stereotypical language in Lamentations might not provide historical 'details of the disaster of catastrophe', it likely conveys the emotional, social, economic and religious impact of Jerusalem's demise.[20]

Stereotypical Language and Historical Referents

In his analysis of the literary character of Lamentations, Iain Provan rightly observes that the book's language is generally stereotypical, tropic (or non-literal), and hyperbolic in character.[21] Provan questions '[w]hether scholars are justified in feeling so confident about the historical background' of Lamentations.[22] He also recognizes the difficulties inherent in attempts to identify actual historical referents in the book.[23] Addressing these difficulties, he

---

[17] Ibid., p. 239. Specifically, Smith-Christopher references the books of Daniel, Esther, and Judith. I believe that his insight is also applicable to the book of Lamentations.

[18] Smith-Christopher, *A Biblical Theology of Exile*, p. 103.

[19] Ibid.

[20] Ibid., p. 104.

[21] See Provan, *Lamentations*, pp. 5–6; see also Provan, 'Past, Present and Future in Lamentations 3:52–66: The Case for a Precative Perfect Reexamined', pp. 164–175; Provan, 'Reading Texts Against an Historical Background: The Case of Lamentations 1', pp. 130–143.

[22] Provan, *Lamentations*, p. 12.

[23] Ibid., pp. 12–15.

asks: '...if it is the case that the language of a poem is frequently and demonstrably hyperbolic, how could we ever know *how much* inexactitude is actually present at any given point?'[24] Moreover, 'How could we know which details could be used for historical reconstruction and which not?'[25] Provan correctly concludes that identifying the precise historical background of the poems comprising Lamentations is very difficult.[26] In fact, he claims, '[t]here does not seem to be...*any* evidence with regard to' establishing a definitive date for the book.[27] In some instances, there are multiple possible referents.[28] His questioning of attempts to assign Lamentations to one specific historical period, or reading the book as a response to one particular set of historical circumstances, is legitimate.[29] Furthermore, his challenge of the scholarly consensus regarding Lamentations' date of composition is necessary to prevent the general assumptions that form the basis of this consensus from masquerading as conclusive or established facts. Assumptions regarding the book's date of composition are just that—*assumptions*.

Nevertheless, Provan's view suffers the (unintended) consequence of diminishing the realities of actual traumatic events that likely informed the composition of Lamentations.[30] Admittedly, as Hillers observers, the book's style 'is deliberately universalizing,

---

[24] Ibid., p. 13, emphasis original.

[25] Ibid.

[26] Ibid.

[27] Ibid., p. 15, emphasis added.

[28] Ibid., pp. 13–14.

[29] See also, Gerstenberger, *Lamentations*, p. 473.

[30] Studies on the functions and power of post-traumatic poetry are insightful in responding to Provan's argument. See, for example, Roland Bleiker's analysis of the poetry of Paul Celan, a Holocaust survivor (R. Bleiker, '"Give it the Shade": Paul Celan and the Politics of Apolitical Poetry', pp. 661–676. Concerning Celan's poetic commentary on the Holocaust, 'Deathfugue', Bleiker asserts: his poetry serves 'as a method of letting the disaster stand out, as a lament in a void of meaning' (ibid., p. 664). While Celan's 'Deathfugue' is certainly not straightforwardly referential, it does echo some of the death-dealing realities of life in a concentration camp in graphic poetic language (ibid., p. 665).

using conventional and traditional descriptions of the fall of a city that, by their very nature and intent, resist efforts to treat them as documentary films of what happened.'[31] Further, while it is possible that the universalizing and conventional language of Lamentations might suggest literary creativity (that is, fiction), it is equally plausible that the book's style and language give voice to the very real suffering of a particular group of ancient Judeans. Lamentations utilizes conventional language to express particular responses and reactions to specific historical events. Smith-Christopher correctly observes the danger in some scholars' tendency to move from 'proper caution in dealing with literary forms of language (i.e., stereotypical language), to open skepticism that such language has any historical referent at all'.[32] The fact that the language of Lamentations is demonstrably stereotypical, tropic, or hyperbolic does not necessarily prevent its poems from conveying *history*, a traumatic history or a history of trauma.[33] The language that Lamentations' poet utilizes conveys the responses of some ancient Judean survivors to very real, traumatizing experiences.[34]

Proper caution and a critical examination of assumptions are essential prerequisites; nevertheless, Lamentations is not ahistorical or devoid of identifiable historical referents. Though latent, signals of the effects of trauma surface at different points in the poems. These signals are evident in the book's tendency towards hyperbole—a tendency especially evident in the frequent mood shifts in the

---

[31] Hillers, *Lamentations* (1992), p. 10.

[32] Smith-Christopher, *A Biblical Theology of Exile*, p. 102. See R. Carroll, 'Exile! What Exile? Deportation and the Discourse of Diaspora', pp. 62–79.

[33] Smith-Christopher, *A Biblical Theology of Exile*, p. 103.

[34] In addressing the challenges inherent in comparing ancient societies with modern ones, Smith-Christopher insightfully asserts, 'In our attempts to carefully and critically remember that ancient societies are *not* modern societies, and that we must be careful in making comparisons, we run the equally serious risk of denying the human reality of traumatizing experiences of fellow humans, even if those humans experienced these events over 2500 years ago' (Smith-Christopher, 'Reading War and Trauma', pp. 253–274).

poems, and the way the book describes the extent of the city's destruction and the plight of mothers and their children.

THE EXTENT OF DAUGHTER ZION'S WOES

Lamentations utilizes hyperbolic language to describe the extent of the catastrophe that befell Daughter Zion and her children. Often these descriptions contradict other statements about the extent of the catastrophe in the book and elsewhere in the Hebrew Bible. For example, Lam 1:3a states that 'Judah has gone into exile'.[35] Here, the use of synecdoche might suggest that the *entire* nation of Judah went into exile. Judah (the whole) stands for (the inhabitants of) Jerusalem. However, even as we recognize synecdoche in the above statement, it is clear elsewhere in Lamentations that *not all* of Judah, or Jerusalem, went into exile (see Lam 2:10, 11–12; 4:5; 5:6, 8–9). The land is not empty. Thus, the statement that 'Judah has gone into exile' is best understood hyperbolically—an exaggeration of actual facts. Within this hyperbolic reference, however, lies an elusive, traumatic experience that is not fully grasped by, or accessible to, the survivors. The statement 'Judah has gone into exile' is not simply poetic; it signals the traumatic experiences that shaped the text. The significance of the use of hyperbole in Lam 1:3a is that it expresses the narrator's sense of the enormity or excessiveness of trauma that informs the text.

Similarly, the hyperbolic statement that Zion's 'maidens' have gone into captivity in Lam 1:18c is in tension with Lam 1:4c, which asserts that Zion's 'maidens' are still in Zion. Lamentations 1:19b indicates that Zion's 'priests' and 'elders' have all died in the city. Statements in Lam 1:4b and 2:10, by contrast, suggest that at least some of Zion's priests and elders are alive in Jerusalem.[36] These hyperbolic references to the fate of two classes of Zion's religious functionaries in the wake of the city's destruction recount a history that is not straightforwardly referential. Did *all* of Zion's priests and elders perish in the city, as Lam 1:19a implies? The text itself indicates that the answer to this question is no. Yet the disruptive

---

[35] See Provan, *Lamentations*, p. 5.

[36] Ibid.

experience of trauma is evident precisely in the tension between these contradictory sentiments. This tension reflects the struggle to bear witness to trauma—to express that which cannot be fully grasped.

The elusiveness of the traumatic experiences that inform the book of Lamentations is also evident in statements that highlight the finality and totality of Zion's demise. For instance, Lam 2:2a states that Adonai has destroyed '*all* of Jacob's dwellings'.[37] He has 'cut down *all* of Israel's might' (Lam 2:3a); and 'like a fire' He has 'devoured Jacob *all* around' (v. 3c).[38] Moreover, Adonai has 'wiped out Israel' and '*all* her strongholds' (v. 5a).[39] While archaeological evidence supports the claim of the *total* (or near total) destruction of Jerusalem and certain areas in its immediate environs following the 586 BCE Babylonian assault on the city, evidence for widespread destruction throughout the rest of Judah is lacking.[40]

The references to 'Jacob' and 'Israel' in the preceding verses are used synonymously with 'Daughter Zion' (vs 1, 4) and 'Daughter Judah' (vs 2, 5). These identifications of 'Daughter Zion' with national entities, or the identification of Zion with the chosen people as a whole ('Jacob'; see Lam 1:17; Isa 10:20; 14:1; 40:27; 41:8, 14; 43:1, 22, 28), use synecdoche in ways that affirm the catastrophe's enormity. That the poet of Lamentations speaks of the destruction of Judah's capital city in terms suggestive of razing of the entire nation is significant. Taken literally, such statements do not correspond to our knowledge of realities of any period of Judah's history. Yet they are not propagandistic in nature. Rather, they highlight the sense of excess typically associated with trauma and its aftermath. While it is possible (even likely) that the poet uses hyperbole as a rhetorical strategy precisely to express the enormity of the debilitating disaster that struck Zion and her children, these hyperbolic statements also bear the imprint of trauma. They witness to an experience that remains beyond mastery. The excessiveness evident in hyperbolic statements draws attention to the enig-

---

[37] Emphasis added.

[38] Emphasis added.

[39] Emphasis added.

[40] See Stern, *Archaeology and the Land of the Bible*, pp. 321–323.

ma of survival. In the wake of the razing of Zion, no one should have survived.

The enigma of survival is poignantly expressed in Lam 2:22: וְלֹא הָיָה בְּיוֹם אַף־יְהוָה פָּלִיט וְשָׂרִיד (*wĕlo' hāyāh bĕyôm 'ap-YHWH pālîṭ wĕśārîd*), 'On the day of YHWH's anger, no one survived, none escaped'. This statement of complete annihilation stands in tension with other references to survival in the book. We have already noted that there were survivors (see Lam 1:4, 11; 2:10–12). Lamentations itself bears witness to the realities of survivors and survival. For many survivors of traumatic events, however, the enigma of survival is experienced as a sensation(s) of being dead while yet alive.[41] Thus, the hyperbolic perspective that in the aftermath of YHWH's anger, there were absolutely no survivors speaks to the impact of trauma. Provan recognizes the use of hyperbole in Lam 2:22,[42] and I agree with his assertion that the hyperbole functions strategically to emphasize the magnitude of the catastrophe. However, the feature of non-referential history that is typical of survivors' testimonies also illuminates other dimensions of the function of this hyperbole. The element of excess reveals the debilitating nature of trauma. In addition, it highlights the incomprehensibility and inaccessibility of the experience such experiences. The catastrophe in question is not only enormous, but also world-shattering and beyond mastery. It is incomparable (Lam 2:13).

THE PLIGHT OF MOTHERS AND THEIR CHILDREN

Lamentations also uses hyperbole in depictions of the plights of women and children, Zion's most vulnerable inhabitants. These hyperbolic depictions highlight the catastrophe's magnitude and bring into sharper focus the enormity of its impact on survivors. Depictions of the miseries endured by mothers and their children disclose a ruptured world. Common norms of decency and civility have been shattered. Basic ideals of altruism have been smashed.

Lamentations 2:11c-12 depict graphic scenes of starving 'children' and 'infants' (עוֹלֵל [*'ôlēl*] and יוֹנֵק [*yônēq*]) in the city squares,

---

[41] See Langer, *Using and Abusing the Holocaust*, p. 2.

[42] See Provan, *Lamentations*, p. 79.

languishing and ultimately dying in their mothers' bosoms. These mothers are unable to nourish or sustain their famished offspring. According to personified Zion, these extreme, traumatic circumstances eventually force desperate mothers to eat their own babies in order to survive (Lam 2:20). Similarly, Lam 4:4 depicts the painful miseries of starving 'infants' and 'children' (יוֹנֵק [*yônēq*] and עוֹלָלִים [*ʿôlālîm*]). As in Lamentations 2, the profound impact of the severe famine associated with the city's demise have forced mothers, who are normally compassionate, to cook their own children in order to survive. Whether or not such cannibalistic activities actually took place during or following the sixth century BCE Babylonian assaults on Jerusalem remains a matter of conjecture. However, while it is conceivable that actual, isolated cases of cannibalism occurred in ancient Jerusalem during the sixth century, the references to wide-spread cannibalism among mothers in Lamentations seem stereotypical and hyperbolic.[43]

References to mothers turning to cannibalism for survival reveal the shattering of the expected maternal instincts to protect and nourish their children. Such ruptures of traditional norms of basic human decency and civility are not simply the result of extreme famine; they also testify to trauma. That the poems repeat and, seemingly, exaggerate such gruesome acts of human cruelty is indicative of the debilitating effects and incomprehensibility of trauma and its aftereffects. The impact of extreme violence and physical need often force survivors to the limits of their humanity. Thus, while references to maternal cannibalism function strategically to heighten the emotional impact of Zion's demise, they also reveal the potentially life-altering impact of trauma. Although these references to cannibalism do not provide verifiable historical information, they bear witness to experiences lying beyond the grasp of those whose voices the book of Lamentations preserves.

---

[43] See Berlin, *Lamentations*, p. 76.

MOOD SWINGS: A PSYCHOLOGICAL ANALYSIS OF LAMENTATIONS

Non-referential history lends credibility to traumatic experiences, which often involve varied emotional expressions—the voicing of pain, hope, fears and agony. Shifts in mood are one of the prominent features in Lamentations' five poems.[44] Graphic descriptions of the psychological state of the survivor-sufferer(s) also are ubiquitous in these poems.[45] Expressions of varied, often conflicting, emotions and graphic depictions of anguish are typical features of trauma survivors' testimonies. At strategic points in each poem, shifts from depictions of tragedy to descriptions of the sufferer's anguish and agony occur.[46] In other instances, the poems describe in gripping language the survivors' experiences of loneliness or abandonment, betrayal, and/or extreme hopelessness.[47] Some poems refer to, or describe, mourning and/or mourning rituals. The poems also highlight experiences of grief and human responses to extreme loss.[48] In sum, Lamentations include vivid accounts of ongoing experiences of trauma, as well as recollections of past traumatic events. These shifts in the psychological or emotional states of the sufferer(s) in each poem focus attention on their dilemma. As Robert L. Cohn asserts, 'Sorrow, anger, bafflement,

---

[44] For a useful analysis of the implications of shifts of mood in Psalms of Laments and other biblical laments see F. G. Villanueva, *The 'Uncertainty of a Hearing': A Study of the Sudden Change of Mood in the Psalms of Lament.* Villanueva argues cogently that the shifts of mood from lament to praise, and back to lament, in many lament psalms signal a sense of the lamenter's uncertainty about whether or not God actually has heard his/her plea. The same motif also appears elsewhere in the Hebrew Bible (Ibid., pp. 213–247). This sense of uncertainty is the dominant mood within the entire book of Lamentations (See ibid., p. 243).

[45] As noted above, the sufferer in Lamentations can be personified Zion, an individual, the poet or another individual, or a community or subgroup of same.

[46] See Lam 1:2a, 12b, 16a; 2:11ab, 18ab; and 3:48.

[47] See Lam 1:1a, 2c, 4cβ, 9bβ, 16b, 17a, 22c; 2:21b; 3:6, 53; 4:9, 18b; 5:20, 22.

[48] See Lam 1:4a; 2:8c, 10; 5:15.

contrition, vengeance, desperation and hope cry forth from [Lamentations] in dizzying succession'.[49] The poems focus not on the *why* of the traumatic experiences, but on the *extent* and *reality* of those experiences.

Lamentations 1

In Lamentations 1, Daughter Zion is depicted as abandoned by her God and her allies. She is bereft of comforters—'there is no one to console her'.[50] The Piel participle of the root נחם (*nḥm*), 'to be sorry', 'to be moved with pity', or 'to have compassion', מְנַחֵם (*mĕnaḥēm*), 'to comfort', or 'to console', appears five times in this poem (see Lam 1:2bβ, 9bβ, 16bα, 17aβ, and 21aβ).[51] Saul M. Olyan notes that the semantic range of the Hebrew verb נחם (*nḥm*), 'to comfort', includes joining mourners in mourning rites (see Job 2:11; Isa 51:19), helping to end the mourner's mourning (see Gen 37:35; 1 Chr 7:22–23; Jer 31:13), and the performance of acts of consolation (see Job 42:11).[52] Each of these meanings of the root נחם (*nḥm*) is evident in Lamentations. Zion has endured unimaginable trauma, and is left alone with אֵין מְנַחֵם לָהּ (*'ên mĕnaḥēm lāh*), 'no one to console her' (Lam 1:9bβ). According to the description of the *marzēaḥ* (mourning rite) in Jer 16:5–9, providing *comfort* or *consolation* to the bereaved was an essential element in ancient Isra-

---

[49] R. L. Cohn, 'Biblical Responses to Catastrophe', p. 269.

[50] See Lam 1:2, 9, 17; Cf. Ps 69:21 [ET, 20].

[51] The participle מְנַחֵם (*mĕnaḥēm*) appears in Gen 37:35 in the context of Jacob mourning over the apparent death of his beloved son, Joseph. His sons and daughters attempt to *console* him, but he is inconsolable. Upon hearing of the death of Nahash, king of the Ammonites, in 2 Sam 10:2 (cf. 1 Chr 19:2–3), King David is said to send envoys to *console* (מְנַחֵם [*mĕnaḥēm*]) Hanun, Nahash' son and successor. In this context, David seems to be sending his *condolences* to King Hanun as a gesture of good will. In Gen 50:21 מְנַחֵם (*mĕnaḥēm*) is used in the sense of offering *reassurance* or *encouragement* (see 2 Sam 12:24; 1 Chr 7:22; Eccl 4:1; Nah 3:7; Zech 10:2). Following the horrendous tragedies that befall Job, his friends come to 'sympathize with him, and to *console* him' (Job 2:11, emphasis mine; cf. Job 21:34; 29:25).

[52] See S. M. Olyan, *Biblical Mourning*, pp. 47–48.

el's mourning rituals.[53] Yet Zion is not afforded even this basic benefit in the aftermath of her great loss. Her trauma is intensified by the absence of sympathizers, who would dare to acknowledge and bear witness to her pain. Not even YHWH seems available to console Zion. The repetition of Zion's abandonment in Lamentations 1 serves to highlight the extent and intensity of her predicament. Thus, the repetition of references to Zion's abandonment functions rhetorically to persuade YHWH to attend to her plight.

Zion's emotional states are also expressed through the poems' graphic representations of despair and distress: 'Sorely she weeps in the night, her tears upon her cheeks' (Lam 1:2a, 16a).[54] In both verses, reference to Zion's uncontrollable weeping precedes a notice of Zion's lack of consolers.[55] There is no one to dry her tears or to offer her sympathy or condolences; hence, she continues to weep. That Zion's trusted political 'lovers' and 'friends' have betrayed her only intensifies her agony (v. 2bc, 19a).

The interruptions introduced by the imperative רְאֵה (*rĕʾēh*; Lam 1:9cα, 11cα, and 20aα) call YHWH's attention to the extent of Zion's woes. Zion implores YHWH to 'see' her 'affliction' (v. 9cα), to 'see' and 'behold' how 'worthless' she has become (v. 11cα), and to 'see' her 'distress' (v. 20aα). Furthermore, Zion has become so desperate that she implores the 'peoples' to 'hear' and 'see' her 'sorrow' or her 'suffering' (v. 18b). Her heart is in 'turmoil' (v. 20aβ), and her 'groaning' gives voice to her unbearable emotional anguish

---

[53] See Philip J. King and Lawrence E. Stager, *Life in Biblical Israel*, pp. 379–380. King and Stager assert that the *marzēaḥ* was typically associated with the cult of the dead. In Jeremiah 16, YHWH forbids Jeremiah from attending the *bêt marzēaḥ* ('house of mourning') and from participating 'in the memorial meals associated with mourning the dead and consoling the mourners' (ibid., p. 379).

[54] Cf. Jeremiah 9:18–19.

[55] There are other similarities between Lam 1:2 and 16. Both verses utilize the root בכה (*bkh*), 'to weep', in the first line. Both refer to 'tears' in line 2, though different expressions are employed. Both end with references to אוֹיֵב (*ʾôyēb*) 'foe' (v. 16; אֹיְבִים [*ʾoyĕbîm*], 'foes', v. 2). The third line in both verses affirms that Zion has 'no one to comfort' her (Lam 1:2bα and 1:16:bα).

(v. 21aα). Zion's 'groans' are many, and her heart is 'sick' (v. 22c). Such striking portrayals of Zion's grief signal experiences of trauma and its aftermath. Emotional expressions and graphic depictions of anguish give voice to survivors' testimonies. Together, they constitute a history consisting of traumatic experiences and their effects. These depictions implore all who hear Zion's cries or see her peril, including YHWH, to stop and sympathize with Zion—to join Zion in bearing witness to her trauma.

Lamentations 2

Lamentations 2 begins with a lengthy description of YHWH's systematic razing of Zion and her religious rites and institutions (Lam 2:1–9). Depictions of her distress interrupt these graphic descriptions of YHWH's onslaught on Daughter Zion. As in Lam 1:4a, the poet uses synecdoche in Lam 2:8c to highlight Zion's plight. YWHW has caused her 'wall' and 'rampart' to be in 'mourning' (אבל [*'bl*]; cf. Lam 1:4a)[56] and to 'languish' (אמל [*'ml*]). The emotions assigned to these non-human entities are typically associated with human experiences of grief. Thus, these descriptions are personifications. Zion's gates have 'sunken (טבע [*ṭbʿ*]) into the ground' (v. 9aα). Since the preceding line (v. 8c) utilizes tropic language to speak of inanimate objects associated with Zion in terms of human emotions of grief, the language here can also be understood metaphorically.[57] The expression highlights Zion's state of depression. The bars on Zion's gates are 'destroyed' (אבד [*'bd*]), completely 'shattered' (שבר [*šbr*]). While this description might refer to the actual conditions of Jerusalem's gates after the Babylonian attack (see Neh 1:3; 2:13), it functions within this literary context as an apt metaphor for Zion's emotional state—she feels 'destroyed' and 'shattered'.

The mourning scene in Lam 2:10 is a poignant depiction of the trauma associated with Jerusalem's destruction:

---

[56] For a critical analysis of the ways אבל (*'bl*), 'mourning', is used in the Hebrew Bible, see Olyan, *Biblical Mourning*, pp. 28–110.

[57] For an example of the metaphorical use of the verb טבע (*ṭbʿ*) 'to sink', see Ps 69:3 and 15 [ET 2, 14]). In these verses, the psalmist uses טבע (*ṭbʿ*) to depict his state of depression.

> They sit on the ground, silent,
> Daughter Zion's elders.
> They have placed dust on their heads
> *And* have clothed themselves with sackcloth.
> The maidens of Jerusalem
> Have bowed their heads to the ground.[58]

While the stereotypical mourning ritual depicted here might have actual historical referents in post-destruction Jerusalem, in its present literary context, this scene functions metaphorically to highlight Zion's psychological state—she is in mourning.[59] The text makes explicit references to Daughter Zion's 'elders' and 'maidens'. Like rulers, priests, and prophets, elders were important leaders in ancient Israel (see Ex 3:16; Lev 4:15; 1 Kings 20:7–8). As representatives of the people (see Ezek 14:1; 20:1), they spoke for them, provided them with advice and guidance, and were involved in decision-making.[60] In the wake of the tragedy that befell Zion, however, these often outspoken leaders sit in silence, engaged in mourning rites. Similarly, maidens have adopted a posture of mourning. The Hebrew word בְּתוּלָה (*bĕtûlāh*), 'maiden' ('young woman', 'virgin'), refers to young women of marriageable age (see Gen 24:16; Deut 22:19). Maidens were among the most vulnerable members of ancient Israelite society (see Judg 19:24; 21:12; 2 Sam 13:1–22). Thus, the reference to 'maidens' in Lam 2:10 indicates that Zion's collapse has affected her most vulnerable citizens. Hence, the references to Zion's 'elders' and 'maidens' can be un-

---

[58] In traditional mourning rituals in ancient Israel, mourners typically sat on the ground and engaged in fasting, weeping, throwing dust on their heads, and wallowing in ashes (see Ezek 27:29–32). See King and Stager, *Life in Biblical Israel*, pp. 372–373.

[59] Jeremiah 41; Zech 7:3, 5; 8:19; Isa 63:7–64:12; and the book of Lamentations points to public occasions of mourning during Judah's exilic and post-exilic periods. See also Hoffman, 'The Fasts in the Book of Zechariah and the Fashioning of National Remembrance', pp. 169–213.

[60] See Provan, *Lamentations*, p. 70.

derstood as a merismus:[61] the former represents Zion's most powerful citizens, while the latter represents her weakest inhabitants. This example of merismus brings into sharper focus the far-reaching impact of Jerusalem's destruction—*everyone* was affected.

References to the narrator's own experience of trauma appear immediately after the mourning scene (Lam 2:11–12). Like Daughter Zion (Lam 1:2, 16), the poet's eyes are 'spent with tears'. The poet is in extreme emotional distress (see Lam 1:20a, 22c) on account of the plight of his beloved people (Lam 2:11b). He is particularly stunned and disturbed by the plights of Zion's most vulnerable inhabitants—the mothers and their infants (vs 11c–12).[62] At this point, the poet shifts from objective narrator of Zion's tragedy to Zion's empathetic companion—an implicated witness. The expression of the narrator's own experience of trauma functions rhetorically to persuade YHWH to attend to Zion's and the narrator's predicaments. Read through the lens of trauma studies, those who dare to pay attention to Daughter Zion's trauma cannot escape the far-reaching impact of their exposure.[63] Thus, even YHWH would experience a change of heart should he dare to attend to Zion's trauma. This change, at least, is what Zion and the narrator seem to hope for (see Lam 2:18–22).

The narrator's sympathy and empathy for Daughter Zion's predicament undergirds the view that Zion's trauma is incomparable and irreparable (Lam 2:13; cf. 1:12). This conclusion is expressed by means of four rhetorical questions: 1). 'How can I bear witness to you [memorialize your trauma]?'[64] Response: *you cannot!*

---

[61] A merismus is a type of synecdoche in which two opposing parts of a thing are used to refer to the whole.

[62] Cf. Jer 9:20–22.

[63] For a discussion of secondary trauma, see D. Laub, 'Bearing Witness or the Vicissitudes of Listening', pp. 57–74.

[64] Some exegetes emend the verb עוד (*ʿwd*), 'to testify', 'warn', 'assure' to read ערך (*ʿrk*), 'to compare'. Parry retains עוד (*ʿwd*), 'to testify', and suggests that it should be understood in the sense of 'memorialize' (See Parry, *Lamentations*, pp. 80–81). Similarly, Adele Berlin states *vis à vis* עוד (*ʿwd*), '[t]he poet wishes to serve as a witness who testifies to the actuality of the destruction and to its enormity' (Berlin, *Lamentations*, p. 66).

2). 'What can I liken to you[*r plight*], O Daughter Jerusalem? Response: *nothing!* 3). 'What can I compare to you *so that* I can comfort you, O Daughter Zion?' Response: *nothing!* 4). 'Who can heal you?' Response: *no one!*[65] Zion's 'demise is as vast as the sea' (v. 13cα). Seemingly, nothing this enormous and calamitous has *ever* happened before.[66] Consequently, all attempts to memorialize Zion's trauma are *a priori* inadequate. Even the poems in Lamentations that commemorate Zion's tragedy through disciplining poetic structures are limited. The narrator feels that Zion's suffering is unrivaled and her grief inconsolable. Moreover, her wounds appear irreparable. The narrator's understanding of Zion's plight echoes Zion's own perspective. By lifting up the sheer enormity and incomparability of Zion's experience of trauma, the poet undercuts certain traditional explanations for suffering.

The next shift in mood occurs in Lam 2:18. Survivors of the onslaught of YHWH's judgment (v. 17) register their anguish: 'Their heart cried out to Adonai' (v. 18aα).[67] This phrase highlights the agony of those who must live in the aftermath of YHWH's wrathful judgment. The survivors did not simply 'weep' or 'cry

---

[65] Cf. Jer 19:10–11.

[66] See Parry, *Lamentations*, p. 81. While this claim can be challenged on historical grounds, those who have survived traumatic experiences can identify with the poet's (and Zion's) perception that their trauma seems incomparable and irreparable.

[67] The verb צָעַק (*ṣāʿaq*), 'cry out', that begins verse 18 is 3rd person masculine singular, unlike the verbs that follow, which are all feminine singular, referring to Zion's wall. Some commentators emend צָעַק to the feminine imperative form, צעקי 'cry out!' While such an emendation is plausible, I do not think that it is necessary. The phrase 'their heart cried out…' refers to the collective of Zion's survivors. Berlin notes that 'the first line of the verse hangs by itself, unattached to the address to the wall that follows' (Berlin, *Lamentations*, p. 74). This structural anomaly is consistent with the seemingly erratic shifts in voice, speakers, and type of speech that are ubiquitous in the book of Lamentations. While grammatically the first line of Lam 2:18 seems to hang by itself, it is clearly thematically connected to the rest of the verse.

out': 'their heart cried out' in distress to Adonai.[68] The use of 'heart' in the singular points to a sense of solidarity among the survivors—they share a common pain. Next, the poet, utilizing synecdoche, addresses 'the wall of Daughter Zion'.[69] I concur with Berlin: '[i]t is especially touching that the wall, the protector of the city that has not been able to provide protection, must now cry for help'.[70] The utter vulnerability and destitution of Zion's wall mirrors the plight of survivors who remained in Jerusalem after 586 BCE. The narrator exhorts Zion to 'let [her] tears run down like a torrent, day and night' (Lam 2:18b; cf. Ps 42:4; Jer 8:23; 14:17). The imagery of unrelenting weeping reflects the depth of Zion's pain. Her own tears mirror the tears of the survivors whom she represents and speaks for, and with whom she identifies.[71] Moreover, the graphic portrayal of unmitigated sorrow resists simple correlations between suffering and sin. Zion has suffered beyond measure and reason.

Zion is inconsolable (cf. Gen 37:34–35; Jer 31:15). Her wall participates in her anguish and is urged to: 'Give yourself no relief, your eyes no rest' (Lam 2:18c). The narrator sees no immediate resolution or relief on her horizon. The narrator further urges 'the

---

[68] Parry correctly observes, 'the Hebrew Scriptures often portray YHWH as the one to whom such cries are directed [Exod 2:23; 3:7; 107:6, 28]' (Parry, *Lamentations*, p. 83).

[69] There is no consensus among biblical scholars regarding the precise meaning of 'the wall of Daughter Zion'. If the phrase is read as a parallel expression for 'to Adonai', with 'the wall of Daughter Zion' qualifying 'Adonai', then Adonai is 'the wall of Daughter Zion'. Alternatively, the phrase can refer to the actual wall of the city, which is symbolically invited to weep. Building on what I have argued regarding Lam 2:8c, I follow the latter option in this study. In her discussion of Lam 2:18, Berlin notes, '[t]he motif of cities or their structures lamenting is common in the Sumerian lamentations….' Further, Berlin argues, it is fitting that the city's fortifications lament in Lam 2:18 since they are victims of YHWH's judgment in the earlier parts of this chapter (Berlin, *Lamentations*, p. 75). See also Parry, *Lamentations*, p. 69, n. 3.

[70] Berlin, *Lamentations*, p. 75.

[71] See Bosworth, 'Daughter Zion and Weeping', p. 228.

wall of Daughter Zion' to 'arise, cry out in the night' (Lam 2:19aα).[72] The typical time for rest has become a time for mourning. Like one who is tormented and agitated, Zion must allow herself no rest. Moreover, Zion is invited to 'cry out' at the 'beginning of each watch of the night', that is, throughout the night.[73] The invitation continues the motif of unrelenting sorrow in the previous verse. Such protracted wailing gives expression of Zion's anguish and raises a desperate plea to Zion's God to pay attention to her perils.

Zion's personified wall is urged to 'pour out [her] heart like water before the face of Adonai' (Lam 2:19b). The razed wall that once offered physical protection is invited to offer emotional support by lamenting before Adonai on Zion's behalf. Zion's wall fulfills the role that comforters should have fulfilled. Symbolically, the poet urges Daughter Zion's wall to become utterly vulnerable in the presence of her deity and to plea desperately for Adonai's attention. The enormity of the evils Zion has endured is too important to allow Adonai, or anyone else, to ignore or gloss over it.[74] Finally, the narrator implores Zion to 'lift up [her] hands to' Adonai in prayer.[75] The poet's imperatives in Lam 2:18b–19cα highlight the urgency of his call to Zion.[76] The horror Zion has survived (Lam 2:1–9, 15–17) and the haunting realities of survival itself (Lam 2:11b–12 and 19c) motivate the narrator's impassioned plea to Zion to give unremitting expression to her anguish. In the aftermath of YHWH's onslaught, those who have escaped exile and

---

[72] The exhortation to the upward move of supplication stands in stark contrast to the downward posture of mourning and sorrow depicted in earlier verses in Lamentations 2. See vs 9a, 10 and Berlin, *Lamentations*, p. 75.

[73] See Berlin, *Lamentations*, p. 75 and Parry, *Lamentations*, pp. 83–84.

[74] See Parry, *Lamentations*, p. 83.

[75] For other examples of lifting hands as a posture for prayer see Pss 63:4 and 141:2.

[76] See Parry, *Lamentations*, p. 83. The imperatives are, 'let your tears run down', 'do not give yourself respite', 'do not allow your eyes to be still', 'arise', 'cry out [in distress]', 'pour out your heart', and 'lift your hands'.

death must endure the slow, painful deaths of Zion's most vulnerable citizens, her 'infants who are feeble because of hunger' (v. 19c). 'At the head of every street' (v. 19cβ; cf. vs. 11cβ and 12bβ), signs of death and dying re-traumatize survivors, reminding them of the tenuousness of their own survival.

The precariousness of life in the aftermath of trauma comes into sharper focus in the poem's final psychological shift (Lam 2:20–22). Zion accepts the invitation that was given to her wall (vs 18–19): to weep without ceasing and pour out her heart in supplication before the face of Adonai. She passionately implores YHWH to pay attention to her plight (v. 20). Zion's most vehement, scathing protest against, and indictment of, YHWH's merciless assault on her follows: mothers desperate to survive have eaten their own offspring (v. 20b); the unburied bodies of religious leaders lie in the sacred precincts of Adonai's sanctuary (v. 20c); and the corpses of Zion's youth and elderly inhabitants also lie unburied in the streets (v. 21). 'On the day of' Adonai's 'wrath', God indiscriminately 'killed' and 'slaughtered' Zion's children 'without pity' (v. 21c): 'on the day of YHWH's anger, none survived, none escaped' (v. 22b). This chilling testimony forms the climax of the description of Daughter Zion's trauma in Lamentations. Her survival in its aftermath is uncertain and precarious. The painful struggle for survival becomes even more bewildering because the 'foe' responsible for Zion's suffering, her own God (Lam 2:22c), also holds the keys to her survival.

Zion longs for YHWH to 'walk in her shoes', identify with her pain, and join with her in bearing witness to her trauma as the sympathetic narrator has done, and as her wall was invited to do. Like Parry, I view Lam 2:20–22 as a prayer of protest in which Zion is noticeably angry with her God. Zion has not broken her relationship with Adonai; she 'continues to speak to him, trying to shock him into action'.[77] Although YHWH has acted as Zion's foe, she still desires a relationship with her deity in the aftermath of trauma. Thus, the emotive and graphic descriptions of agony in Lamentations 2 (like those in Lamentations 1) function rhetorically

---

[77] Parry, *Lamentations*, 84.

both to draw attention to Zion's anguish and to persuade YHWH to take note of the enormity of her suffering.

Lamentations 3

The narrator's trauma depicted in Lam 3:1–20, mirrors the collective trauma of Zion in Lamentations 1 and 2. Lamentations 3 also holds YHWH responsible for the victim's predicament (See Lam 1:14–15, 21; 2:1–9, 17, 20–22; cf. Lam 3:1–16). The sufferer has experienced עֳנִי (*ʿŏnî*) 'affliction' (3:1a), and feels rejected by YHWH—a sentiment repeated in Lam 5:22. Emotionally, the sufferer is sated with 'bitterness' (מרר [*mrr*]), which appears in semantic parallelism with לַעֲנָה (*laʿănâ*), 'wormwood' (3:15). Both 'well-being' (שָׁלוֹם [*šālôm*]) and 'prosperity' (טוֹבָה [*ṭôbâ*]) are absent from the sufferer's life (3:17). The victim had resigned himself to hopelessness and helplessness (3:18). Recollections of past suffering have resulted in feelings of anguish (3:19–20). While Lam 3:1–20 depicts the survivor's plight, the focus is on his emotional state, rather than on specific descriptions of actual traumatic experiences.

The first prominent mood sift in Lamentations 3 appears in verses 21–24.[78] In these verses, the victim shifts from the dominant, melancholic tone of preceding verses to affirmation of confidence in YHWH, a common feature in many individual lament Psalms.[79] Rising from the depths of despair, the sufferer confidently affirms, 'I have hope' (v. 21b). This confidence is grounded in the belief that 'YHWH's covenantal loyalty' or 'fidelity' (חֶסֶד [*ḥesed*]) 'is relentless'; 'compassion' for, or 'loving feelings' רַחֲמִים [*raḥămîm*]) toward his people 'have not been exhausted' (v. 22).[80] In fact, YHWH's 'tender mercies (רַחֲמִים [*raḥămîm*]) are fresh (or 'renewed') every morning; great is [his] steadfastness (אֱמוּנָה [*ʾĕmûnâ*])' (v. 23). The sufferer's affirmation of confidence in YHWH's covenant fidelity, compassion, and steadfastness provides the basis for exuber-

---

[78] See Villanueva, *The 'Uncertainty of a Hearing'*, pp. 213–247.

[79] See Gerstenberger, *Psalms,* 492–494. Gerstenberger classifies Lam 3:19–36 as an 'affirmation of confidence'.

[80] See discussion in Parry, *Lamentations*, pp. 100–102.

ant exclamations of hope. A didactic, sapiential voice takes up and expands this note of hope in the following verses (vs 25–39).[81]

The note of hope and affirmation of confidence in YHWH is short lived, however. Immediately following the sapiential voice in vs 21–39, we hear a communal voice. This communal speaker shifts to a somber tone, urging the community to 'search and examine' their 'ways, and turn back to YHWH' (v. 40). Next, the communal voice shifts to a tone of despair and hopelessness (vs 41–47). The sufferer is now a community, which is reminiscent of the depictions of Daughter Zion in Lamentations 1 and 2. Stark contrasts between the hopeful tones of the individual victim and didactic, sapiential voice on one hand, and the community's stand-in speaker on the other, bring the community's predicament into sharper focus. YHWH has acted out of character, contrary to expectations. Instead of experiencing YHWH's 'covenant fidelity' and 'compassion', YHWH has 'not pardoned' them (v. 42b). Rather than 'fresh mercies every morning' and an 'abundance of faithfulness', YHWH has 'covered' himself 'in anger' and has 'pursued' them and 'slain' them 'without mercy' (v. 43; cf. Lam 2:21–22). YHWH has 'covered' himself with 'a cloud'—a permanent barrier against all prayers ascending from his people (v. 44). YHWH seems to have defaulted on his covenant fidelity in his dealings with the suffering community (vs 45–47).

Not only has YHWH acted as a foe, but also he appears to have no interest in restoring a relationship with the suffering community. The call to penitence in Lam 3:40 is undercut in Lam 3:42 with the statement that YHWH has 'not pardoned', despite the people's acknowledgement of their culpability. Similar to Zion's sympathetic narrator in Lam 2:19, the communal speaker urges the community to 'lift up' their 'heart' and their 'hands to God in heaven" (3:41). The tenacious hope of the individual sufferer (3:21–24),

---

[81] I discuss this section in greater detail below. There are striking similarities between the sapiential perspective in these verses and the perspectives of Job's friends in the book of Job (see Job 4; 8; 11; 15; 18; 20; 22; and 25). The sapiential voice affirms the direct causal relationship between sin and punishment on one hand, and virtue and reward on the other, though YHWH can choose to act otherwise.

and the didactic, sapiential speaker's perspective on divine forbearance, function rhetorically in Lamentations 3 to draw attention to the severity of the suffering community's plight. The community lacks the hope that the individual sufferer proclaims. Further, the community's lived experience of God's relentless wrath contrasts with the didactic voice's perspective. Juxtaposing the community's experience of trauma with perspectives of hope and divine forbearance brings the community's trauma to the forefront.[82] The psychological shifts in this text are strategically employed to highlight the intensity of the community's suffering. Hopelessness cancels out simple retreats to their traditions of hope.[83] The nature and extent of suffering depicted thus far in Lamentations 3 resist any simple, causal explanations of suffering.

In Lam 3:48–51, the poem shifts from depictions of the community's plight to the narrator's response to his people's predicament. Much like Zion's sympathetic interlocutor in Lam 2:11–14, 18–19, a sympathetic voice attends to the community's perils in Lam 3:48–51. 'Streams of water will flow down my eyes, over the crushing of my dear people' the sympathetic voice laments (3:48).[84] 'My eyes will overflow without relief, without respite' (3:49). While the sympathetic narrator in Lam 2:18–19 urges Daughter Zion to grieve fully for her loss, the sympathetic voice in Lam 3:48–49 is grief stricken. Here, the narrator identifies so completely with his crushed people that he takes up a lament over the fate that has befallen them. The narrator's willingness to attend to his people's plight, which is consistent with other mood shifts in Lamentations, functions to persuade YHWH to view the trauma of his people from their perspective.[85] The trauma evident in the sympathetic narrator's experience is precisely what Daughter Zion hopes YHWH will experience—YHWH must risk being affected by daring fully to pay attention to the effects of his crushing of '*his* dear people'. The sympathetic narrator promises to bear witness to the

---

[82] See Villanueva, '*The Uncertainty of a Hearing*', pp. 242–243.

[83] See Gerstenberger, *Psalms,* pp. 11–14

[84] Cf. Jer 14:17. See O'Connor, *Lamentations*, pp. 1015–1016.

[85] See John F. Hobbins, 'Zion's Plea that God See Her as She Sees Herself: Unanswered Prayer in Lamentations 1–2', pp. 149–176.

enormity of his people's perils 'until YHWH looks down and sees from heaven' (3:50).

In Lam 2:11, the sympathetic narrator expresses intense anguish 'over the crushing of [his] dear people'. He is evidently traumatized by his exposure (attending) to the harrowing realities of ancient siege warfare and its debilitating consequences (see Lam 2:11c-12; cf. 2:20; 4:3–5, 9–10; 5:8–9). The posture and position of the sympathetic narrator in relation to Daughter Zion function strategically to invite YHWH to follow suit—YHWH must risk doing what the sympathetic narrator dares to do (identifying with the victims). The narrator and Daughter Zion hold out hope for YHWH to 'look down and see' the trauma of *his* dear people from *their* vantage point. It is precisely from this vantage point of trauma that the narrator in Lam 3 states, 'my eye[s] vex me because of all the daughters of my city' (3:51).[86] The poet's eyes do not simply cause him grief; what the poet has witnessed assaults or vexes his very being. He is traumatized. He is assaulted and afflicted at the core of his being because of what he dares to *witness* and *bear witness to*—the plight of his people, particularly the maidens of his city. By implication, if YHWH dares to witness and bear witness to the victims' anguish, he also will be assaulted by the sight of their trauma.

Lamentations 3:52–66 shifts back to the earlier perspective of the individual sufferer in Lam 3:1–24. As in the earlier, individual lament section, in Lam 3:52–66 coalescing of melancholic and hopeful confidence in YHWH occurs. The sufferer, who most likely is the sympathetic narrator of Lam 3:41–51, begins by describing his own experience of trauma (vs 52–54). The survivor's 'enemies hunted' him down 'like a bird, without a cause' (v. 52). He describes his life as having been put to an 'end' by his foes (v. 53).[87]

---

[86] The precise meaning of this phrase is unclear. See Parry, *Lamentations*, p. 90; Dobbs-Allsopp, *Lamentations*, pp. 125, 126).

[87] Cf. Lam 2:22bc; 4:18b. Allusions to and scenes of death and dying are ubiquitous in Lamentations (see 1:11, 16c, 19bc, 20c; 2:11–12, 19c, 20–22; 3:6, 16, 47, 53, 55; 4:4–5, 9–10, 18b; 5:9, 12, 15). Though the survivors of the 586 BCE destruction of Jerusalem 'missed' their encounter with death, it seems evident that many were further traumatized by the

The sufferer's depiction of himself as being dead while yet alive highlights the reality and extent of his experience of trauma. He feels hopeless and helpless.

In verses 55–66, the poem's tone shifts from depiction of anguish to addressing YHWH. The victim recounts pleading with YHWH to pay attention to his predicament from the depths of anguish and despair. In Lam 3: 57–66, the sufferer shifts to affirmation of confidence in YHWH—confidently declaring that YHWH has and will intervene in his situation. YHWH has seen and heard his peril, YHWH will defend his cause and vindicate him, and YHWH ultimately will deal with his foes. The community of Lam 3:41–51, by contrast, has experienced YHWH as hidden and distant. He has screened himself off with a cloud, blocking prayers from penetrating (3:44). In the context of Lamentations 1–2, neither Daughter Zion nor her interlocutor has experienced YHWH as one who 'draws near' in response to prayer. YHWH is the foe.

Lamentations 4

'Alas!' (אֵיכָה [*ʾêkâ*]), the exclamation of anguish that introduces and sets the psychological tone for Lamentations 1 and 2, also appears in Lam 4:1. In Lamentations 1, אֵיכָה (*ʾêkâ*) precedes a graphic depiction of Daughter Zion's dramatic reversal of fortunes: she is destitute and mournful (Lam 1:1–11). In Lamentations 2, it introduces a vivid description of YHWH's systematic razing of Daughter Zion and her political and theological pillars (Lam 2:1–10). As in Lamentations 1, the particle expresses anguish that such atrocities have befallen Daughter Zion. In both chapters, אֵיכָה (*ʾêkâ*) conveys the speaker's astonishment over what has befallen his beloved city.

In Lamentations 4, אֵיכָה (*ʾêkâ*) introduces graphic descriptions of Zion's drastic reversal of fortunes (4:1–5). In verse 2bα, the poet uses it to highlight that Zion is not what/who she used to be. 'Even jackals provide *the* breast to nurse their cubs; *but* my dear

---

haunting death-ridden realities of survival itself—they were dying among the dead.

people have become cruel, like ostriches in the desert' (v. 3). At first glance, this depiction of Daughter Zion appears to portray her as a deranged, unfit mother—Zion 'has become cruel'. However, the dire conditions described in verses 4–5 and 8–10 are consistent with the realities of ancient siege warfare and its painful aftermath. The poet's uses emotive language to convey victims' extreme suffering: enfeebled mothers are unable to nourish their babies (v. 4); formerly elite inhabitants have become common vagrants (v. 5); survivors face imminent death from starvation (v. 9); and compassionate mothers resort to cannibalism to survive (v. 10a).[88] Through poignant depictions of Zion's reversal fortunes, the poet insists that her calamity demands attention. The strategic, rhetorical purpose of the book of Lamentations reaches its peak in Lamentations 4. The enormity of Zion's predicament, her drastic reversal of fortunes, resists simple explanations. She has fallen to her lowest possible state—utterly destitute and nearly insane.

As in Lam 2, the reference to the plight of Zion's most vulnerable inhabitants undercuts any simple justification for YHWH's wrathful onslaught. The imagery of mothers who, in desperation, are driven to cannibalism is horrifying. Maternal instincts are generally associated with nurturing, protecting, defending, and providing for offspring. It seems anathema that a mother, in her right mind, would resort to eating her own child. These graphic images of the plight of enfeebled mothers and their helpless infants are intended to shock, to disturb, and to persuade to action. Trauma can drive its victims to the limits of sanity, and the threshold of absurdity.[89]

In Lam 4:17, a communal voice describes the community's experience of disappointment. They have hoped, and continue to hope, for deliverance from a political ally (cf. Jer 34:21; 37:5–11). But the suffering community did not escape destruction (v.18). They were no match for their 'pursuers' (v. 19). Ultimately, their last strand of hope, 'YHWH's anointed' and 'the breath of our nostrils', was captured by their pursuers (v. 20). Much like Daughter

[88] Cf. Lam 2:11–12, 19c, 20.

[89] See Anthony P. Morrison, *et al*, 'Relationships between Trauma and Psychosis: A Review and Integration', pp. 331–353.

Zion in Lamentations 1 and 2, the survivor-community in Lamentations 4 is desolate, destitute, and bereft of hope.

Lamentations 4 concludes with an oracle-like unit (4:21–22). While the overarching mood of the preceding sections is melancholic, a sudden shift to confidence reappears. In ironic, mocking tones, Daughter Edom is urged to 'rejoice and be glad' while she still can, for Zion's 'cup' of judgment will soon be hers to drink (v. 21).[90] Edom will be so drunk with judgment that she will expose her 'nakedness' (v. 21bβ; cf. 1:8); ultimately, YHWH 'will punish [her] iniquity' and 'expose [her] sins' (v. 22b). By contrast, Zion's 'punishment is completed' and YHWH 'will not add to [her] exile'; her time of exile is over (v. 22a; cf. Isa 40:2).[91] The promised judgment of Edom mirrors Zion's plea in Lam 1:21–22. Zion wants YHWH to deal with her foes as he has dealt with her. Ultimately, however, hope that YHWH will punish Zion's foes and bring an end to her punishment and exile is not the book's last word. The hopeful tone of Lam 4:22 gives way to a description of the extent of the suffering community's predicament in Lamentations 5. Affirmation of confidence in YHWH in Lam 4:21–22 is undercut by affirmation of the continuation of suffering in Lamentations 5. Vacillation between hope and despair is a significant feature of survivor testimonies. Because the debilitating effects of trauma typically cause survivors to feel hopeless and helpless, despondency often overshadows attempts to affirm hope.

In Lamentations 3, affirmations of confidence in YHWH (3:21–40, 58–66) do not actually address the enormity of the individual victim's predicament (3:1–20) or the suffering community's perils (3:41–47). Similarly, passing the cup of judgment to Daughter Edom, exposing her nakedness and sins, and ending Daughter Zion's exile neither address nor cancel out the traumatic extremes confronting her enfeebled mothers and their infants. Reading Lam 4:21–22 as ultimately hopeful ignores Daughter Zion's calamity and misses the goal of her pleas—persuading YHWH to regard her

---

[90] See Salters, *Lamentations*, p. 335.

[91] This reference to the end of exile may suggest a later date for the composition (or addition) of this verse (cf. Isa 40:1).

trauma from her vantage point and to identify with her plight (see Lam 2:20a).

Lamentations 5

Three imperatives set the tone for Lamentations 5. A survivor-community makes an impassioned plea to YHWH: 'Remember...what has become of us!'; and 'Look, and see our disgrace!' (v. 1). This plea echoes Zion's previous pleas in the book (see 1:9c, 11c, 20a; 2:20a; cf. 3:50, 56). The community's urgency indicates that they continue to experience YHWH as absent and indifferent to their perils. This feeling of divine indifference is ubiquitous in Lamentations.[92] YHWH is depicted as ravaging Zion in a fit of rage (see Lam 2:1–9, 17; 3:43–45; 4:11); God has turned away and refuses to look at the destruction he has caused, and Zion's repeated pleas for YHWH to attend to her predicament testify to her feelings of god-forsakenness.

Survival conditions for the suffering community have been precarious (Lam 5:2–14), leaving them bewildered and destitute. They must now risk their lives to get food (5:9). Post-siege and post-catastrophe conditions have left them bereft of any sense of normalcy (5:13). Life as they knew it has been shattered (5:14). The survivors' melancholy is poignantly voiced in their terse lament: 'The joy of our heart has ceased, our dancing has turned to mourning' (v. 15; cf. Ps 30:11). The experience of trauma and its aftermath has left '[their] heart sick' and '[their] eyes dimmed' (v. 17).[93] Moreover, the physical desolation of Mount Zion (v. 18) mirrors the sufferers' emotional and physical destitution (5:2–16). These are the realities that the suffering community wishes YHWH to 'remember,' 'look' at, and 'see'.

---

[92] The motif of 'divine abandonment' is a common feature in the Psalter's individual and communal laments. See C. C. Broyles, *The Conflict of Faith and Experience in the Psalms: A Form Critical and Theological Study*, pp. 67–80.

[93] See Provan, *Lamentations*, p. 132. For Provan, the reference to the sufferers' eyes being 'dimmed' implies that '[t]he events described have sapped the people's vitality, their joy in living'.

Lamentations 5:19 shifts suddenly to an affirmation of confidence in YHWH: 'You, O YHWH, sit *enthroned* forever, your throne endures from generation to generation'. Yet this note of confidence is immediately subverted by a reference to the survivors' painful experiences. The affirmation of confidence in YHWH conflicts with how the community has experienced him. They ask, 'Why have you forgotten us indefinitely, abandoned us for such a long time?' (v. 20). Hence their initial plea to YHWH to 'remember', 'look', and 'see'. The conflict between the survivors' beliefs and their experiences is destabilizing. Depictions of the victims' psychological state draw attention to and invite sympathy for their plight. For this reason, the affirmation of confidence does not have the final say. In Lam 5:21, the community pleads with YHWH to restore their former relationship completely. The desperation of this plea is apparent in the repetition of שוב (*šwb*) '*Bring us back* to you, and let us *return*'. Such a restoration of relationship will, of necessity, require that YHWH risks exposure to Zion's trauma. Experiencing YHWH as a merciless foe and an indifferent patron deity traumatizes Zion in ways that resist glib responses.

The victimized community's last words are unsettling: 'Indeed you have rejected us, *and* are extremely angry with us' (v. 22). Lamentations 5 opens up the dreadful possibility that the chasm between YHWH and his people is irreparable. Hope is flickering and fleeting. YHWH appears to have 'forgotten' his people 'indefinitely'; he seems to have 'forsaken' them indeterminately (5:20). 'Indeed, [he] has forsaken [them]', remains 'extremely angry with [them]', and continues to keep silent. Daughter Zion's plight is perplexing: she has endured unimaginable trauma at the hands of her seemingly absent, indifferent deity. While she is privileged to have a sympathetic interlocutor, she longs for YHWH, her covenant partner, to identify and sympathize with her plight.

SUMMARY

The book of Lamentations presents a history that is not straightforwardly referential. It is a history of trauma—a history shaped through traumatic experiences and poetically expressed through unfiltered emotions, and dizzying shifts in mood. The book's use of hyperbole to register the enormity of the tragedies that have befallen Zion bear the imprint of trauma. Its use of stereotypical and metaphoric language bears witness to experiences that remain beyond the survivors' grasp and mastery. Their experience of overwhelming violence is elusive. The graphic descriptions of the plights of mothers and their children reveal the bewildering excesses and extremes of the impact of trauma. Vacillations between hope and despair, affirmation of confidence in YHWH and recognition of the experience of god-forsakenness, testify to the debilitating effects of trauma and its aftermath. Verifiable, datable truth claims are not ubiquitous in the book. However, Lamentations bears witness to voices, responses, cries, testimonies and experiences of trauma likely associated, directly or indirectly, with Jerusalem's demise.

Lamentations 1–5 teem with mood shifts and graphic depictions of agony. These psychological dimensions of the book's five poems are significant for understanding the plight of the survivors whom Daughter Zion represents, speaks for, identifies with and intercedes for. She and her inhabitants have endured far more than a sequence of undesirable experiences; they have experienced trauma and its crippling effects. The circumstances of Jerusalem's fall and its aftermath were limit events—tragic and disastrous. Historically, it is likely that certain Judean survivors of Jerusalem's demise experienced, responded to, and interpreted these events differently.[94] Nevertheless, Lamentations echoes those perspectives that highlight the enormity of Zion's trauma and creates poetic spaces for voicing survivors' overwhelming suffering. Cohn is correct when he asserts that in biblical responses to catastrophe like those expressed in the book of Lamentations, 'one can hear the tormented emotions of the survivors, the outraged protests against the suffering of the innocent, and the herculean efforts to buttress the faith of the decimated'.[95] By giving voice to the survivors' conflicting emotions, 'biblical poets exorcise the demons of disaster'.[96]

In this chapter, I have argued that the notion of non-referential history in trauma theory provides an important interpretive lens for construing the contents and functions of Lamenta-

---

[94] See my discussion in chapter 2 and Ackroyd, *Exile and Restoration*, pp. 39–61.

[95] Cohn, 'Biblical Responses to Catastrophe', p. 268.

[96] Ibid.

tions' poems. The book is an example of writing trauma. Basic features of non-referential history have informed my psychological analysis; and from this analysis, I have gleaned four major insights. First, the psychological and mood shifts in the poems typically function to foreground the extent and intensity of the survivors' perils, be they Daughter Zion (Lamentations 1, 2 and 4), an individual victim (Lam 3:1–20, 52–56), or a suffering community (Lam 3:41–47; 4:17–19; 5:1–10). Through vivid expressions of raw emotions—grief, anguish and suffering—the book unequivocally asserts that Zion's trauma is incomparable (Lam 1:12bβ; 2:13).

Second, the psychological and mood shifts also function to persuade YHWH to pay attention to Daughter Zion's predicament and to *see* her suffering as she sees it from her vantage point—the site of trauma. Through the graphic portrayals of the predicaments of Daughter Zion, her surviving children, and an individual sufferer, the poet seeks to change YHWH's heart toward his people. Nevertheless, hope in the possibility of such a change in YHWH remains tenuous and uncertain throughout the book. Third, Daughter Zion's sympathetic narrator mirrors how she wishes YHWH to response to her trauma. In general, the narrator in each poem adopts a sympathetic view of Zion, bearing witness to her plight. The poet, often through the voice of the narrator, *pays attention* to, *looks* at, *remembers*, and *sees* her plight from her perspective (Lam 2:11–13, 18–19; 3:48–51). Hence, the narrator dares to identify with Zion's predicament. Both entities bear witness to the experience of trauma. Like her sympathetic narrator, Zion expects YHWH to risk exposure to and identify with her trauma.[97] However, these are not the only responses that Zion expects from her deity. She also tentatively holds out hope for the restoration of her relationship with YHWH.

Fourth, the poems' psychological and mood shifts undercut simple moves towards hopeful affirmations of confidence in YHWH in order to bring the realities of Zion's trauma into sharper focus. Confident hope does not have the final word in Lamenta-

---

[97] Passages like Hosea 11 and Jer 12:7–13 highlight God's ability to experience deep emotions and even a change of heart. Thus, Zion's expectations are not farfetched.

tions; it is contrasted with graphic depictions of the enormity of the survivors' suffering. This feature in the poems asserts the view that the lived experiences of the people stand in stark contrast to the character of YHWH as described in the sections that affirm confidence in him. The survivors' beliefs about YHWH's character contradict their experience of YHWH.[98] This disjuncture between belief and experience undergirds the melancholic overtones of cognitive dissonance that pervades the entire book.

---

[98] See Broyles, *The Conflict of Faith and Experience in the Psalms.*

CHAPTER 5. THE RHETORIC OF THE TRAUMA PROCESS AND THE BOOK OF LAMENTATIONS

INTRODUCTION

This chapter analyzes various aspects of Lamentations' poems utilizing insights from studies on how individuals and collectivities that have survived traumatic experiences typically seek to reconstitute themselves and re-organize their worlds in the aftermath of extreme tragedies. How might Lamentations have functioned for its earliest readers and hearers? This is one of the key questions that guides the analyses in this chapter. Specifically, I explore protest as one of the book's major strategic, rhetorical functions.[1] Edkins observes that traumatic events typically strip away the 'commonly accepted meanings by which we lead our lives'.[2] Such events bring into question 'settled assumptions about who we might be as human and what we might be capable of'.[3] Consequently, trauma survivors' testimonies 'can challenge structures of power and au-

[1] By 'protest', I am referring to overt aspects of the poems that question the justice or fairness of God's actions (see Lam 2:20–22). By 'protest', I am also referring to the covert aspects of the poems that depict the victims' suffering as excessive and unparalleled. Through these overt and covert protests, the poems challenge and seek to change the status quo in order to chart a course for Zion's future in the wake of Jerusalem's destruction.

[2] Edkins, *Trauma and the Memory of Politics*, p. 5.

[3] Ibid.

thority'.[4] Challenging structures of power and authority is a prominent feature of the trauma process. 'Trauma process' refers to the ways victims, whether directly or indirectly affected by limit events, choose to represent, reconstruct, and memorialize their traumatic experiences.

The Rhetoric of the Trauma Process

The testimonies of trauma victims are very significant for reconstructing their lives and communities in the aftermath of toxic events. Whether in the form of oral testimonies, memorials, narratives, art, poetry, or other mediums, these testimonies help victims to bridge the chasm between pre-catastrophe and post-catastrophe conditions. Pre-catastrophe ideologies are typically re-examined and modified, if needed, in the light of traumatic experiences. Social, religious and political structures or institutions that sustained life in pre-catastrophe times, often give way to radically different or new structures and institutions in the aftermath of traumatic events. Individual/group identities, beliefs systems, social networks, available economic and institutional resources, and other factors tend to shape responses to, perceptions, and experiences of trauma.[5] Thus, different individuals and collectivities construct trauma in very different ways.[6] The ways survivors choose to represent, reconstruct, bear witness to, and memorialize their experiences of extreme violence is the trauma process.

This process of constructing and representing trauma, especially for survivor-groups, often entails rhetorical dimensions. These testimonies seek to inspire change or garner support for victims.[7] The culture creators who represent or signify these testimonies include novelists, painters and poets.[8] Such witnesses to trauma have the potential to exert extraordinary influence on the reorganizing and re-structuring of social worlds in the aftermath of

[4] Ibid.

[5] See Saul, *Collective Trauma, Collective Healing*, p. 8.

[6] See Moffatt, *Survivors*, pp. 1–24; and Saul, *Collective Trauma, Collective Healing*, pp. 1–18.

[7] Alexander and Breese, *Narrating Trauma*, p. xxvii.

[8] Ibid., p. xxii.

trauma. The process of representing trauma has the capacity to protest against and subvert oppressive structures and ideologies.[9] The ultimate goal of these culture creators is typically to bring about changes in pre-catastrophe status quos.[10] In order for such changes to occur, survivors must retain control of the trauma creation process.[11] Through this process of trauma creation and protest, victims are able to reassert their humanity and reshape their identity.

In the book of Lamentations, the trauma process is especially evident in the ways the poems address the following themes: culpability and suffering; God and suffering; and hope and suffering, I will address the latter in Chapter 6. While the poems clearly affirm Zion's culpability, they ultimately subvert or undermine direct correlations between her sin and her plight (see Lam 1:5, 18, 20, 22; 2:13–14; 4:6–7, 13; 5:7, 16). Further, the poems depict YHWH, and not a historical, political foe, as the active agent of most of Zion's woes, and seek to persuade God to pay attention to her predicament (see Lam 2:1–8).[12] Ultimately, Zion's future hinges on her patron deity experiencing a change of attitude towards her (see, Lam 5:21–22). Although the poems include rays of hope (see, Lam 3:21–24, 29), Zion's future remains uncertain and elusive. In the end, God remains silent, and confidence that God will hear and respond to Zion continues to be tentative. In reconstructing and re-ordering life in the aftermath of Jerusalem's demise, the five poems that constitute the book of Lamentations subvert or significantly adapt certain ancient Israelite perspectives of judgment, God, and hope.

---

[9] Edkins, *Trauma and the Memory of Politics*, p. 5; see also Tal, *Worlds of Hurt: Reading the Literatures of Trauma*, p. 7.

[10] Tal, *Worlds of Hurt: Reading the Literatures of Trauma*, p. 7.

[11] Ibid.

[12] This feature of assigning responsibility for a city's destruction to its patron deity also appears in other laments in the Hebrew Bible (e.g., Pss 44:10–11; 60:12; 74:19; 79:4–5; 89:39–42) and in other ancient Near Eastern collections. See Dobbs-Allsopp, *Weep*, pp. 52–65; Ferris, *Genre*, pp. 54–57; Bouzard, *We Have Heard*, pp. 78–91, 129–38.

CULPABILITY, PENITENCE, AND PROTEST: RESISTING JUDGMENT

In his ground-breaking work, *Studies in the Book of Lamentations*, Norman K. Gottwald argues that the key to the theology of Lamentations lay in 'the tension between Deuteronomic faith and historical adversity'.[13] The Deuteronomic teaching of reward and retribution insisted upon a direct correspondence between right actions (obedience to YHWH's commands) and rewards (blessings) on the one hand, and sin (covenant disobedience) and retribution (punishment) on the other.[14] Gottwald asserts that the Deuteronomic view of the direct, causal relationship between virtue and reward and sin and punishment informs the theological tension evident in Lamentations. King Josiah's sweeping religious reforms, which were influenced by Deuteronomic ideology (2 Kings 23; 2 Chr 34–35) preceded the historical events in Judah that ultimately led to its fall and the demise of its temple-city, Jerusalem. This series of events, Gottwald posits, would have lead survivors to question how the nation could suffer such enormous tragedy not long after the implementation of Josiah's religious reforms. In his view, this tension between faith, particularly Deuteronomic faith, and lived experience, the horrific fall of Judah, shapes the book's theology.[15] Thus, Gottwald's thesis presupposes that the survivors were convinced that they actually were faithful to YHWH's precepts prior to the life-altering catastrophes associated with Jerusalem's destruction.[16] This view of survivors' perspective ignores depictions of Judah's broken relationship with YHWH in the prophets (see Jer 1–6 and Ezek 4–10) and the book of Lamentations itself (see Lam 1:5, 8, 18, 20, 22; 2:14; 3:39–40; 4:6, 13, 22; 5:7, 16). Based on these accounts, Zion is not an innocent sufferer. The central concern in Lamentations is not the veracity of Zion's cul-

---

[13] Gottwald, *Studies in the Book of Lamentations*, pp. 52–53.

[14] The contours of this teaching are exemplified in Deuteronomy 28.

[15] See Gottwald, *Studies in the Book of Lamentations*, pp. 47–53.

[16] Albrektson comes to a similar conclusion (Albrektson, *Studies*, p. 218).

pability, but the validity of her excessive, disproportionate suffering.

In his analysis of communal laments in the Hebrew Bible, Walter C. Bouzard, Jr., observes that penitential elements and references to sin or forgiveness are typically absent from these laments.[17] Though Bouzard does not identify any of Lamentations' poems as a true communal lament, his insights are useful for analyzing the relationships between culpability and suffering in these poems.[18] Bouzard notes that in communal laments, the psalmists typically suggest divine inattention or rejection as the ultimate cause of the victims' perils.[19] These laments usually ignore the possibility that the people's culpability might have precipitated God's disfavor.[20] The psalmists were more inclined to protest the people's innocence.[21] In Lamentations, by contrast, affirmation of culpability is ubiquitous, especially in Lamentations 1. There is no pretention or protestation of innocence in the book's poems. Unlike the typical communal laments, however, penitential features are absent from the poems.

Drawing on Murray J. Haar's study, Bouzard observes that the major concern in communal laments is not forgiveness of sin, but the distress of the suffering community.[22] This conclusion is convincing. The psalmists urge God to recognize that God's 'relationship to Israel is greater than any sin that might have been committed'.[23] It is on the basis of this relationship that the psalmists implore YHWH to deliver or bring salvation to Israel.[24] In order to

---

[17] See Bouzard, *We Have Heard*, pp. 115–118, 142–145. I understand penitence as showing sorrow or regret for sin. Penitence typically involves the wrong doer repenting of her/his sins, and seeking forgiveness.

[18] Bouzard does recognize that there are some communal lament features in the book of Lamentations, especially in Lamentations 5.

[19] Bouzard, *We Have Heard*, p. 133. See Pss 44:8, 10, 24–25; 60:3, 12; 74:1, 23; 79:11; 89:39–40, 49.

[20] Psalm 79 may be an exception.

[21] Bouzard, *We Have Heard*, p. 134. See Ps 44:18–19, 21–22.

[22] Ibid., 144. See Haar, 'The God-Israel Relationship', p. 92–93.

[23] Haar, 'The God-Israel Relationship', p. 92.

[24] See Pss 44:23–26; 60:10–12; 74:20; 80:3, 7, 14, 19.

accomplish this goal of divine intervention for Zion, the book of Lamentations subverts the Deuteronomic understanding of punishment and rewards by juxtaposing affirmations of culpability with depictions of the enormity or extent of victims' suffering. Acknowledgement of culpability does not lead to penitence, but to more descriptions or expressions of pain.[25] Thus, the book downplays judgment or retribution—the view that Zion's suffering is just punishment for her sins, or that her calamity is commensurate to her culpability. In this sense the book resists or protests against judgment, at least the Deuteronomic view of this motif. Resisting or protesting judgment by juxtaposing assertions of culpability with depictions of excessive suffering prominently appears in Lamentations. In the instances where the poet utilizes this rhetorical strategy, neither penitence nor repentance follows acknowledgement of guilt.

Resisting Judgment in Lamentations

Lamentations 1:5

The gripping portrayal of Daughter Zion's widowhood, desertion, destitution, and disconsolation in Lam 1:1–5a is an affront to the view that her affliction is deserved. The portrayal is momentarily interrupted with a challenging theological reflection: 'For YHWH has caused her grief because of the multitude of her transgressions' (Lam 1:5b). Zion's tragedy is YHWH's doing—*he* has 'caused her grief'—but YHWH's acts of judgment appear as a direct, proportionate response to Zion's unfaithfulness. Thus, a direct correspondence is posited between Zion's transgressions and her suffering. The severity of Daughter Zion's punishment corresponds to the 'greatness of her transgressions (פְּשָׁעֶיהָ [*pĕšāʿêhā*])'. The doctrine of retributive punishment is a core tenet of Deuteronomic thinking.[26] According to this perspective, YHWH acts such that right-

[25] Expressions of penitence following acknowledgments of guilt is a significant motif in the Hebrew Bible (see Psalm 51; Jer 14:19–22; Dan 9:7–19; Neh 1:5–11; cf. Ps 38.

[26] See Deut 4:25–28, 4, 28; Josh 7:1; Judg 2:11–23; 3:7–8, 12–13; 4:1–2; 6:1–6; 10:6–8; 2 Kings 17:5–23; 21:10–16.

eousness or virtue is always rewarded, while unrighteousness or rebellion always leads to punishment (though YHWH can choose to be gracious and not mete out deserved punishment).[27] In Lam 1:5b, the narrator asserts Zion's culpability, which appears to indicate that her punishment is commensurate with her crimes against YHWH. The term פשע (*pāšaʿ*) asserts Zion's rebellion against her benefactor. She has violated the terms of her covenant agreement with YHWH. House notes, 'Zion's rebellions were not sporadic, rash acts that disrupted a general pattern of obedience. Disobedience eroded God's patience with their activity over a long period of time'.[28]

D. Bergant also argues that the term פשע (*pāšaʿ*) indicates that Zion did not merely make a 'mistake' or violate a 'social or ritual prescription': Zion has broken off her prior allegiance to YHWH.[29] Consequently, Bergant insists, 'it would not be correct to say that God has been excessive in punishing' Zion.[30] Her punishment was commensurate to her serious offenses.[31] Nevertheless, a close analysis of this reference to Zion's 'great transgressions' in its literary context does not support Bergant's claim. While the text makes only a passing reference to Zion's culpability and does not specify her crimes, it goes into great detail to describe the enormity of her plight (see Lam 1:1–5a, 5c–7).[32] Parry's observation is insightful: the reference to Zion's 'sin is brief, general, and in a context designed to elicit compassion from YHWH and the implied reader. The narrator does not want the focus to be on her sin, nor does he wish to minimize or ignore it'.[33]

Immediately following the acknowledgement of Zion's guilt (Lam 1:5b), the narrator returns to depictions of Zion's extreme circumstances (v. 5c). The reference to the exile of 'her infants'

---

[27] See Dobbs-Allsopp, 'Tragedy, Tradition, and Theology in the Book of Lamentations', p. 46. See also Provan, *Lamentations*, p. 23.

[28] House, *Lamentations*, p. 351.

[29] D. Bergant, *Lamentations*, p. 34.

[30] Ibid.

[31] Ibid.

[32] See Dobbs-Allsopp, *Lamentations*, p. 61.

[33] Parry, *Lamentations*, p. 48.

(עוֹלָלֶיהָ [*ʿôlālêha*]) in Lam 1:5cα highlights the fate of Zion's most vulnerable citizens, 'her babes', or 'little ones'.[34] Juxtaposing affirmations of her guilt with the enormity of her perils serves to mitigate the apparent, causal link between Zion's sin and her fate.[35] Among those who have suffered are infants incapable of acts of unrighteousness and disobedience. Is the displacement of babes a justifiable punishment for (their parent's) sin? Bergant's reflections are insightful, '[t]hey were suckling infants, totally dependent upon her. Snatched from her embrace and her protection and forced into exile, they are now captives of the enemy. The loss of children is not only a present tragedy, but it also signifies the forfeiture of the city's future'.[36] Does the 'greatness' of Daughter Zion's sins really correspond to the enormity of her suffering? The magnitude of her tragedy appears to obscure the 'greatness of her transgressions' (v. 5bβ). Dobbs-Allsopp observes that the ethical vision—that virtue is rewarded, and vice is punished—functions primarily as a foil for the 'poet's more tragic take on the situation'.[37] While the poet does not, and need not, overtly criticize the ethical vision, he suffuses it with 'arresting and manifold images of human suffering'.[38]

The depiction of Daughter Zion's dramatic reversal of fortunes (Lam 1:1–5a, 6–7) alludes to some of the punishments or curses for disobedience in Deuteronomy 28 (cf. Lev 26:14–39).[39] For example, both Deuteronomy 28 and Lamentations 1 allude to the exile or captivity of YHWH's people (Deut 28:41, 64; Lam 1:3a, 5c, 18c; cf. Lev 26:33); both texts point at reversal of political status (Deut 28:13, 44; Lam 1:5a; cf. Lev 26:17); both indicate a state of restlessness in captivity (Deut 28:65; Lam 1:3a); and both refer to derision by foes (Deut 28:37; Lam 1:7c, 8a-b, 9cβ). On the surface, these allusions appear to support the view that Zion's tragedy is

---

[34] The noun עוֹלֵל 'child' or 'infant', also appears in Lam 2:11, 19, 20; and 4:4. In each instance, the poet emphasizes Zion's most vulnerable and defenseless citizens.

[35] See Dobbs-Allsopp, *Lamentations*, p. 61.

[36] Bergant, *Lamentations*, pp. 34–35.

[37] Dobbs-Alsopp, 'Tragedy, Tradition, and Theology', p. 47.

[38] Ibid.

[39] See Albrektson, *Studies*, pp. 231–237.

just punishment for her sins. In Lamentations, however, they are framed by Zion's dire circumstances, which evoke sympathy and pity, rather than affirmations of the justice of YHWH's actions. The allusions to punishment also appearing in Deuteronomy 28 are used not only as indications of just penalties, but also as evidence of the extent and enormity of Zion's perils. The poet undermines the ethical view of judgment by downplaying penitence in favor of graphic depictions of suffering. As Dobbs-Allsopp observes, the portrayal of Zion's transgressions is 'flattened, spare, and does not readily seize the reader's imagination, especially in comparison to the many and finely painted pictures of suffering that appear elsewhere in the poem'.[40] The primary concern of Zion and her sympathetic narrator is to draw attention to her predicament. By contrasting affirmations of Zion's guilt with YHWH's violent assaults on Zion—he 'caused her grief'—including the harrowing realty of 'her little ones' going into 'captivity before the enemy' (v. 5), the poet invites careful, sympathetic attention to the enormity of Zion's desperate circumstance.

Lamentations 1:8

In Lam 1:8, the poem's structure is again interrupted by an acknowledgement of Zion's irrefutable culpability: חֵטְא חָטְאָה יְרוּשָׁלַםִ (*ḥēṭ' ḥāṭĕ'â yĕrûšālaim*), 'Jerusalem has gravely sinned'. As in Lam 1:5, the narrator highlights the flagrancy of Zion's sin. Her violations of her covenant stipulations are extensive and long-lived. 'Consequently', עַל־כֵּן (*ʿal-kēn*), 'she has become a mockery;[41] those who *once* honored her *now* despise her, because they have seen her nakedness, עֶרְוָתָהּ (*ʿerwātāh*); she groans aloud[42] and turns away' (v.

[40] Dobbs-Allsopp, *Lamentations*, p. 61.

[41] Here I follow Hillers in reading נידה, 'a shaking of head', in the sense of an object of mockery. Thus, Zion's misery continues and intensifies from the previous verse (v. 7), where her enemies gloat over her demise. Now, even her former admirers deride her (see Hillers, *Lamentations* [1992], pp. 85–86).

[42] See Hillers, *Lamentations* (1992), pp. 70–71; and Dobbs-Allsopp, *Lamentations*, p. 65.

8). In addition, Jerusalem's 'uncleanness (טֻמְאָה [*tum'â*])[43] is on her skirts; she did not consider her future,[44] therefore her demise was horrendous, *and* there was none to console her' (v. 9a–b). Dobbs-Allsopp's view that the depiction of Jerusalem in verses 8–9 seems to draw from the motif of 'besieged cities and countries metamorphized as sexually assaulted women'[45] in prophetic literature is valid. The graphic portrayal of Jerusalem's sexual attack, experience of public insensitivity, and utter humiliation is unsettling.[46] Honestly confronting such brutality, yet remaining unsympathetic, is inhumane. The poet skillfully shifts the focus from Jerusalem's egregious sins to her gruesome situation in the aftermath of YHWH's indiscriminate, wrathful response to her unspecified infractions.

Now, not only her enemies (Lam 1:7d), but also Zion's former admirers loathe her (Lam 1:8b) because her 'nakedness' has been exposed.[47] In agony, Jerusalem 'groans aloud' and 'turns away' (v. 8c). Here, Jerusalem is depicted as just as vulnerable and defenseless as her 'babes that were forced into exile' (v. 5). The painful evidence of the violence against her remains 'on her skirts' (v. 9a).[48] According to Lev 20:17–21, inappropriately 'seeing' or 'uncovering' a woman's 'nakedness' results in her defilement and disgrace (see

---

[43] The word טמא (*ṭm'*), to 'be' or 'become unclean', 'unclean', in its verbal and adjectival forms, is used, especially in the Priestly material, to refer to both ritual and moral impurity and defilement. In the context of Lam 1:9, the impurity or uncleanness on Zion skirts might not refer metaphorically to Jerusalem as a menstruant (this does not fit the context), or to the results of Jerusalem's sexual misconduct (see Berlin, *Lamentations*, p. 54); rather, it may refer to the results of Jerusalem's assault.

[44] See Hillers, *Lamentations* [1992], p. 86. Lam 1:9aα is best understood as a continuation of the poet's depiction of personified Jerusalem's plight in Lam 1:8.

[45] Dobbs-Allsopp, *Lamentations*, p. 63. See also G. Baumann, *Love and Violence: Marriage as Metaphor for the Relationship between YHWH and Israel in the Prophetic Books*, pp. 167–174.

[46] See Hillers, *Lamentations* [1992], p. 86; Salters, *Lamentations*, p. 61.

[47] See Dobbs-Allsopp, *Lamentations*, pp. 63–65; Hillers, *Lamentations* (1992), pp. 85–86; and Berlin, *Lamentations*, pp. 53–54.

[48] See Berlin, *Lamentations*, p. 55; Salters, *Lamentations*, pp. 62–63.

also Ezek 22:10). Even if Zion has 'played the harlot' (see Ezek 16:15–36), her assault is not justified. The depiction of Jerusalem's helplessness and vulnerability in Lam 1:8–9 seems reminiscent of Jerusalem's metaphoric portrayal as YHWH's brazenly unfaithful wife in Ezek 16:37–43 and Ezekiel 23. A key difference is that while Ezekiel 16 and 23 detail Zion's offences against YHWH, Lamentations 1 does not identify Zion's specific sins.

According to Ezekiel 16, YWHW will respond to Zion's brazen harlotry by assembling all of Jerusalem's 'lovers' against her and exposing 'her nakedness' (v. 37; *NJPS*).[49] Furthermore, YHWH in his fury will 'inflict upon [Zion] the punishment of women who commit adultery and murder' (v. 38; *NJPS*), and 'deliver [her] into' the hands (v. 39; *NJPS*) of 'all the lovers to whom [she] gave [her] favors, along with everybody [she] accepted and everybody [she] rejected' (v. 37, *NJPS*). This group of hoodlums will 'throw down [Zion's] platform and break down [her] lofty places; they shall strip [Zion] of [her] clothes and take [her] beautiful objects and leave [her] naked and bare' (v. 39; *NRSV*). Ultimately, 'a mob' will be assembled 'against [Zion] to pelt [her] with stones and pierce [her] with their swords' (v. 40; *NJPS*). According to Ezekiel 16, Zion's plight is the result of YHWH's murderous, vengeful judgment. While Ezekiel uses these graphic descriptions of Zion's assault to justify her punishment, the depiction of Zion's assault in Lamentations 1 functions to question its validity. Jerusalem is not guiltless, but her suffering is excessive and inappropriate.

While the use of harlotry metaphors to describe Israel's and Judah's religious infidelity to YHWH is prominent in some prophetic collections,[50] the depiction of Jerusalem in Lam 1:8–9c is not of a wanton whore, but of a woman who has been sexually assaulted as part of a vengeful reaction to her unspecified infractions. The issue is not whether or not Jerusalem is innocent, but whether the extent of her punishment is warranted. While a cursory reading of Lam 1:8–9c indicates that Zion's severe punishment fits the grievousness of her sins, here, as in the previous assertion of

---

[49] See Darr, *The Book of Ezekiel: Commentary and Reflections*, pp. 1234–1235.

[50] See Hos 2–3; Jer 2–3; and Ezek 16; 23.

guilt in Lam 1:5, the poet juxtaposes the assertion of guilt with graphic depictions of Zion's suffering resulting in a downplaying of the former (the guilt) and an accentuation of the latter (the suffering). In Lam 1:8–9c, the narrator adopts the perspective of the 'victim herself'.[51] In so doing, the poet intends to 'communicate horror at the violence that was committed against this one woman'.[52] In Jerusalem's unfaithfulness to YHWH, 'she did not consider her future' (v. 9aβ)—that YHWH's response could be so violent—'her demise was horrendous' (v. 9bα). Moreover, she is left 'naked' and bereft of consolers (v. 9bβ). Zion is stunned by the cruelty and enormity of her situation, and all of her conscientious observers should be as well. Zion's posture and position in these verses invites sympathy and solidarity and resist simple correlations between her sin and her suffering, bringing the justness of her punishment into question.

In response, Jerusalem neither repents nor seeks forgiveness (confessional or penitential prayer); rather, she interrupts the narrator's graphic depictions of the extent of her predicament to implore YHWH to 'see' her 'misery; for the enemy boasts' (Lam 1:9c). Here, Zion echoes the narrator's sentiments in Lam 1:7, which states that her enemies 'mocked' her 'over her demise'. The insensitive responses of Zion's (former) friends (Lam 1:8b) and foes (Lam 1:7d, 8cβ) only intensify her anguish. In Deut 28:37, one of the curses for disobedience to YHWH is: 'You shall become an object of horror, a proverb, and a byword among all the peoples where the Lord will lead you' (*NRSV*). However, Zion seems not to agree that such responses to her suffering are appropriate and just. To the contrary, the cruel, heartless response of her foe only deepens her 'misery'.[53] To boast about, laugh at, or even mock Zion's tragic violation and demise is reprehensible and wounds her afresh, but more deeply and severely. Zion calls YHWH to attend to and respond to this 'misery' appropriately.

Thus, the tenor of Zion's response undermines the Deuteronomic correspondence between sin and punishment, virtue and

---

[51] Dobbs-Allsopp, *Lamentations*, p. 65.

[52] Ibid.

[53] The poet does not identify the specific 'foe' in question.

reward. Zion does not seek to refute the narrator's claims regarding her culpability. She does not assert her innocence, or lift up her virtue as grounds for YHWH to respond. Lamentations 1 makes clear that both of these characteristics—innocence and virtue—are sadly lacking in Daughter Zion. Instead, she seeks to motivate YHWH to act by lifting up *what* she has endured—the repulsive nature of the foe's response to her demise—and the one against *whom* such evil was directed—Zion herself, who still clings tentatively to the hope that her special relationship with YHWH might yet persuade God to intervene on her behalf.

A graphic depiction of what Zion has suffered at her foe's hand follows. She has been assaulted by her foe (Lam 1:10);[54] her sanctuary has been looted. She has been invaded by nations that Deuteronomic law prohibited from entering the assembly of YHWH's people (see Deut 23:3; cf. Ezra 10:10–44; Neh 13:1–3, 23–27); and her words are theologically charged: 'You [YHWH] forbade [these nations] to enter into Your [YHWH's] assembly' (see Ps 79:1). YHWH has uncharacteristically acted against his own word and some of Zion's ostensibly God-given, traditional beliefs. Though Zion has indeed 'sinned gravely' (1:8aα) and 'did not consider her future' (1:9aβ), she refuses to link her culpability to the tragedies she has endured at her foe's hands. Zion is not penitent; to the contrary, she insists that she has been wronged and repeatedly attempts to rouse YHWH to vindicate her. The poet steadfastly resists establishing a direct, causal connection between her guilt and suffering.

Lamentations 1:14

In Lam 1:11, Zion again interrupts a description of her dire straits (1:11a-b) to entreat YHWH to 'see' and 'look at' her plight (1:11c). Zion's agony is incomparable (1:12b), and YHWH has 'caused [her] grief' or 'afflicted [her]' on the day of his wrathful fury (1:12c),

---

54 Some commentators see here another reference to Zion being sexually violated. See F. W. Dobbs-Allsopp and T. Linafelt, 'The Rape of Zion in Lam 1:10', pp. 77–81; see also Dobbs-Allsopp, *Lamentations*, pp. 65–67. Given the references to Zion's assault in Lam 1:9, it is likely that Lam 1:10 continues that motif.

viciously attacking her, deserting her, and leaving her in a state of constant decrepitude (1:13). Zion depicts YHWH's judgment as excessive; her graphic portrayal of YHWH's brutality far overshadows passing references to her culpability.

In Lam 1:14, Zion acknowledges her culpability for the first time: פְּשָׁעַי (*pěšāʿay*), 'my transgressions'. The verb פשע (*pāšaʿ*) means to 'rebel' or 'transgress'. It can describe the 'revolt' of a vassal nation against its suzerain (see 2 Kings 1:1; 3:5,7; 8:22) or 'rebellion' against God (see Isa 43:27; 59:13; Jer 2:8, 29; Ezek 2:3; 20:38). In the absolute sense, פשע (*pāšaʿ*) can be used to describe 'rebels' and 'transgressors' (see Isa 1:28; 48:8; 53:12; Hosea 14:10).[55] Zion acknowledges her rebellion against YHWH. Like the narrator, however, she does not specify her crimes. The way Zion describes her rebellion is paradoxical: 'The *yoke* of my transgressions is *bound, woven together* by his hands, he *forced* them on my neck; he caused my strength to be *exhausted.* The Lord *gave* me into the hands of those *I cannot withstand.*'[56] Adonai has intentionally refused to relieve Zion of her transgressions. Instead, God has used them to inflict significant violence on her, ignoring God's special relationship with her. Although Zion is not completely innocent, YHWH's actions are presented as excessive and unjust. Her acknowledgement of guilt is itself a divine assault. Her affirmation evokes sympathy, rather than antipathy. Consequently, her guilt is overshadowed by still another description of YWHW's brutal assault on her (1:15). YHWH has acted as an enemy of his people.

Lamentations 1:18

In Lam 1:18, another assertion of Zion's guilt appears. She affirms the justice of YHWH's actions: כִּי פִיהוּ מָרִיתִי (*kî pîhû mārîtî*), 'For I have been disobedient to his command' (1:18a). Her astonishing acknowledgement that past rebelliousness invited YHWH's actions against her appears to exonerate God of wrong-doing. Yet, even this poignant confession of culpability is not followed by statements and/or acts of penitence, or by requests for divine for-

---

[55] See F. Brown, S. Driver, and C. Briggs, 'פשע (*pāšaʿ*)', p. 833.

[56] Emphasis added.

giveness. Rather, Zion calls on the 'peoples' to 'hear' and 'see' her 'suffering' (1:18b); her 'young women and first-born sons have gone into captivity' (1:18c; cf. 1:5c). This reference to the captivity of Zion's youthful, vulnerable children, who are not explicitly accused of sins in this context, serves subtly to undermine Zion's earlier statement about the 'righteousness' or 'justness' of YHWH's actions. Yes, Zion has disobeyed YHWH's command, but is the captivity of her 'maidens' and 'first-born sons' just punishment for *her* crimes? According to Deut 28:32, 41, the captivity of Israel's sons and daughters is one of the multiple curses Israel will incur for disobedience to YHWH. However, Zion lifts up her loss of children not as just punishment, but as an example of her extensive pain and suffering. Zion's confession that *she* has disobeyed YHWH's commandments implies that her *children* are innocent. To add to Zion's anguish, her friends have betrayed her (1:19a); and her religious leaders have perished from severe famine (1:19b-c). Thus, assertions of guilt function strategically to foreground Zion's predicament.

Lamentations 1:20

The same rhetorical strategy reappears in Lam 1:20b, where Zion asserts her culpability only to subvert her confession with a depiction of the enormity of her suffering: 'In the street the sword bereaves, in the house it is like death'. Her disorientation is obvious; Zion regards YHWH's punitive actions as extreme and shocking. On one hand, she acknowledges her guilt; on the other, she cannot reconcile her beliefs about YHWH with her experience of her divine enemy. How could YHWH, her beloved deity, sworn protector, and defender, inflict and permit the gruesome atrocities she has suffered?

Lamentations 2:14

In Lam 2:14bα, the narrator insists that Zion's seers failed her because they did not uncover or expose her 'iniquity'. However, he neither specifies her infractions, nor calls upon Zion to repent. Dobbs-Allsopp argues that the charge against Zion's seers can refer either to the failure of prophets to warn Zion, prior to the disaster, so that the catastrophe could be averted, or to the inability of 'present-day' prophets to see visions that might comfort Zion, or both.[57] In Parry's view, the phrase might 'refer to the *present* failure of the prophets in the midst of the sorrow: they do not point Judah to the covenant way of living that could reverse their current plight'.[58] If covenant fidelity were the solution to Zion's predicament, however, why would the narrator not point Zion to this solution? If the narrator is convinced that covenant living is the key to reversing Zion's present perilous circumstances, why does he not call upon Zion to acknowledge her sins, repent, and experience restoration? Through subtle omissions, the poet draws attention to the enormity of Zion's suffering, thus undermining the fairness of YHWH's retributory actions. No simple solution to Zion's suffering exists. Her trauma is not simply a consequence of her failures: her suffering is extreme. Restoration of Zion's fortunes depends more on YHWH experiencing a change of heart than on a change in her heart. Her pre-catastrophe seers have failed her,[59] and her surviving seers are unable to see comforting visions.

In graphic terms, the narrator describes Zion's reversal of fortunes (Lam 2:15–16). Passersby deride her and are amazed[60] at what has become of a city once called 'perfect in beauty, joy of all the earth' (cf. Ps 48:1–4 [ET 1–3]). In his view, Zion's guilt pales in comparison to her drastic circumstances. What is more, since Zion's pre-catastrophe seers failed her through their deceptive oracles (v. 14), she is not wholly to blame for her perils. Thus, her fate seems undue and unfair. Zion has become an object of scorn and ridicule because she foolishly heeded the oracles of those who falsely claimed to be YHWH's spokespersons.

---

[57] Dobbs-Allsopp, *Lamentations*, p. 97.

[58] Parry, *Lamentations*, p. 81; emphasis original.

[59] Prophets like Isaiah and Jeremiah warned Israel/Judah of YHWH's impending judgments on Zion and called upon the people to turn from their rebellion (see, e.g., Isa 2:5–22; 3; 29:1–16; Jer 2; 3–4; 6; 7; 13:15–27; 15:1–9; 17:1–4). Apparently, other prophets opposed this message of woe (see, e.g., Jeremiah 28). Jeremiah denounces false prophets who delude the people with their deceptive visions (see Jer 23:14–40).

[60] For a discussion of the meaning of the gesture of 'hand clapping', see N. Fox, 'Clapping Hands as a Gesture of Anguish and Anger in Mesopotamia and in Israel', pp. 49–60.

Lamentations 3:1–20

Lamentations 3 continues the motif of questionable or underserved suffering. The individual sufferer of Lam 3:1–24 neither acknowledges culpability nor establishes a direct correlation between sin and punishment. This sufferer has 'seen' affliction under God's rod of wrath (v. 1). Provan observes that the expression רָאָה עֳנִי (*rāʾāh ʿŏnî*), 'to see affliction', is typically used only of God paying attention to the plights of others (see Lam 1:9; Exod 3:7).[61] The use of this expression in Lam 3:1 is unusual in the book in two respects: a human being is the subject of the verb *rāʾāh*, 'see'; and the verb is used in the sense of 'experiencing, knowing', as opposed to 'seeing' in the physical sense.[62] This choice of phrase, Provan rightly asserts, highlights the severity of the narrator's situation: YHWH has chastised him, rather than sympathizing with him.[63] That the poet of Lamentations 3 has 'known' (*rāʾāh*) affliction first hand might indicate that he is able to identify and sympathize with Zion's afflictions. This perspective fits well with the view of the sympathetic narrator that I have identified in previous chapters. That the poet knows the experience of attending to misery, a quality typically reserved for God, also accords with my argument that the sympathetic narrator in Lamentations exemplifies what Zion expects from YHWH—he identifies with her affliction.

YHWH has not acted like the Divine Shepherd of Psalm 23. Rather than serving as a source of comfort (Ps 23:4), YHWH's rod is a rod of wrath (Lam 3:1). Rather than leading into 'green pastures' (Ps 23:2), YHWH has driven the sufferer into utter darkness (Lam 3:2). The sufferer's misery seems distinctly excessive (Lam 3:1–17); God seems intent on annihilating him without cause (Lam 3:7, 9, 12, 13; cf. Job 6:4). [64] This motif of excessive suffering challenges the Deuteronomistic view of a correlation between virtue and reward on one hand, and sin and punishment on the other. In

---

[61] Provan, *Lamentations*, p. 84.

[62] Ibid.

[63] Ibid.

[64] For a discussion of the Job-like features in Lamentations 3, see Villanueva, 'The Uncertainty of a Hearing', pp. 230–233.

this sense, the poet's experiences of God unjustly inflicting excessive suffering upon him (without a cause) parallel Zion's own experiences of YHWH's capriciousness.

Lamentations 3:25–39

Lamentations 3:25–39 affirms the Deuteronomistic view of retribution: YHWH rewards piety (3:25) and punishes unfaithfulness (3:32, 39). 'Weal and woe' come from YHWH's hands (3:37). Moreover, there is always a just basis for suffering (3:33); and YHWH is willing to pardon sinners (3:32). These perspectives are not sustained in the poem; and they appear unsustainable in light of the graphic depictions of 'innocent suffering' in Lam 3:1–20. YHWH has not strictly followed the law of retribution in the experience of the one who has 'seen affliction'. YHWH has intentionally caused misery (3:6–15), *contra* the statement in Lam 3:33. Likewise, the communal lament that follows in verses 40–54 overshadows the thrust of the wisdom unit (Lam 3:25–39). While guilt is asserted (v. 42a), YHWH's actions seem excessive and cruel (vs 43–47); and God has refused to pardon victims (v. 42b). Depictions of relentless weeping and protracted mourning in response to YHWH's judgments (vs 48–51) invite sympathy, not condemnation, for the sufferers.

Lamentations 4:6, 13

Graphic scenes of death and dying, painful struggles for survival, and evidence of human trauma dominate Lam 4:1–5, 7–10. In the midst of these depictions of extreme anguish, the narrator asserts Zion's culpability: her guilt exceeds the iniquity of Sodom, the paradigmatic wicked city.[65] Her many sins seem proportionate to her excessive suffering. Nevertheless, recognition of culpability is ameliorated by references to suffering, innocent infants (4:4; cf. Lam

[65] Sodom and Gomorrah were paradigmatic wicked cities that YHWH destroyed (see Gen 19:1–29; Deut 29:23; 32:32; Jer 23:14; 49:18; 50:40; Amos 4:11). Sodom and Gomorrah are also associated with utter destruction (see Isa 1:9). Isaiah chides Israel by addressing its leaders as 'rulers of Sodom' and its people as 'people of Gomorrah' (Isa 1:10).

2:11b-12) and to desperate mothers driven to cannibalism (4:10; cf. Lam 2:20; Lev 26:29). Are such traumatic experiences just punishment for iniquity, or is Zion's suffering disproportionate to her sins? YHWH's actions against Zion seem extreme, devoid of mercy and compassion (Lam 4:11; cf. Lam 3:22–23, 32).

In Lam 4:13, the narrator blames Zion's suffering on the sins of her priests and prophets (cf. 2:14). This pair of Israel's religious leaders is the subject of scathing criticisms in the book of Jeremiah (see Jer 6:13–15; 23:11); indeed, they are the dominant antagonists in Jeremiah's ministry (see Jeremiah 26–29). It is possible that the author of Lamentations was familiar with these Jeremianic traditions. Lamentations 4:13 charges Zion's priests and prophets with shedding innocent blood. Unlike previous references to Zion's guilt in the book, the narrator specifies the religious leaders' crime: they shed the blood of the righteous. Yet, all of Zion's inhabitants, including innocent children and compassionate mothers (4:4–5, 10), are made to suffer for the crimes of these religious leaders. Zion's agony seems unmerited and unreasonable. Protest, rather than penitence, seems to be the most appropriate response to such a travesty of justice.

Lamentations 5:7, 16

Traces of the ethical view, or Deuteronomistic understanding of retributive justice, appear in Lam 5:7, 16. In the first instance (v. 7), the sufferers' ancestors are guilty of sin, yet the suffering community must bear the consequences of their ancestors' guilt (cf. Ezek 18:2b; Jer 31:29b). From this vantage point, the community's suffering seems undeserved. Moreover, this assertion of guilt evokes neither penitence nor confession, but further descriptions of the community's woes. A similar phenomenon appears in Lam 5:16b. The community acknowledges its own, collective culpability; nevertheless this admission is also subverted.

The Day of YHWH Tradition and Resisting Judgment

Another theological tradition that Lamentations' poet manipulates in order to resist the ethical understanding of judgment and to protest Zion's unmerited suffering is the Day of YHWH tradition. The traditional understanding of the Day of YHWH in ancient Israel affirmed that at some future point, YHWH would intervene in history to fight against and defeat his enemies (see Isaiah 13).[66] YHWH's triumph over these enemies would ultimately benefit his people (see Isa 14:1–4), since Israel's enemies were YHWH's enemies. The prophet Amos turned this positive view, which his audience embraced, on its head, insisting that Israel was not exempt from judgment on the Day of YHWH (Amos 5:18–20). Dobbs-Allsopp rightly observes: 'Israel, too, can be numbered among Yahweh's enemies'.[67] Israel was numbered among YHWH's enemies on the day of his visitation because of its protracted unfaithfulness to its patron deity (Amos 5:1–17, 21–24). Judgment against Israel on the Day of YHWH would be just punishment for its sins.

Isaiah 13 includes typical, recurrent features of the Day of YHWH motif in the Hebrew Bible: an initial call to weep (Isa 13:6); a day of battle (Isa 13:2, 4–5); YHWH envisioned as a Divine Warrior (Isa 13:3–5); references to divine anger (Isa 13:1, 5, 9, 13); darkness and gloom (Isa 13:10); acknowledgement of sin (Isa 13:11); references to the haunt of wild animals (Isa 13:19–22); and responses to the destruction (Isa 13:7–8). Other passages also include references to fire (Ezek 30:8, 14, 16; Joel 2:3, 5; Zeph 1:18).[68] The recurrent features of the Day of YHWH tradition appear prominently in the entire book of Lamentations, but especially in Lamentations 2.[69] Conspicuously missing from the features of this tradition in Lamentations 2 is the attribution or acknowledgement of sin.[70] Downplaying culpability focuses attention on Zion's underserved punishment. In the following analyses, I concentrate on passages in Lamentations that directly refer, or allude, to the Day of YHWH.

Lamentations 1:12, 21

In Lam 1:21, Zion's wounds are foregrounded by her enemies' repulsive responses (cf. Lam 1:7d; 19c): they 'rejoice', שָׂשׂוּ (*śāśû*) when they hear of her predicament (v. 21b). Her foes also have

[66] Dobbs-Allsopp, 'R(az/ais)ing Zion', p. 27.

[67] Ibid.

[68] Ibid., p. 28.

[69] Ibid., p. 27–40.

[70] Ibid., p. 37.

concluded that her painful ordeal is YHWH's doing (v. 21bβ). Resentment surfaces in her agonizing acknowledgement that YHWH has 'brought on the day [he] proclaimed' (v. 21cα). Here, the Day of YHWH tradition found in some prophetic collections makes its second appearance in the book.[71] Zion already alluded to this day in Lam 1:12 ('On the day of his anger'). According to Lam 1:12c, the Day of YHWH is not a future event: it has already occurred. Zion uses this tradition to highlight YHWH's vicious assault on her (v. 13). A cursory reading of Zion's reference to the Day of YHWH tradition in Lam 1:21 suggests that she acknowledges her suffering as just punishment for her sins. [72] Nevertheless, Zion does not use the Day of YHWH tradition to bolster her acknowledgement of guilt, or to affirm the appropriateness of her suffering. Instead, she takes up this liturgical tradition to implore YHWH to inflict a similar fate on her foes (vs 21cβ–22).[73] Zion wants YHWH to punish her enemies, thereby relieving her of their repugnant taunts. Despite her admission that the suffering she endures is punishment for her sins, she does not acknowledge that this suffering comports with the prophets' reversal of conventional expectations for the Day of YHWH, that is, that it is/will be a time of 'darkness for Israel', not 'light'. She utters no words of penitence or repentance (see v. 12).[74] Zion is not concerned about the Day of YHWH as such, but about the opportunity that this tradition creates for articulating the more pressing concern of her extreme suffering.

---

[71] See also Isa 2:12; 13–23; Jer 46–51; Ezek 7; Amos 1–2, 5; Joel 2; Zeph 1. See Dobbs-Allsopp, 'R(az/ais)ing Zion', pp. 27–39.

[72] See, Ezek 7:3–9; Amos 5:21–24. These passages turn the Day of YHWH tradition on its head, depicting it as a time when YHWH will punish Israel's unfaithfulness, rather than defeating its enemies.

[73] See Isaiah 13–23; Jeremiah 46–51; and Amos 1:3–2:3. Parry notes that these passages highlight the 'universal scope of the Day of YHWH' (Parry, *Lamentations*, p. 65).

[74] For examples of penitence and repentance following acknowledgements of divine judgment and culpability, see Dan 9:4–19; Ezra 9:5–15; and Neh 1:4–10; 9.

Defeating the Foe

As noted above, the reprehensible responses of Zion's enemies to the suffering she has endured intensifies her anguish.[75] An equally prominent feature in the poems is holding YHWH responsible for the enormity of her plight.[76] Thus, Zion is concerned not only about her political foes' actions (Lam 1:22), but also about her deity's actions (Lam 2:4–5, 22; 5:20, 22). While Parry's assertion that Zion's plea in Lam 1:22 is a call 'for God to notice *all* evils and not merely *her* evils'[77] is correct, her plea seeks to accomplish more than that single purpose. By implication, '*all* evils' include those evils that YHWH has allegedly perpetrated. The fact that Zion is convinced that her foes are guilty of punishable offenses, including their reprehensible responses to her tragedy, does not remove the onus from YHWH, who has neither punished nor defeated her enemies. How can YHWH's judgments be equitable under her present circumstances? Who will hold YHWH accountable for God's injustices? YHWH cannot deal justly with Zion's earthly enemies'

---

[75] In Lam 1:2, her former allies have 'become her foes'; in 1:5, 'her foes have become her masters'; in 1:7, her people have fallen into the hands of foes, who celebrated her demise; in 1:9, her foes mockingly laugh at her plight; in 1:10, her foe has assaulted her, laying hands on her and invading her sacred sanctuary; in 1:16, her foe has prevailed over her; in 1:17, YHWH has enlisted the foes against his people; and in 1:21, the foes unsympathetically celebrate Zion's plight.

[76] According to Lam 1:5, the elevation of Zion's foes is a direct result of YHWH's punitive actions against her: כִּי־יְהוָה הוֹגָהּ (*kî-YHWH hôgāh*), 'because YHWH has caused her grief'; according to 1:12, Zion's incomparable agony was 'dealt to' (עוֹלַל [*'ôlal*]) her when 'YHWH brought grief' to her (הוֹגָה יְהוָה [*hôgāh YHWH*]) on the day of his wrathful fury; in 1:13, it is YHWH who has assaulted Zion; according to 1:14c, Adonai has 'given' Zion 'into the hands of those' she is 'unable to withstand'. In Lam 1:15, it is Adonai 'in the midst' who has spurned Zion's 'valiant ones'. Further, 'as in a wine press', 'Adonai' has 'trodden on' Daughter Zion; according to 1:17, YHWH has gathered foes against his people. According to Lam 1:21, Zion's predicament is YHWH's doing. In general, the chapter depicts Zion as abandoned by YHWH. See Lam 1:1–2, 10.

[77] Parry, *Lamentations*, p. 65.

traumatizing actions against her without first addressing God's trauma-inflicting actions and inactions in dealings with her. The latter (YHWH's inactions) are the ultimate reasons why Zion became vulnerable to her earthly foes' assault. Thus, while acknowledging, yet again, her own 'transgressions' (v. 22bβ), she overshadows that acknowledgement with descriptions of her crushing agony (v. 22c). Zion wants YHWH to punish her foes for their transgressions as well.

Lamentations 2:17

In Lam 2:17, the poet lifts up the Day of YHWH motifs, including an invitation to weep incessantly (vs 18–19), with further depictions of the plight of Zion's most vulnerable inhabitants, her infants (v. 19c-d). The invitation to weep is a prominent feature of the Day of YHWH motifs in the Hebrew Bible. For example, the prophet Isaiah implores his audience to 'howl' or 'wail' for the imminent יוֹם יְהוָה (*yôm YHWH*), 'Day of YHWH' (Isa 13:6). Similarly, Ezek 30:2 (MT), Joel 1:15, 13, and Zeph 1:11 include a call to 'wail' in anticipation of, or in response to, the *yôm YHWH*. This call to wail can double as a cry of terror or a cry of astonishment (see Ezek 30:2; Joel 1:15; Amos 5:18) in response to the extensive destruction meted out on the Day of YHWH.[78] The invitation to weep in Lam 2:18–19 is a call to mourn that refuses consolation due to the enormity of the loss. David A. Bosworth persuasively argues that the personification of Zion as a weeping daughter and mother in Lamentations 1 and 2 heightens the poem's emotional pathos and impact.[79] The imagery of the 'wall of Daughter Zion' (v. 18a) utilizes synecdoche to highlight personified Zion's vulnerability. Her symbol of security is invited to mourn on her behalf, to weep unremittingly over the wide-ranging catastrophes Daughter Zion has endured (vs 1–16). Through the use of synecdoche, Zion is invited to intercede in the presence of Adonai for the lives of her languishing children (v. 19cd). This depiction of a defenseless

---

[78] See Dobbs-Allsopp, 'R(az/ais)ing Zion', pp. 28–35.

[79] Bosworth, 'Daughter Zion and Weeping in Lamentations 1–2', pp. 217–237.

'Mother' Zion weeping over her famished infants, who lie 'at every street corner' (v. 19d), undermines the view that the murderous results of the *yôm YHWH* are appropriate or just. Thus, the poet strategically lifts up elements of the Day of YHWH motif to resist the Deuteronomic understanding of retribution as an adequate explanation for Zion's extreme suffering.

Although the Day of YHWH has come to Zion, the poet does not urge her to weep for her sins. Rather, he urges her to weep for her helpless infants (Lam 2:19cd). What Zion has suffered is not proportionate to her sins; it is excessive. The poet uses the Day of YHWH motif to evoke sympathy for Zion's cause, rather than to excoriate her. The imagery of starving infants compels the text's readers and listeners to sit down 'at a distance' with Hagar and exclaim, 'Let me not look on as the child dies'. 'And sitting thus afar,...burst into tears' (Gen 21:15, 16, *NJPS*).

Lamentations 2:22

Zion's address to YHWH in Lam 2:20–22 demonstrates that she resists the view that the trauma her mothers and their children endure constitutes just punishment for her sins. Bosworth argues that as personified mother and daughter, Zion can utter the woes of surviving mothers and children in Jerusalem. She can identify with the mothers who were brutalized and lost precious children in the catastrophe. As daughter, she can also identify with the children who endure the traumatic events associated with Jerusalem's demise.[80] Thus, Bosworth asserts, '[t]he audience that identifies with personified Zion understands her pain and violation as their own. This empathy for the personified figure both draws on and reinforces empathy for the individual victims'.[81] By lifting up the enormity of her suffering, Zion—and ultimately the poet—questions some of the assumptions surrounding the Deuteronomic doctrine of retribution and the Day of YHWH tradition. Are the extremities of post-siege warfare just punishment for sin? Even if Zion incurred YHWH's wrath and was numbered among his ene-

---

[80] Bosworth, 'Daughter Zion and Weeping', pp. 218, 226–230.

[81] Ibid., p. 228.

mies for her unspecified infractions, 'should women [be driven to] eat their own offspring, the new-born for whom they have cared?' (v. 20).

RESPONSIBILITY, SUFFERING, AND JUSTICE: RESISTING GOD

In communal laments within the Psalter, psalmists typically recognized that national tragedies challenged the 'elemental beliefs upon which they understood Israel's relationship with God to rest'.[82] National catastrophes, brought about by God's direct actions or inaction, jeopardized fundamental assumptions about God's power and covenant relationship with Israel.[83] The attack on these assumptions, more than the physical assaults inflicted by political foes, accounts for the bewilderment evident in these laments.[84] Dissonance arises between the psalmists' faith assumptions and their people's experiences of defeat, destruction, and some other national calamities.[85] This dissonance appears also in Lamentations'

---

[82] Bouzard, *We Have Heard*, p. 134.

[83] Ibid. See also Broyles, *The Conflict of Faith and Experience in the Psalms*, pp. 135–139, 150–173, 214–215. Broyles identifies three dominant fundamental presuppositions that informed communal laments: divine warrior traditions (e.g., Psalms 44 and 60); Royal Zion traditions (Psalms 74, 79, and 89), and exodus/conquest traditions (e.g., Psalm 80).

[84] Bouzard, *We Have Heard*, p. 134. See T. N. D. Mettinger, 'The Name and the Glory: The Zion-Sabaoth Theology and Its Exilic Successors', pp. 1–24. Mettinger draws on L. Festinger, *A Theory of Cognitive Dissonance* and R. P. Carrol, 'Prophecy and Dissonance: A Theoretical Approach to the Prophetic Tradition', pp. 108–119. Carrol argues that during the exilic era, there was a clash between the Zion-Sabaoth theology ('YHWH's royal presence in Zion') and the reality of political history ('the conquest of Jerusalem and the destruction of the temple'), which created a situation of 'cognitive dissonance' for the survivors. He further suggests that the Deuteronomic Name theology and the Priestly Kabod theology represent hermeneutical attempts to offer developments of, or alternatives to, the old Zion-Sabaoth theology.

[85] This element of cognitive dissonance appears also in individual laments (see Psalm 88).

poems. Zion theology is a dominant cause for cognitive dissonance in the book.[86]

Bertil Albrektson argues that Zion theology/traditions is a major theological key to interpreting Lamentations.[87] In his view, Zion traditions, rather than the Deuteronomic perspective that Gottwald proposes, stands in tension with the historical adversity described in Lamentations.[88] Paul R. House concedes the considerable achievement of Albrektson's study; nevertheless, he notes that Albrektson either overstated, or understated, various aspects of the book's theology.[89] House posits that Albrektson's chief overstatement pertains to Jerusalem's inviolability.[90] In his view, it is debatable whether the 'inviolability of Zion and the impregnability of Jerusalem' are identical concepts in the Hebrew Bible. Unquestionably, Zion was YHWH's dwelling place and was believed to be inviolable (Pss 46; 48; 76; and Isa 25). Jerusalem, by contrast, 'is the place where God has chosen to put his name (see Deut 12:8–12; 1 Kings 9:3…).'"[91] Nevertheless, if the people rebel, 'Jerusalem can be destroyed' (1 Kings 9:6–9; Jer 7 and 26).[92]

House's contrast between Zion on one hand, and Jerusalem on the other, is unconvincing and unnecessary. The two terms are used in hendiadys and as synonyms in the book of Lamentations (see Lam 1:17; and 2:10, 13), suggesting that they refer to the same geographical and geo-political entity.[93] The designations 'Zion' and

---

[86] Zion theology refers to the view that YHWH had a special relationship with Zion, which was home to the temple and the capital city of Davidic Kings, YHWH's earthly vice-regents. Zion traditions affirmed the city's inviolability on the basis of this unique relationship between YHWH and Zion.

[87] Albrektson, *Studies*, pp. 219–231 and passim.

[88] Ibid., p. 30.

[89] House, *Lamentations*, p. 318.

[90] Ibid.

[91] Ibid.

[92] Ibid., p. 319.

[93] See Isa 10:12; 24:23; Joel 2:32; see also 1 Kings 8:1//2 Chr 5:2; 2 Kings 19:21, 31; Ps 51:20 [ET, 51:18]; 102:22 [ET, 102:21]; 128:5; 135:21;

'Jerusalem' are used interchangeably. Ultimately, Jerusalem will share in Zion's future glory (see Joel 3:17). Jerusalem (the city) is inseparable from the implications of Zion theology.

House is correct in his assertion that the view of Zion's inviolability expressed by the people and some of their enemies in Lamentations might not necessarily represent the poet's views.[94] Nevertheless, judging from the trauma process evident in the book, the culture creator utilizes and adapts various aspects of Zion tradition to bear witness to Daughter Zion's trauma. Both Isaiah and Jeremiah challenged the popular view of Zion's/Jerusalem's unconditional inviolability (see, Isa 3:16–4:1; Jer 4, 6, and 7). For these prophets, the city's inviolability is contingent on the people's covenant faithfulness. Davidic/Zion theology is among the most prominent motifs in Lamentations. The poet skillfully utilizes and adapts this theology to question the fairness of God's actions. Zion traditions are also one of the bases for motivating YHWH to respond in the book.

Contours of Davidic/Zion Traditions

While biblical scholars dispute the exact origins of Zion traditions in ancient Israel,[95] most agree on these traditions' basic contours. The exact origins of the Zion traditions, whether in pre- or early Israelite, Canaanite, or monarchic antecedents, is not pertinent to the present study. Nevertheless, understanding the basic tenets and presuppositions of these traditions is necessary for an analysis of the cognitive dissonance survivors of Jerusalem's destruction experienced, including the torching of the Jerusalem temple and the Babylonians' capture of the reigning Davidic monarch.

147:12; Isa 2:3; 4:3; 4:4; 31:9; 37:22, 32; 40:9; 41:27; 52:2; 64:10; Jer 51:35; Amos 1:2; Micah 3:10; 4:8; and Zeph 3:14, 16.

[94] House, *Lamentations*, p. 319.

[95] See J. J. M. Roberts, 'The Davidic Origin of the Zion Tradition,' pp. 313–330; Roberts, 'Zion in the Theology of the Davidic-Solomonic Empire', in *The Bible and the Ancient Near East: Collected Essays*, pp. 331–347. See also Jon D. Levenson, 'Zion Traditions', pp. 1101–1102; John H. Hayes, 'The Tradition of Zion's Inviolability', pp. 417–426.

The assertion that YHWH is the 'great king' is fundamental to Zion theology (see Ps 48:3; 47:3).[96] The enthronement of YHWH as head of the pantheon and sovereign ruler of Israel underpins passages such as Deut 32:8,[97] 33:4–5,[98] and Ps 82.[99] YHWH's victory over cosmic and earthly enemies (Ps 48; 74:12–17) serves as the basis for affirmations of his invincibility, sovereignty, and reliability.[100] YHWH's kingship also is grounded in his roles as creator (see Ps 89:9–19)[101] and defender/redeemer of Israel.[102] Closely related to the kingship of YHWH is the view that he has chosen David (and his 'house' ['dynasty']) as his vice-regent and adopted son.[103] During the Davidic monarchy, YHWH became suzerain over the entire earth 'with vassal states who actually acknowledged his suzerainty'[104]—a belief alluded to in Psalms 2 and 47.[105] In sum, YHWH, the 'Great King' and suzerain of the whole earth, chose David and his descendants as his earthly representatives.

Another key element in Zion traditions is that YHWH has chosen Jerusalem, specifically Mount Zion, as his permanent dwelling place.[106] Mount Zion is sometimes identified with Mount Zaphon, Baal's dwelling place in Canaanite mythological traditions.[107] 'As the dwelling-place of Yahweh, creator of the cosmic

---

[96] See Ben C. Ollenburger, *Zion, The City of the Great King*, pp. 23–80.

[97] See Roberts, 'The Davidic Origins of Zion Tradition', pp. 324–325.

[98] Roberts, 'Zion in the Theology', p. 334.

[99] See Simon B. Parker, 'The Beginning of the Reign of God: Psalm 82 as Myth and Liturgy', pp. 532–559.

[100] Levenson, 'Zion Traditions', p. 1099.

[101] Ollenburger, *Zion, The City of the Great King*, pp. 54–55.

[102] Ibid., p. 57.

[103] Levenson, 'Zion Traditions', p. 1099.

[104] Roberts, 'Zion in the Theology', p. 336.

[105] See Roberts, 'The Religio-political Setting of Psalm 47', in *The Bible and the Ancient Near East*, pp. 266–272.

[106] See, for example, Pss 46:4–6; 48:2–9; 78:68; 87:2; and 132:13.

[107] It is evident, as J. J. M. Roberts notes, that the biblical Zion traditions may have adapted several elements of Canaanite and Babylonian

order and defender of Israel, Zion functions pre-eminently as a symbol of security'.[108] YHWH's presence in Zion makes the city inviolable (Ps 46:6);[109] the city is protected from attacks by enemy kings.[110] Zion itself is a symbol of security for those who completely trust in YHWH.

Further, the temple-city was a visible symbol 'of the futility of wars and weapons when they are directed against the master of all that is'.[111] YHWH will protect his temple-city and those who dwell in it. Thus, peace also is a prominent aspect of Zion traditions. Finally, as a result of God's 'beneficence', Zion is associated with infinite beauty and joy—'beautiful in elevation…the joy of all the earth' (Ps 48:2).[112]

YHWH's choice of Zion as his dwelling place also bears significant implications for its inhabitants: '[O]nly those who meet God's righteous standards can live in his presence (Isa 33:13–16; Ps 24:3–4)'.[113] Ultimately, the fit inhabitants of Zion will 'rejoice in the security and abundant life that Yahweh's presence brings'.[114]

The key components of Zion theology can be summarized as follows:

1. YHWH is the Great King of the whole earth;

---

mythology (see Roberts, 'Zion in the Theology', 336; Roberts, 'The Davidic Origin', pp. 316–322).

[108] Ollenburger, *Zion*, p. 66.

[109] See Hayes, 'The Tradition of Zion's Inviolability'.

[110] Ollenburger, *Zion*, p. 66.

[111] Levenson, 'Zion', p.1101.

[112] Ollenburger suggests that joy is often associated with enthronement (Ollenburger, *Zion*, pp. 34–35). Levenson notes that it is 'not unusual for a king upon his accession or the anniversary of it to give his subjects a very tangible cause for joy by issuing a decree that would cancel debts, release prisoners, repatriate prisoners of war, and the like' (Levenson, 'Zion', p. 1099). It seems likely that the enthronement of YHWH was envisioned in very similar ways. YHWH's reign brings 'justice and righteousness' for Zion's inhabitants (ibid).

[113] Roberts, 'Zion in the Theology', p. 342.

[114] Ibid., p. 343.

2. YHWH is the defender of Israel;
3. YHWH, the Great King and suzerain, has chosen David and his house (dynasty) as his earthly representatives in perpetuity;
4. YHWH has chosen Zion, the temple city, as his permanent dwelling place;
5. Zion is secure because of YHWH's abiding presence;
6. YHWH's presence in Zion significantly benefits the inhabitants of the city, who enjoy peace, joy, and security.

Resisting God in Lamentations

Zion traditions, among the most prominent theological influences in Lamentations, figures most conspicuously in Lamentations 2.[115] As Dobbs-Allsopp has convincingly argued, Zion is both 'razed' and 'raised' in Lamentations 2. In this chapter, Zion traditions, 'especially Yahweh's presence in Zion and the inviolability of Jerusalem...are encountered most forthrightly'.[116] While Lamentations 1 focuses especially on depictions of Zion's traumatic misfortunes, Lamentations 2 shifts attention to the architect of Zion's calamities—YHWH. Daughter Zion is portrayed as the helpless victim of her angry guardian, who has punished her beyond reason. Zion traditions are inverted in this chapter: YHWH is Zion's adversary, not her protector; YHWH's presence in Zion has murderous implications, not salvific ones. Ultimately, these rhetorical strategies serve to highlight the extent of Zion's woes and to challenge the actions of her patron deity.

---

[115] On Zion tradition and its significance in Lamentations, see Albrektson, *Studies*, pp. 219–239. See also Dobbs-Allsopp, 'R(az/ais)ing Zion in Lamentations 2', pp. 21–68. I believe that the significance of Zion traditions as one of the theological filters of Lamentations has been sufficiently and recognized in Biblical scholarship. It is not my aim here to restate or critique all the scholarly arguments that have already been established on this issue; rather my discussion will focus on issues relating to Zion's trauma, particularly the trauma process, as I have conceived it thus far in this study.

[116] Dobbs-Allsopp, 'R(az/ais)ing Zion in Lamentations 2', p. 21.

Lamentations 2:1–5

Lamentations 2:1–5 contains a gripping description of YHWH's merciless bulldozing of Zion (traditions). Prominent in these verses is the undeniable acknowledgement of YHWH's unbridled fury against Zion. 'In his anger' (בְּאַפּוֹ [*bĕʾappô*]), Adonai has 'covered Daughter Zion with a cloud' of dishonor (v. 1a). 'On the day of his anger (אַפּוֹ [*ʾappô*])',[117] Adonai 'did not remember his footstool' (v. 1c).[118] Further, according to verse 2a, Zion's deity has 'destroyed without compassion' (לֹא חָמַל [*loʾ ḥāmal*]). 'In his rage' (בְּעֶבְרָתוֹ [*bĕʿebrātô*]), he has leveled fortifications (v. 2b); in 'fiery anger' (בָּחֳרִי-אַף [*bāḥŏrî-ʾap*]), he has cut off all the 'strength of Israel' (2:3a). Moreover, Adonai has 'poured out his rage like fire' (שָׁפַךְ כָּאֵשׁ חֲמָתוֹ [*šāpak kāʾēš ḥămātô*]; v. 4b); and 'he has burned in Jacob like a flaming fire, devouring round about' (v. 3). Ultimately, Zion's deity has acted toward her as an avowed enemy would act (vs 4aα, 4aβ, 5a). Dobbs-Allsopp insightfully asserts: 'That a Judean poet could call God 'enemy' is a telling sign of the deep distress and unparalleled suffering brought on by the catastrophe'.[119] Beyond drawing attention to Zion's enormous anguish, saying that God has acted like an enemy serves to resist or question God's actions. Adonai's incendiary, wrathful onslaught on Daughter Zion is excessive: God's fury seems out of control. K. M. O'Connor correctly notes that God's presence is a consuming fire.[120] Furthermore, 'God has lost control, turned into a mad deity….'[121] In Lam 2:1–5, the poet does not attempt to justify Adonai's violence against Zion. In order to bear witness to Daughter Zion's trauma, the poet chooses to resist God's wrathful actions. He depicts God's furious attacks on Zion as unjustifiable and unreasonable. In so doing, the poet creates a context for survivors to assert their humanity and retain some control of the trauma process. The chilling depictions

---

[117] This statement refers to the Day of YHWH as a day of wrath. See Dobbs-Allsopp, *Lamentations*, p. 80.

[118] Here and elsewhere in the book, the Hebrew text uses the divine name 'Adonai' instead of 'YHWH'.

[119] Dobbs-Allsopp, *Lamentations*, p. 83.

[120] O'Connor, *The Book of Lamentations*, p. 1038.

[121] Ibid.

of YHWH's wrath unequivocally affirm the enormity of Zion's predicament—her own deity has betrayed her and become her antagonist.

Zion traditions typically affirmed that YHWH's presence in Zion ensured security for its inhabitants, though the prophets warned that without covenant obedience, this belief was deceptive and could foster a false sense of security (see Jer 7–11; 26).[122] The prophets' relentless attempts to modify or clarify Zion traditions on this point reflect this popular belief's far-reaching grip. The belief that YHWH's special presence in Zion meant security for the city and its inhabitants, along with the accompanying belief in Zion's inviolability, is crucial for understanding the cognitive dissonance, astonishment, and trauma that characterize Lamentations' poems, particularly Lamentations 2. According to Lam 2:1–5, Zion's fortunes have been negatively reversed as a result of YHWH's rage (v. 1). The fact that neither the 'splendor of Israel' (v. 1b) nor YHWH's 'footstool' were spared 'on the day of his anger' (v. 1c) strikes a deadly blow to the heart of Zion traditions.[123] Adonai has

---

[122] That obedience is essential for Zion's security is evident in, for example, in Jer 7:4–11, 14; 9:11; 26:4–6, 18.

[123] While the text is ambiguous at some points, scholars agree that the epithet 'splendor of Israel' refers to the city of Jerusalem or its temple, and Adonai's 'footstool' refers to the temple. Thus both epithets refer to personified Daughter Zion. See Dobbs-Allsopp, *Lamentations*, p. 81; Provan, *Lamentations*, pp. 59–60; Berlin, *Lamentations*, pp. 67–68; Hillers, *Lamentations* (1992), pp. 96–97; House, *Lamentations*, pp. 376–377; Bergant, *Lamentations*, pp. 57–58; Parry, *Lamentations*, pp. 73–74. While Salters agrees that the 'footstool' is a reference to the temple, he argues that the 'splendor of Israel' is a reference to 'Israel's illustrious past' (Salters, *Lamentations*, p. 114). This interpretation of 'the splendor of Israel', Salters posits, comports well with the radical reversal of Zion's fortunes depicted in the text. While this interpretation is intriguing, in most of the prophetic collections in the Hebrew Bible, as well as in the book of Lamentations itself, Israel's past is anything but illustrious (see Jer 11:1–17; Ezek 16:1–58; 23). According to Jer 2:1–3, the wilderness generation was devoted to YHWH; however, subsequent generations were rebellious (vs 4–37). Thus, against the backdrop of Zion traditions, the view that the 'splendor

intentionally and systematically decimated all of Zion's outlying areas (v. 2aβ),[124] the city's fortifications (vs. 2bβ, 5bβ), the royal domain and its officials (v. 2β), the nation and its fortified palaces (v. 5a-b), and the 'strength of Israel' (v. 3aβ). Zion's radical reversal of fortunes reflects YHWH radically new relationship with the temple-city—God's presence no longer means security for Zion, or God has abandoned God's dwelling place (see Ezek 10). Zion has been ravaged and forsaken by her God.

Moreover, Adonai has 'withdrawn his right hand' from Zion, leaving her completely vulnerable to the whims of her earthly foe.[125] These depictions of God's razing of Zion (traditions) suggest that God 'has truly turned away from' Zion.[126] Unlike the Exodus narratives, his fire no longer serves as a symbol of his protection but as a manifestation of God's destructive wrath (see Ex 13:21–22; 15:6, 12).[127] Even more striking is the imagery of Adonai as a warrior, bow drawn, who indiscriminately launches deadly arrows in the onslaught on Zion (traditions).[128] YHWH is no longer Zion's defender or guardian; instead, God has become her vicious archenemy. God's rancorous actions have increased Daughter Judah's[129] 'mourning and moaning' (Lam 2:5c). The enormity of Zion's predicament results from the enormity of her deity's murderous onslaught—hence the cognitive dissonance evident in Lam

---

of Israel' refers to Zion, the temple-city, is the more appropriate interpretation based on context.

[124] Based on archaeological and historical evidence this statement is clearly hyperbolic. See discussion in Chapter 2.

[125] See Dobbs-Allsopp, *Lamentations*, p. 82.

[126] Provan, *Lamentations*, p. 62.

[127] Ibid.

[128] Dobbs-Allsopp notes that, 'The divine warrior is portrayed with bow and arrow (2 Sam 22:15; Hab 3:9; Ps 7:14). In Ps 7:13 and Lam 3:12 Yahweh is imagined bending (*drk*) his bow as here (cf. Zech 9:13)' (Dobbs-Allsopp, 'R(az/ais)ing Zion', p. 33, n. 46).

[129] This epithet is used interchangeably with 'Daughter Zion' and other epithets in Lamentations to refer affectionately to the personified city of Jerusalem and/or her inhabitants as a woman. See Hillers, *Lamentations* (1992), pp. 30–31.

2:1–5, as well as elsewhere in the book. By questioning the appropriateness of YHWH's actions, the poet highlights Zion's precarious plight and sets the stage for her survival and re-construction of identity in the aftermath of tragedy.

Lamentations 2:6–7

YHWH's assaults on Zion (traditions) continue in Lam 2:6–7. References to YHWH's destruction of 'his booth' (שֻׂכּוֹ [*śukkô*]; See Pss 27:5; 76:3) and 'his tabernacle' (מוֹעֲדוֹ [*môʿădô*], and rejection of 'his altar' (מִזְבְּחוֹ [*mizbĕḥô*]) and 'his Sanctuary' (מִקְדָּשׁוֹ [*miqdāšô*])—all metaphorical references to Zion—further shatter important assumptions within Zion traditions that the book presupposes. YHWH has brought an end to religious festivals and the Sabbath, important symbols of Israel's special covenant relationship with YHWH (see Ex 31:12–17; Lev 23). God has spurned 'king' and 'priest', both important functionaries within Zion traditions. Daughter Zion's traditions, which promised her security, have been breached in the face of the earthly foe's (and divine) assaults on her city and precious children. She indicts YHWH for this breach in Zion traditions.

Lamentations 4:17–20

Lamentations 4:17–20 highlights the anguish of those abandoned. They have hoped in vain for deliverance (v. 17), but their political allies have refused to intervene on their behalf. YHWH's anointed, a veiled reference to the Davidic king (probably Zedekiah), has been captured (see 2 Kings 25:7). These verses depict the suffering community's vulnerability. YHWH has not intervened to save them. They are left to rely on earthly political powers, yet they too have failed them. Furthermore, the Davidic king, an important pillar of Zion traditions, has been apprehended. According to Dobbs-Allsopp, YHWH's control of history is one of the literary/religious traditions that the poet adapts in the book of Lamentations.[130] The tradition asserts that victory in war was a palpable sign of YHWH's

---

[130] Dobbs-Allsop, 'Tragedy, Tradition, and Theology', p. 50.

control over Israel and its enemies[131] and this view is maintained even though the Babylonians have defeated Zion. For the poet, neither the Babylonian army nor its gods are responsible for Zion's fate. YHWH alone is responsible. God withdrew God's protective presence from Zion and fought against God's own people.[132] Interestingly, the community's desperate complaint must be understood as addressed to YHWH. Thus, the motifs of divine indifference, abandonment, and absence (*Deus absconditus*) serves to draw attention to the survivors' hopeless plight and to indict YHWH for the atrocities they have endured.

Lamentations 5:1–16

In Lam 5:1–16, the poet continues to adapt and manipulate certain facets of Davidic/Zion traditions. The suffering community has been abandoned to the whims and devices of foreigners and slaves (Lam 5:2, 8), conditions in Zion have become perplexing (5:3–5; 9–15), and food is scarce (5:4, 6, 9–10). These conditions suggest that YHWH's reign in Zion has become punitive. Here, as elsewhere in the book, the poet does not question the reality of YHWH's reign. Rather, he questions the effects and implications of God's reign. This modification of Zion traditions functions strategically to draw attention to the vastness of Zion's suffering—YHWH has left her and her children at the mercies of foreigners and slaves. The poet also lifts up these traditions as the basis for imploring YHWH to address Zion's situation. YHWH should 'remember!', 'look!', and 'see!' Zion's disgrace, upholding Davidic/Zion traditions and restoring Zion's former status, inheritance, prosperity, security, and crown.

The book of Lamentations indicts YHWH for Zion's suffering: God is responsible for 'administering punishment that is unjust in its excessiveness'.[133] The book resists God's wrathful actions against Zion by questioning the justice and proportionality of those actions. The indictment of YHWH functions strategically to draw

[131] Ibid.

[132] Ibid.

[133] Lee, *Singers*, p. 36.

attention to Zion's suffering, and to ensure her survival. If YHWH bears ultimate responsibility for Zion's fate, then YHWH has survived the Babylonian assaults on Jerusalem. If YHWH survived, then Zion also has a chance to survive. Accordingly, the poet adapts various aspects of Davidic/Zion traditions in order to better register the extent of Zion's perils and to set the stage for reconstructing her identity and re-ordering her worlds in the wake of her trauma. While the book of Lamentations does not undertake these tasks (re-construction and re-ordering), it provides the platform on which subsequent generations of Israelites can reconstruct Zion's identity and re-order her worlds (see, for example, Isa 40:1–2; 49:8–26; 51:3–8, 17–23; 53:1–12; 54:1–17; 60:1–22; 62:1–12; 66:6–16).[134] Ultimately, Zion will be comforted, restored, and vindicated; and her scattered children will return home. YHWH will uphold Zion traditions and restore God's special relationship with Zion.

SUMMARY

The book of Lamentations provides a framework for Daughter Zion's survival in the aftermath of Jerusalem's demise. The poet (culture creator) skillfully adapts, adopts, and manipulates various aspects of certain ancient Israelite traditions regarding judgment, God's relationship with Zion, and hope, to ensure the possibility of survival. Lamentations' poems resist the Deuteronomic perspective of retribution and reward by highlighting Zion's excessive suffering. However, this perspective also serves as a basis for beseeching YHWH to intervene on her behalf—God can punish her foes and vindicate her cause. The book of Lamentations also resists certain popular assumptions concerning Zion traditions, and especially regarding YHWH's covenant relationship with her. YHWH has acted as Zion's foe and not as her guardian. The razing of Zion traditions in Lamentations, and especially in Lamentations 2, is God's doing. Nevertheless, assigning responsibility for Zion's de-

[134] See Linafelt's discussion of how Second Isaiah (Isaiah 40–55) responds to the demands for survival in Lamentations (Linafelt, *Surviving*, pp. 62–79).

mise to her patron deity becomes the foundation for her survival. If Zion's deity is responsible for her current fate (her destruction), then her deity has survived her fate. So long as YHWH's reign persists beyond Zion's defeat, the possibility of a future for Zion lingers.

CHAPTER 6. HOPE AND RESILIENCE IN LAMENTATIONS

INTRODUCTION

The focus on hope as an important motif in the book of Lamentations is well documented in biblical scholarship. Typically, this focus is based on giving structural or theological prominence to Lamentations 3.[1] Nevertheless, a close critical reading of Lamentations 3 supports neither the centrality of hope in this poem, nor its presence throughout the book as a whole.[2] Hope is not entirely absent from Lamentations; rather, the book's traces of hope are faint and serve to highlight Zion's feelings of hopelessness and despair, and provide a theological context for her survival.

DAUGHTER ZION'S RESILIENCE: THE MEANING OF HOPE IN LAMENTATIONS

Hope is a critical aspect of survival in trauma's aftermath. The shattering of identity and its supporting structures and institutions (for example, familial, communal, religious, political, and institutional) results in a loss of meaning that can exert debilitating effects on trauma survivors. Coping skills and responses undoubtedly vary

---

1 See Assis, 'The Alphabetic Acrostic'; and Johnson, 'Form and Message'.

2 See Provan, *Lamentations*, p. 22; Dobbs-Allsopp, 'Tragedy, Tradition, and Theology in the Book of Lamentations', pp. 47–48; Villanueva, 'The Uncertainty of a Hearing', pp. 213–233.

from person to person and community to community.[3] Nevertheless, finding or affirming hope following traumatic experiences is crucial for constructing meaning. Psychologist Gregory K. Moffatt states, 'Hope gives us focus and something to live for'.[4] Loss of hope often precedes loss of meaning.[5] The resilience of persons or communities in the wake of traumatic events is linked to their ability to affirm hope (a vision of a future) and construct meaning (something or someone to live for). In her study of resilience in families, family therapist and psychiatrist Froma Walsh asserts that belief systems play powerful roles in these processes:[6] 'we cope with crisis and adversity by making meaning of our experience: linking it to our social world, to our cultural and spiritual beliefs, to our multigenerational past, and to our hopes and dreams for the future'.[7] Although Walsh's conclusions are based on modern, empirical, multicultural studies, her work serves as a useful heuristic tool for evaluating aspects of resilience in Lamentations. Walsh identifies three aspects of belief systems that influence resilience:

---

[3] Some scholars have proposed the politics of grief as a viable approach to rebuilding and reshaping shattered individual and collective identities, especially in post-war contexts. The politics of grief involves intentionally acknowledging and working through the painful emotions associated with post-conflict traumas, including fear, anxiety, anger, humiliation, and guilt. Its ultimate goal is to help survivors and surviving communities cultivate empathy and compassion. See E. Hutchison and R. Bleiker, 'Grief and the Transformation of Emotions after War', in *Emotions, Politics and War*, pp. 210–221; Hutchinson and Bleiker, 'Emotional Reconciliation: Reconstituting Identity and Community after Trauma', pp. 385–403. For detail analyses of practices for resilience and meaning-making in response to natural and human-made disasters, see Ani Kalayjian and Dominique Eugene, eds, *Mass Trauma and Emotional Healing Around the World: Rituals and Practices for Resilience and Meaning-Making*.

[4] Moffatt, *Survivors*, p. 43.

[5] Ibid.

[6] F. Walsh, *Strengthening Family Resilience*, p. 49.

[7] Ibid.

making meaning of adversity; positive outlook (hope); and transcendence and spirituality.[8]

MAKING MEANING OF ADVERSITY

In the book of Lamentations, the poet affirms Zion's culpability. Nevertheless, focus falls on the disproportionality of her punishment. The poet does not ignore the reason for Zion's suffering. Rather, he draws attention to the extent of her calamity. God remains responsible for Zion's woes, and, as such, references to her culpability and retribution function to subvert God's justice or fairness. The book creates meaning out of adversity by affirming what Zion's suffering *does not* mean: it does *not* mean that YHWH is no longer in control; it does *not* mean that her suffering is proportionate punishment for her sins. Having affirmed what her adversity does *not* mean, the poet asserts its meaning: Zion's deity, YHWH, though present, has withdrawn protective covering from her; her suffering is YHWH's own doing; and YHWH's attack on Zion's children, inheritance, temple, and king is excessive. The poet constructs meaning by adapting motifs of divine presence, rejection, and indifference. Since God is responsible for Zion's woes, her only hope lies in the hands of her deity.

YHWH permitted Zion's foes to defeat and ravish her. To conclude otherwise would threaten the foundation of Zion's identity, because her identity was closely linked to her special relationship with YHWH, her divine patron. The poet affirms Zion's identity by asserting that, contrary to appearances, Zion's patron deity remains in control of history. The enemy was permitted to ravage Zion because of YHWH's actions and inactions. Furthermore, YHWH acted like a foe and is responsible for *most* of the destruction that Zion suffered. The poet uses the enormity of Zion's ruin to affirm the sovereignty and (abusive) power of her deity. Thus, YHWH survives the demise of Jerusalem; and if YHWH survives, then Zion has a chance to survive as well.

The poet assures YHWH's survival by asserting that Zion's pleas, prayers, and protests must be directed to her estranged pa-

---

[8] Ibid., pp. 54–82.

tron deity. YHWH is called to witness and attend to suffering (see Lam 1:9b, 11c, 20a; 2:20a; 5:1). The narrator and Zion insist that YHWH is neither dead nor defeated. They doggedly insist that YHWH still reigns; and God, rather than the Babylonians, has conquered and razed Zion. As O'Connor rightly observes, '[s]peakers in Lamentations tenaciously persist in trying to engage God. They make claims on God, demand attention, and beg for a future. They do this even as God walks away and silently closes the door to them'.[9] The sufferers in Lamentations refuse to give in to the pessimistic perspective that God is dead. However, they do not blindly construct meaning at the expense of their human dignity—they do not embrace the notions of silent submission and resignation as encouraged by the voice of wisdom (Lam 3:26–29). The sufferers do not put their mouths in the dust (Lam 3:29). They speak loudly, they protest, and they cry out in defiance. As O'Connor further notes, 'God may hide, but they [the sufferers] stand in plain view. They berate God, protest God's work, and dare to ask for more than patent cruelty'.[10] For the book's lamenters, YHWH is not dead; God must be roused to conscientious action on behalf of God's people.

POSITIVE OUTLOOK

Lamentations holds out hope that YHWH might respond, acknowledge God's own excesses, right the wrongs done to Daughter Zion, and restore relationship with God's people. In Walsh's words: '[a] positive outlook has been found to be vitally important for resilience'.[11] The hopeful aspect of resilience is not passive. Survivors must dare to act on their conviction that their actions can make a difference in their situation—they can contribute to the future they envision. They must be willing to struggle and persist in the face of overwhelming adversity. A strong determination to persevere in spite of adverse conditions is crucial for

---

[9] O'Connor, *Tears of the World*, p. 127.

[10] Ibid.

[11] Walsh, *Strengthening Family Resilience*, p. 65.

survival.[12] Psychologist Jack Saul adds that hope is how survivors cope with adversity, their source of strength.[13] But because '[t]rauma survivors who carry a sense of shame or guilt often feel undeserving of a promising future',[14] they must move beyond shame and guilt in order to affirm hope in the aftermath of trauma.[15]

While the book of Lamentations does not affirm an overwhelmingly optimistic outlook, it preserves some glimpses of hope. The survivors are future-oriented; they are resilient, not passive. They act on their conviction that a better future is possible. The most prominent affirmations of hope and confidence in the book, first by the individual sufferer in Lam 3:21–24, and then by the didactic sapiential voice in Lam 3:25–39, are undercut by graphic descriptions of suffering. Nevertheless, resilience persists in the book. Hope rears its head from the rubles of despair and forges a path through adversity. The poet undermines traditional perspectives on hope in order to construct a vision of hope that is more consistent with the community's extreme suffering (Lam 3:40–51). The anguished community has not experienced God or hope along the lines of either the individual sufferer (Lam 3:21–24) or traditional wisdom (Lam 3:25–39). Nevertheless, through their pleas and protest (3:42–47), and the cries of their representative (3:48–51), they resist absolute pessimism and absurdity. Hope remains that God will look down and see their plight (3:50). God can experience a change of heart and chose to attend to Daughter Zion's trauma. As O'Connor observes, '[t]he speakers' excess passion beats upward to God's throne…. They batter God with insistence and accusation. They refuse God's refusal. In the midst of their collective midnight they cry out, reveal themselves, open outward'.[16] The sufferers in Lamentations do not abandon hope; they reframe it to survive beyond, and in excess of, the death of hope.

---

[12] Ibid., p. 69.

[13] J. Saul, *Collective Trauma, Collective Healing*, pp. 48–49.

[14] Ibid., p. 48.

[15] For a discussion of guilt and shame in the aftermath of trauma see discussion by Ruth Leys, *From Guilt to Shame: Auschwitz and After.*

[16] O'Connor, *Tears of the World*, 127.

Such a radical, necessarily flickering, affirmation of hope resists impositions of guilt and shame. While Zion is brought to shame, publicly exposed (Lam 1:8, 9), and judged as culpable (Lam 1:5, 8; 2:14), and though she acknowledges her guilt (Lam 1:22; cf. 5:16), she does not permit guilt and shame to cripple or undermine her hope. This hope cannot be sustained through penitence or repentance. It is, rather, akin to what is found in the book of Job—hope survives by means of resistance to and protests against God's unjust actions, and the expectation of a divine response. But unlike Job, who is characterized as blameless (Job 1:1), Zion is guilty, though her punishment is presented as disproportionate to her sins. No divine response appears in the book of Lamentations; nevertheless, the expectation of a divine response persists. Thus, hope lingers beyond the uncertainty of the book's final words (Lam 5:22). The book's ending is ambiguous—neither wholly negative, nor completely positive.[17]

Each of the first four poems in Lamentations ends with a reference to the survivors' foe(s). The foe motif also appears in Lam 5:21–22. The plea for YHWH to restore and renew his relationship with the suffering community 'as of old' (v. 21) is consistent with the perspective in the previous poems that YHWH has acted as an enemy. The disorientation implicit in this verse presupposes YHWH's covenant relationship with Israel, a relationship central to Davidic/Zion traditions. Reference to YHWH's enthronement and reign in verse 19 alludes to Zion traditions, while the question raised in verse 20 points to the dissonance between certain aspects of these traditions on one hand and the people's experiences of YHWH's apparent indifference and abandonment of Zion on the other. The survivors' desperate plea in verse 21 presupposes the faith-assertion in verse 19, and their ominous statement (cry) in verse 22 mirrors their perplexing question in verse 20. Lamentations 5:22 is a strategic affirmation of the community's collective bewilderment. The foe in question is YHWH, their patron deity. YHWH has acted and continues to act as Zion's enemy: 'For indeed, you have rejected us, sorely angry with us' (similarly, *NJPS*).

---

[17] See Gordis, *The Song of Songs and Lamentations*, p. 198; Gordis, 'The Conclusion of the Book of Lamentations (5:22)', pp. 470–471.

This statement about YHWH's enemy-like behavior toward Zion, read against the backdrop of Zion traditions, raises doubts about Zion's future and her relationship with her God. This concluding verse of the poem (and of the book) is a protest against YHWH, whose wrathful actions are excessive. Nevertheless, this negative note also provides the basis for Zion's flickering hope (positive note): perhaps YHWH will restore Zion along the lines of (popular) Zion traditions; perchance God may vindicate Zion's cause and renew God's covenant relationship with her.

TRANSCENDENCE AND SPIRITUALITY[18]

There is value in Walsh's assertion that '[t]ranscendent beliefs provide meaning, purpose, and connection beyond ourselves, our families, and our troubles'.[19] Our need for deeper meaning, especially in the wake of tragedy, is 'most commonly met through spiritual faith and cultural heritage'.[20] Philosophical, ideological, and/or political convictions also can help to fulfill the need for greater meaning.[21] For Walsh transcendent beliefs provide clarity for our lives and comfort in the face of our adversities. These beliefs help us cope with unexpected events and navigate situations that we cannot change.[22] Also useful are Walsh's insights regarding the significance of transcendent beliefs and spirituality for survivors' resilience in the aftermath of calamities. Particularly relevant for analysis of Lamentations is the view that certain ideological/spiritual convictions and beliefs can help survivors cope with and work through unprecedented experiences.

One transcendent belief that no doubt informed the trauma process for survivors of Jerusalem's demise is the belief that

[18] Here, I understand 'transcendence' in the basic sense of that which is beyond the physical level, or that which is divine. Thus, belief in a sovereign deity lies within the semantic rage of my understanding of 'transcendence'. 'Spirituality' refers to practical applications of belief in transcendence, i.e., piety and devotion.

[19] Walsh, *Strengthening Family Resilience*, p. 72.

[20] Ibid.

[21] Ibid.

[22] Ibid.

YHWH—though silent and possibly indifferent—remains in control of history. YHWH is God beyond Jerusalem's fall, beyond lamentations over its destruction. YHWH remains God despite the loss of city, temple, and Davidic rule. Exile, economic collapse, and depopulation due to famine, pestilence, and military assaults cannot undermine YHWH because they are all God's doing.

The poems of Lamentations reveal the poet's deep spirituality. Ancient Israel's rich, religio-cultural heritage acts as the lens through which the poet views (and then expresses) Zion's pain. Walsh correctly argues that spiritual 'beliefs may become harmful if they are held too narrowly, rigidly, or punitively'.[23] Lamentations' poet adopts, adapts, and even manipulates a number of Israel's religious traditions in order to create theological space for Zion's survival. Through creativity and innovation,[24] the poet ensures both YHWH's and Zion's survival. He affirms the eternal reign of YHWH (5:19), insisting that Jerusalem's demise did not dethrone its God. Zion's God transcends Jerusalem and its religio-political institutions. Jerusalem's destruction and its attending calamities took place within, not outside of, YHWH's reign. This belief that YHWH still rules over history becomes the basis for the poems' flickering hope that YHWH can act to validate Zion and to restore God's special relationship with her. The possibility of renewed relationship with YHWH persists in, throughout, and beyond the devastation of Zion's children, monumental structures, and religio-political systems.

SUMMARY

To ensure the possibility of hope, the poet subverts traditional perspectives on hope in order to construct a vision of hope consistent with the brutal realities of Daughter Zion's trauma. Thus, Zion protests against YHWH's actions (and inactions) and against religious perspectives that would seek to justify her suffering as proportionate punishment for her sins. Zion is defiant and resilient in the face of God's silence and seeming indifference, and the appar-

---

[23] Walsh, *Strengthening Family Resilience*, p. 74.

[24] See ibid., pp. 76–77.

ent death of hope. The book stands between the complete collapse of Zion's foundational pillars (traditions) and her identity as YHWH's covenant partner on one hand, and the (potential) re-construction of her pillars and re-constitution of her identity in trauma's aftermath on the other. The book creates theological space for survivors to wrestle with the harrowing realities of existence in the wake of unparalleled, world-shattering suffering. Lamentations clings tentatively to the possibility of a divine hearing and response.

CONCLUSIONS

The literary features of the book of Lamentations highlighted in this study are well attested in scholarship: structural and generic complexity; emotive excesses; and the religious significance of its poems. Nevertheless, trauma studies contributes important insights for understanding these features. In the aftermath of trauma, survivors struggle to grasp and bear witness to realities that usually lie beyond their mastery. Survivors' testimonies typically reflect a history that is not straightforwardly referential. Their experiences remain elusive, yet trauma imposes itself through the repetition compulsion in dreams and in the literature that survivors and their descendants produce. The experience of excess inherent in traumatic realities distinguishes these realities from other experiences of suffering. Trauma shatters life; it is caesura in life, a breach in memory and time, and a collapsing of identity-shaping worlds, networks, institutions and assumptions. Bearing witness to traumatic realities, while complex and perplexing, allows survivors, their descendants, and their empathetic partners (historians, poets, musicians, artists, etc.) to construct survival and meaning in the aftermath of these limit events.

Bearing witness permits survivors, both individuals and collectivities, to attempt to reintegrate their ruptured lives, reshape their identities, re-constitute surviving relationships and institutions, re-order their worlds, and re-configure assumptions—about themselves, others, their God, their community, their future, and the ways these entities intersect. The perilous necessity of bearing witness to the excesses of trauma ultimately challenges systems and ideologies of violence and their perpetrators; resists totalizing assumptions; protests simple explanations for suffering; creates space for justice and accountability; and potentially paves the path toward survival, truth and reconciliation in relationships with one's self, one's community, others, and God.

The sixth century BCE destruction of Jerusalem and fall of Judah offers the most plausible historical backdrop for the book of Lamentations. The book likely was written during the decades following these events, and it evokes many of the realities that survivors likely endured. Both archaeological and textual evidence support this viewpoint. The events associated with Jerusalem's demise did not affect all Judeans in identical ways, that is, not all survivors were necessarily traumatized, at least not in the same ways. Not all communities were destroyed, or lost inhabitants to forced deportation. Nevertheless, the religious and psychological significance and implications of these events were no doubt bewildering, debilitating and world shattering for many survivors. For some, these catastrophic events signaled a conformation or fulfillment of prophetic teachings regarding the promised Day of YHWH. For others, YHWH had finally judged his unfaithful people—the Deuteronomic doctrine of rewards and punishment was confirmed. Nevertheless, Lamentations' poet skillfully adopted, adapted, manipulated and re-engaged these theological traditions to construct a future for those whose testimonies the book echoes.

For the survivors whom Daughter Zion represents, Jerusalem's fall created consternation. After all, it shattered optimistic perspectives associated with certain religious traditions. The popular view of Davidic/Zion traditions affirmed Zion's inviolability and impregnability, and promised security for the city's inhabitants based on YHWH's (unconditional) alliance with the Davidic dynasty and covenant relationship with Zion—God's dwelling place. In the opinion of many survivors, Jerusalem's demise, capture of the Davidic king, razing and desecration of YHWH's temple, and decimation/deportation of much of Jerusalem's population shattered these ancient traditions. For others, however, acknowledging their fate as God's just punishment for their sins and the sins of their ancestors' threatened the possibility of their survival as individuals and as a community. The poet of Lamentations, propelled by the excesses of trauma itself, dares to give raw, uncensored and seemingly blasphemous voice to trauma. Survival demanded facing the sufferers' traumatic realities head-on and resisting the tendency to capitulate to penitence.

The disorientation, horror and chaos of life in the aftermath of trauma are evident in the poems. Whether performed or read in private settings, public memorials, or in other mourning rituals, these poems bear witness to trauma. Through the process of giving voice to suffering, survivors can begin to create and discover new meaning from the fractured realities of trauma. While authorial intentionality is likely present in Lamentations, the reality of trauma evident in the poems lies beyond the mastery or control of the poet, who is also likely a survivor. The poet, along with ancient and modern readers and audiences who dare to be exposed to Daughter Zion's trauma, construct a foundation for survival beyond, and in excess of, the death of hope. Lamentations invites readers to take a second look at extreme suffering, not solely for the purpose of theological contemplations, but for survival.

This study highlighted certain aspects of trauma studies that shed light on various features within the book of Lamentations. These aspects include rupture in memory, non-referential history, and the rhetoric of the trauma process. Utilizing insights from these features of trauma studies, it was shown that the disciplining structures of the alphabetic acrostics in Lamentations 1–4 and of the alphabetic allusion in Lamentation 5 are simply façades. They cannot control, order, or contain Zion's trauma. They also cannot contain or proscribe the excess and elusiveness of traumatic experiences. Trauma ruptures these rickety poetic scaffoldings and renders them ineffective. At best, the alphabetic acrostics provide a frail framework for the traumatic experiences that gave rise to the five poems comprising Lamentations.

The book of Lamentations invites readers into the generic worlds of communal laments, dirges, city-laments, individual laments and wisdom sayings, to expose the enormity of Zion's trauma. Its adaptations and juxtapositions of genres open opportunities to express more fully the severity and extent of Zion's anguish. Lamentations' cacophony of voices and perspectives resists totalizing viewpoints—multiple survivors can hear their voices and perspectives in its poems. Mothers, children and men who survived the fall the Jerusalem hear their cries, consternation, and struggles within its verses. The various sufferers in Lamentations utter the pleas of real survivors, empathize with their experiences, and pleads with God on their behalf.

Another important insight of this study is that the poetic façades of Lamentations' five poets are ruptured through dramatic structural and generic breaks, mood shifts and theological interjections. These shifts or breaks in the poems bear witness to the trauma of Daughter Zion and of those on whose behalf she speaks and pleads. They give voice to trauma, allowing survivors (ritually) to express their suffering. Furthermore, these dramatic breaks create theological spaces for expressing and working through trauma. Moreover, these ruptures in the poems serve to motivate YHWH and his defenders to attend to Daughter Zion's trauma, including the plight of all sufferers, from her (their) vantage point, the site of trauma. Ruptures in the façades of Lamentations also highlight the enormity of Zion's trauma. Acknowledgements of culpability in the book lead to graphic depictions of suffering, not to penitence. Descriptions of anguish undermine direct, causal links between Zion's sin and her predicament.

The poems preserve testimonies (retellings of suffering) that are not straightforwardly referential. The poet uses stereotypical, tropic, and hyperbolic language to voice the enormity of Zion's loss. Furthermore, Zion's cries for YHWH to 'see' (recognize and acknowledge) her afflictions function both as painful pleas and as powerful protests. One of the book's primary aims is to motivate YHWH to attend to Zion's plight from her vantage point and reverse her fortunes. As protest, the call to attend to Zion's perils challenges YHWH to reconsider if her suffering is just and proportionate. Both the poet and personified Zion hope that YHWH will acknowledge that Zion's agony is excessive, recognize that he has gone too far, and change his attitude toward his covenant partner. [1]

This study has asserted that trauma informed readings of biblical texts should be intentionally self-critical, recognizing the limitations of this interpretive lens, yet applying its insights in ways that affirm the texts' complex compositional histories. The realities of biblical texts and the worlds they evoke should inform applications of trauma studies in interpreting these texts. Trauma oriented readings of biblical literature do not replace more traditional historical-critical considerations. Rather, they should build upon and move beyond insights gleaned through the applications of traditional methods and approaches. Trauma studies can provide a path beyond some of the limits of traditional approaches, including the

---

[1] Interestingly, both Isa 40:2 and 47:6 YHWH seems to acknowledge that Zion's suffering was excessive.

tendency to identify 'ruptures' in texts as problems that need 'fixing'.

Trauma sensitive readings of biblical literature also can help to make this literature more relevant and accessible to modern readers and audiences. Nevertheless, caution and delicate balances between ancient and modern worlds are necessary in order for such ventures to be legitimate and meaningful. Interpreters must avoid attempts to make these ancient texts 'fit' into uniquely modern systems and categories. We dare not be insensitive to the perspectives and cries of the ancient voices that biblical texts echo. Nevertheless, modern theories, like trauma studies, can shed light of some of the experiences and realities of ancient witnesses.

Biblical studies can help to nuance trauma studies as well. By analyzing ancient catastrophes that qualify as traumatic by modern standards, and by exploring the testimonies and responses of ancient survivors of these events, we broaden our understanding of trauma and its potential effects. The ways by which ancient trauma survivors re-constructed and re-integrated their worlds, their identities, their communities, and their religious beliefs in the wake of trauma are particularly suggestive for modern-day readers and interpreters. Examples of resilience among our ancient counterparts can potentially inspire and shape our own responses to contemporary mass disasters. Hence, the means by which various ancient individuals and groups coped with traumatic events can serve as heuristic tools for modern trauma victims. Daughter Zion and her sympathetic poet provide modern readers with examples of how to frame political and national disasters in religious language. Contrary to appearances, Zion's fate is God's doing; and this radical belief grounds the possibility of her survival. Zion's God can choose to act in precisely those ways that most trouble ancient and modern readers of Lamentations. Trauma studies stands to benefit from more critical analyses of ancient examples of resilience and coping with trauma.

This study challenges modern people of faith intentionally to create theological and liturgical space for lament without hasty retreats to penitence and praise. Lament is just as appropriate an expression of worship as penitence and praise. In the wake of personal and national tragedies, pausing in the midst of (ostensible) divine silence and indifference and venting unbridled anguish is cathartic. Inviting sympathy, empathy and solidarity with victims of unimaginable suffering is a necessary component of worship, especially in the aftermath of trauma. In the face of unmitigated violence, honest protest is an acceptable religious posture. Lamentations opens vistas to a theology that is both constructive and *de*-structive—constructive in the sense of creating meaning that abets the survival of faith individuals and communities in trauma's deadly aftermath, and *de*structive in the sense of canceling out old or outmoded meanings in order to honor and give voice to that which resists and transcends dogmas and propositional truths, refuses to be framed and/or systematized, and of necessity remains mysterious, ineffable, and absurd. That a survivor is able to utter the words 'on the day of YHWH's wrath, no one survived, none escaped' is absurd. Yet, this very absurdity grounds the pleas and protests Zion addresses to her God in hope of giving herself and her children a chance at survival.

Future trauma oriented analyses of the book of Lamentations can benefit from closer attention to the book's poetic features, including analyses of poetic parallelism and meter. Future studies also stand to benefit from more thorough comparative analyses of laments within the Hebrew Bible and from its wider ancient Near Eastern contexts. Finally, combining insights from trauma studies and from contemporary liturgical and ritual studies could inform and enrich contemporary performances and applications of the book of Lamentations.

BIBLIOGRAPHY

PRIMARY TEXT

Schäfer, R. 'Lamentations'. *Biblia Hebraica Quinta.* General Introduction and Megilloth. Germany: Deutsche Bibelgesellschaft, Stuttgart, 2004.

DICTIONARIES AND LEXICONS

Brown, F., S. R. Driver, and C. A. Briggs. *The Brown-Driver-Briggs Hebrew and English Lexicon.* Peabody, MA: Hendrickson Publishers, 1996.

Freedman, David Noel, editor-in-chief. *The Anchor Bible Dictionary.* 6 vols. New York: Doubleday, 1992.

The Diagnostic and Statistical Manual of Mental Disorder: DSM-IV-TR. Fourth Edition, Text Revision. Washington, D.C.: American Psychiatric Association, 2000.

VandenBos, Gary R., ed. *APA Dictionary of Psychology.* Second Edition. Washington, DC: American Psychological Association, 2015. ProQuest ebrary. Accessed July 9, 2015.

http://site.ebrary.com.ezproxy.bu.edu/lib/bostonuniv/reader.action?docID=11033030.

COMMENTARIES AND MONOGRAPHS

Albrektson, Bertil. *Studies in the Text and Theology of the Book of Lamentations: With A Critical Edition of the Peshitta Text.* Studia Theologica Lundensia 21. Lund: CWK Gleerup, 1963.

Allen, Leslie C. *Liturgy of Grief: A Pastoral Commentary on Lamentations.* Grand Rapids, MI: Baker Academic, 2011.

Bergant, Dianne. *Lamentations.* AOTC. Edited by P.D. Miller, *et al.* Nashville, TN: Abingdon Press, 2003.

Berlin, Adele. *Lamentations: A Commentary*. OTL. Edited by W. P. Brown, *et al.* Louisville, KY: Westminster John Knox Press, 2002.

Boase, Elizabeth. *The Fulfillment of Doom: the Dialogic Interaction Between the Book of Lamentations and Pre-exilic/early-exilic Prophetic literature.* London: T & T Clark, 2006.

Dobbs-Allsopp, F. W. *Weep, O Daughter Zion: A Study of the City-Lament Genre in the Hebrew Bible.* Biblica et Orientalia 44. Rome: Editrice Pontificio Istituto Biblico, 1993.

———. *Lamentations.* Interpretation. Louisville, KY: Westminster John Knox, 2002.

Gerstenberger, Erhard S. *Psalms Part 2 and Lamentations.* FOTL 25. Edited by R.P. Knierim, *et al.* Grand, Rapids, MI: Eerdmans, 2001.

Gordis, R. *Song of Songs and Lamentations.* New York: KTAV, 1974.

Gottwald, Norman K. *Studies in the Book of Lamentations.* Studies in Biblical Theology. London: SCM Press, 1954.

Hillers, Delbert R. *Lamentations: A New Translation with Introduction and Commentary.* Second, Revised Edition. The Anchor Bible. New York: Doubleday, 1992.

House, Paul R. *Lamentations.* Vol. 23b, WBC. Nashville, TN: Thomas Nelson, 2004.

Hunter, Jannie H. *Faces of a Lamenting City: The Development and Coherence of the Book of Lamentations.* BEATAJ 39. Frankfurt: Peter Lang, 1996.

Lee, Nancy C. *The Singers of Lamentations: Cities under Siege, from Ur to Jerusalem to Sarajevo.* Biblical Interpretation Series 60. Leiden: Brill, 2002.

Lee, Nancy C., and C. Mandolfo, eds. *Lamentations in Ancient and Contemporary Cultural Contexts.* SBLSymS 43. Edited by V. H. Matthews. Atlanta, GA: Society of Biblical Literature, 2008.

Linafelt, Tod. *Surviving Lamentations: Catastrophe, Lament, and Protest in the Afterlife of a Biblical Book.* Chicago: The University of Chicago Press, 2000.

Mandolfo, Carleen. *Daughter Zion Talks Back to the Prophets: A Dialogic Theology of the Book of Lamentations.* SBL Semeia Studies 58.

General editor, Gale A. Yee, Atlanta, GA: Society of Biblical Literature, 2007.

O'Connor, Kathleen M. *The Book of Lamentations: Introduction, Commentary, and Reflections*. Vol. 6, NIB. Edited by L.E. Keck, *et al.* Nashville, TN: Abingdon Press, 2001.

———. *Lamentations and the Tears of the World.* Maryknoll, NY: Orbis, 2003.

Parry, Robin. *Lamentations*. The Two Horizons Old Testament Commentary. Grand Rapids, MI: Eerdmans, 2010.

Parry, Robin, and Thomas Heath A., eds. *Great is Thy Faithfulness? Reading Lamentations as Sacred Scripture.* Eugene, OR: Pickwick, 2011.

Provan, Iain. *Lamentations*. New Century Bible Commentary. Grand Rapids, MI: Eerdmans, 1991.

Re'emi, S. P. "The Theology of Hope: A Commentary on the Book of Lamentations." In *God's People in Crisis*, 73–134. ITC. Grand Rapids, MI: Eerdmans, 1984.

Salters, Robert B. *A Critical and Exegetical Commentary on Lamentations*. ICC. Edited by G. I. Davies, *et al.* London: T& T Clark, 2010.

Westermann, Claus. *Lamentations: Issues and Interpretation.* Translated by Charles Muenchow. Minneapolis, MN: Fortress Press, 1994.

SECONDARY SOURCES

Ackroyd, Peter R. *Exile and Restoration: A Study of Hebrew Thought of the Sixth Century B.C.* Philadelphia, PA: The Westminster Press, 1968.

Albertz, Rainer. *A History of Israelite Religion in the Old Testament Period: From the Exile to the Maccabees.* Vol. 2. OTL. Edited by J.L. Mays, *et al.* Translated by J. Bowden. Louisville, KY: Westminster John Knox Press, 1994.

———. *Israel in Exile: The History and Literature of the Sixth Century B.C.E.* Translated by D. Green. SBL Studies in Biblical Literature 3. Atlanta, GA: Society of Biblical Literature, 2003.

Albrektson, Bertil. 'The Background and Origin of the Theology of Lamentations'. In *Text, Translation, Theology: Selected Essays on the Hebrew Bible*, pp. 9–34. *SOTSM*. Farnham: Ashgate, 2010.

Assis, Elie. 'The Alphabetic Acrostic in the Book of Lamentations'. *CBQ* 69, no. 4 O (2007): pp. 710–724.

———. 'The Unity of the Book of Lamentations'. *CBQ* 71, no. 2 (2009): pp. 306–329.

Barstad, H. M. *The Myth of the Empty Land: A Study in the History and Archaeology of Judah during the "Exilic" Period.* Symbolae Osloensis Fasc. Suppl. 28. Oslo: Scandinavian University Press, 1996.

———. *History and the Hebrew Bible: Studies in Ancient Israelite and Ancient Near Eastern Historiography*. Forschungen zum Alten Testament 61. Edited by Bernd Janowski, *et al.* Germany: Mohr Siebeck, 2008.

Barton, John. 'Form Criticism'. *ABD*, vol. 2, pp. 838–841. Edited by D. N. Freedman. New York: Doubleday, 1992.

Bautch, Richard J. *Developments in Prayer Between Post-exilic Penitential Prayers and the Psalms of Communal Laments*. SBL Academia Biblica 7. Atlanta, GA: Society of Biblical Literature, 2003.

Becking, Bob and Dirk Human, eds. *Exile and Suffering.* OTS 30. Leiden: Brill, 2009.

Becking, Bob and Marjo C. A. Korpel, eds. *The Crisis of Israelite Religion: Transforming of Religious Tradition in Exilic and Post-Exilic Times.* Leiden: Brill, 1999.

Berges, Ulrich. 'The Violence of God in the Book of Lamentations'. In *One Text, a Thousand Methods*, pp. 21–44. Boston: Brill, 2005.

Betlyon, J. W. 'Neo-Babylonian Military Operations Other Than War in Judah and Jerusalem'. In *Judah and the Judeans in the Neo-Babylonian Period*, pp. 263–283. Edited by O. Lipschits and J. Blenkinsopp. Winona Lake, IN: Eisenbrauns, 2003.

Blenkinsopp, J. 'Bethel in the Neo-Babylonian Period'. In *Judah and the Judeans in the Neo-Babylonian Period*, pp. 93–107. Edited by O. Lipschits and J. Blenkinsopp. Winona Lake, IN: Eisenbrauns, 2003.

Boase, Elizabeth. 'The Characterization of God in Lamentations'. *ABR* 56 (2008): pp. 32–44.

———. 'Constructing Meaning in the Face of Suffering: Theodicy in Lamentations'. *VT* 58, no. 4–5 (2008): pp. 449–468.

Boda, Mark J. 'The Priceless Gain of Penitence: From Communal Lament to Penitential Prayer in The "Exilic" Liturgy of Israel'. *HBT* 25, no. 1 (2003): pp. 51–75.

Boer, Roland. *Bakhtin and Genre Theory in Biblical Studies*. SBLSemeia Studies 63. Atlanta, GA: Society of Biblical Literature, 2007.

Bosworth, D. A. 'Daughter Zion and Weeping in Lamentations 1—2'. *JSOT* 38, no. 2 (2013): pp. 217–237.

Bouzard, Walter C., Jr. *We Have Heard With Our Ears, O God: Sources of the Communal Laments in the Psalms*. SBL Dissertation Series 159. Atlanta, GA: Scholars Press, 1997.

Brug, J. F. 'Biblical Acrostics and Their Relationship to Other Ancient Near Eastern Acrostics'. In *Scripture in Contexts*, vol. 3, *The Bible in the Light of Cuneiform Literature*, pp. 283–304. Edited by W. W. Hallo, *et al.* New York: Edwin Mellen, 1990.

Broyles, Craig C. *The Conflict of Faith and Experience in the Psalms: A Form-Critical and Theological Study*. JSOTSup 52. Edited by D. J. A. Clines and P. R. Davies. Sheffield: Sheffield Academic Press, 1989.

Budde, K. 'Das hebräische Klagelied'. *ZAW* 2 (1882): pp. 1–52.

———. 'Poetry (Hebrew)'. In *A Dictionary of the Bible*. Edited by J. Hastings. New York: Scribner's, 1902.

Buss, Martin J. *Biblical Form Criticism in its Context*. JSOTSup 274. Sheffield: Sheffield Academic Press, 1999.

Carroll, R. 'Exile! What Exile? Deportation and the Discourse of Diaspora'. In *Leading Captivity Captive*, pp. 62–79. Edited by L. L. Grabbe. JSOTSup 278. Sheffield: Sheffield Academic, 1998.

Carter, C. E. 'Ideology and Archaeology in the Neo-Babylonian Period: Excavating Text and Tell'. In *Judah and the Judeans in the Neo-Babylonian Period*, pp. 301–322. Edited by O. Lipschits and J. Blenkinsopp. Winona Lake, IN: Eisenbrauns, 2003.

Cody, Aelred. 'The Forms and Genres of the Book of Lamentations'. *Bible Today* 43 (2005): pp. 79–82.

Cohen, C. 'The "Widowed" City'. *JANES* 5 (1973): pp. 75–81.

Cohen, Mark E. *Balag-Compositions: Sumerian Lamentation Liturgies of the Second and First Millennium B.C.* Malibu, California: Undena Publications, 1974.

———. *The Canonical Lamentations of Ancient Mesopotamia.* Vols 1–2. Bethesda, MD: CDL Press, 1988.

Dobbs-Allsopp, F. W. 'Tragedy, Tradition, and Theology in the Book of Lamentations'. *JSOT* 74 (1997): pp. 29–60.

———. 'Linguistic Evidence for the Date of Lamentations'. *JANES* 26 (1998): pp. 1–36.

———. 'The Enjambing Line in Lamentations: A Taxonomy, Part 1'. *ZAW* 113, no.1 (2001): pp. 219–239.

———. 'The Effects of Enjambment in Lamentations, Part 2'. *ZAW* 113, no. 2 (2001): pp. 370–385.

———. 'R(az/ais)ing Zion in Lamentations 2'. In *David and Zion: Biblical Studies in Honor of J.J.M. Roberts*, pp. 21–68. Edited by Batto, Bernard F. and K. L. Roberts. Winona Lake, IN: Eisenbrauns, 2004.

Eidevall, Göran. 'Spatial Metaphors in Lamentations 3:1–9'. In *Metaphor in the Hebrew Bible*, pp. 133–137. Leuven: Leuven University Press; Peeters, 2005.

Faust, Avraham. *Judah in the Neo-Babylonian Period: The Archaeology of Desolation.* SBLABS 18. Edited by T. Schneider. Atlanta, GA: Society of Biblical Literature, 2012.

Ferris, Paul Wayne, Jr. *The Genre of Communal Lament in the Bible and the Ancient Near East.* SBL Dissertation Series 127. Edited by J.J.M. Roberts and P. Perkins. Atlanta, GA: Scholars Press, 1992.

Gerstenberger, E. 'Elusive Lamentations: What are They About?'. *In* 67, no. 2 (2013): pp. 121–132.

Gordis, Robert. 'The Conclusion of the Book of Lamentations (5:22)'. *JBL* 93 (1974): pp. 289–293.

Gottwald, Norman K. 'The Book of Lamentations Reconsidered'. In *The Hebrew Bible in its Social World and in Ours*, pp. 165–173. Edited by Gottwald, N. K. Atlanta, GA: Scholars Press, 1993.

Gous, Ignatius Gert Pertrus. 'A Survey of Research on the Book of Lamentations'. *OTE* 5 (1992): pp. 184–205.

Greenstein, Edward L. 'The Wrath at God in the Book of Lamentations'. In *The Problem of Evil and Its Symbols in Jewish and Christian Tradition*, pp. 29–42. Edited by Henning Graf Reventlow and Yair Hoffman. JSOT Supplement Series 366. London: T & T Clark, 2004.

———. 'The Book of Lamentations: Response to Destruction or Ritual or Rebuilding?' In *Religious Responses to Political Crisis*, pp. 52–71. New York: T & T Clark, 2008.

Grossberg, Daniel. *Centripetal and Centrifugal Structures in Biblical Poetry*. SBLMS 39. Atlanta, GA: Scholars Press, 1989.

Gunkel, Hermann. *The Psalms: A Form Critical Introduction.* Translated by Thomas M. Horner. Facet Books Biblical Series 19. Philadelphia, PA: Fortress Press, 1967.

Gwaltney, William C. 'The Biblical Book of Lamentations in the Context of Near Eastern Lament Literature'. In *Scripture in Context, II*, pp. 191–211. Winona Lake, IN: Eisenbrauns, 1983.

Hallo, W. W. 'Lamentations and Prayers in Sumer and Akkad'. In *Civilizations of the Ancient Near East*, pp. 1871–1881. Edited by Jack M. Sasson. Peabody, MA: Hendrickson Publishers, 2000.

Heater, Homer, Jr. 'Structure and Meaning in Lamentations'. *BSac* 149, no. 595 (1992): pp. 304–315.

Hecke, Pierre van. 'Lamentations 3:1–6: An Anti-psalm 23'. *SJOT* 16, no. 2 (2002): pp. 264–281.

Heim, Knut. 'The Personification of Jerusalem and the Drama of Her Bereavement in Lamentations'. In *Zion, City of Our God*, pp. 129–169. Edited by Richard Hess and Gordon Wenham. Grand Rapids, MI: Eerdmans, 1999.

Hobbins, John F. 'Zion's Plea that God See Her as She Sees Herself: Unanswered Prayer in Lamentations 1—2'. In *Daughter Zion: Her Portrait, Her Response*, pp. 149–176. Edited by M. J. Boda, C. J. Dempsey, and L. S. Flesher. SBLAIIL 13. Edited by S. L. McKenzie. Atlanta, GA: Society of Biblical Literature, 2012.

Hoffman, Y. 'The Fasts in the Book of Zechariah and the Fashioning of National Remembrance'. In *Judah and the Judeans in the Neo-Babylonian Period*, pp. 169–218. Edited by O. Lipschits and J. Blenkinsopp. Winona Lake, IN: Eisenbrauns, 2003.

Houk, Cornelius B. 'Multiple Poets in Lamentations'. *JSOT* 30, no. 1 (2005): pp. 111–125.

House, Paul R., ed. *Beyond Form Criticism: Essays In Old Testament Literary Criticism.* Winona Lake, IN: Eisenbrauns, 1992.

Jahnow, Hedwig. *Das hebräische Leichenlied im Rahmen der Völkerdichtung.* BZAW 36. Giessen: Alfred Töpelmann, 1923.

Johnson, Bo. 'Form and Message in Lamentations'. *ZAW* 97 (1985): pp. 58–73.

Joyce, Paul. 'Lamentations and the Grief Process: A Psychological Reading'. *BibInt* 1 (1993): 304–320.

———. 'Sitting Loose to History: Reading the Book of Lamentations Without Primary Reference to its Original Historical Setting'. In *In Search of True Wisdom*, pp. 246–262. Sheffield, England: Sheffield Academic Press, 1999.

Klein, Ralph W. *Israel in Exile.* OBT. Philadelphia: Fortress Press, 1979.

Knoppers, G. N., *et al*, eds. *Exile and Restoration Revisited: Essays on the Babylonian and Persian Periods in Memory of Peter R. Ackroyd.* Library of Second Temple Studies 73. Edited by L. L. Grabbe. London: T&T Clark, 2009.

Kramer, S. N. *Lamentation Over the Destruction of Ur.* Assyriological Studies 12. Chicago: University of Chicago, 1940.

———. 'A Sumerian Lamentation: The Lamentation over the Destruction of Ur'. In *Ancient Near Eastern Texts to the Old Testament.* Third Edition. Edited by J.B. Pritchard. Princeton: Princeton University Press, 1969.

Labahn, Antje. 'Wild Animals and Chasing Shadows: Animal Metaphors in Lamentations as Indicators for Individual Threat'. In *Metaphor in the Hebrew Bible*, pp. 67–97. Leuven: Leuven University Press, 2005.

———. 'Fire from Above: Metaphors and Images of God's Actions in Lamentations 2:1–9'. *JSOT* 31, no. 2 (2006): pp. 239–256.

Lanahan, William F. 'The Speaking Voice in the Book of Lamentations'. *JBL* 93, no. 1 (1974): pp. 41–49.

Lee, Archie C. C. 'Mothers Bewailing: Reading Lamentations'. In *Her Master's Tools?*, pp. 195–210. Atlanta: SBL, 2005.

Lee, N. C. 'The Singers of Lamentations: (A)Scribing (De)Claiming Poets and Prophets'. In *Lamentations in Ancient and Contemporary Cultural Contexts*, pp. 33–46. Edited by N. C. Lee and C. Mandolfo. SBLSymS 43. Edited by V. H. Matthews. Atlanta, GA: Society of Biblical Literature, 2008.

Linafelt, Tod. 'Margins of Lamentation, or, the Unbearable Whiteness of Reading'. In *Reading Bibles, Writing Bodies*, pp. 219–231. London: Routledge, 1997.

———. 'Surviving Lamentations'. In *Feminist Companion to Reading the Bible*, pp. 344–357. Sheffield: Sheffield Academic Press, 1997.

———. 'The Impossibility of Mourning: Lamentations after the Holocaust'. In *God in the Fray*, pp. 279–289. Minneapolis: Fortress Press, 1998.

———. 'Zion's Cause: the Presentation of Pain in the Book of Lamentations'. In *Strange Fire*, pp. 267–279. New York: New York University Press, 2000.

———. 'The Refusal of a Conclusion in the Book of Lamentations'. *JBL* 120, no. 2 (2001): pp. 340–343.

Lipschits, O. *The Fall and Rise of Jerusalem: Judah under Babylonian Rule*. Winona Lake, IN: Eisenbrauns, 2005.

———. 'Demographic Changes in Judah Between the Seventh and the Fifth Centuries B.C.E.', In *Judah and the Judeans in the Neo-Babylonian Period*, pp. 323–376. Edited by O. Lipschits and J. Blenkinsopp. Winona Lake, IN: Eisenbrauns, 2003.

Lipschits, O., and J. Blenkinsopp, eds. *Judah and the Judeans in the Neo-Babylonian Period*. Winona Lake, IN: Eisenbrauns, 2003.

Mandolfo, Carleen. 'Dialogic Form Criticism: An Intertextual Reading of Lamentations and Psalms of Lament'. In *Bakhtin and Genre Theory in Biblical Studies*, pp. 69–90. Atlanta: SBL, 2007.

McDaniel, T.F. 'The Alleged Sumerian Influence upon Lamentations'. *VT* 18 (1968): pp. 198–209.

Middlemas, Jill . *The Troubles of Templeless Judah*. Oxford: Oxford University Press, 2005.

———. *The Templeless Age: An Introduction to the History, Literature and Theology of "Exile."* Louisville, KY: Westminster John Knox Press, 2007.

———. 'The Violent Storm in Lamentations'. *JSOT* 29, no. 1 (2004): pp. 81–97.

Miller, C. W. 'The Book of Lamentations in Recent Research'. In *Currents in Biblical Prayer*, pp. 9–29. Minneapolis: Fortress, 1994.

———. 'Reading Voices: Personification, Dialogism, and the Reader of Lamentations 1'. *BibInt* 9, no. 4 (2001): pp. 393–408.

Mintz, Alan. 'The Rhetoric of Lamentations and the Representation of Catastrophe'. *Proof* 2 (1982): pp. 1–17.

O'Connor, Kathleen M. 'Prayer in the Book of Lamentations'. *Bible Today* 39, no. 1 (2001): pp. 138–144.

Oded, B. 'Where is the "Myth of the Empty Land" to be Found?: History versus Myth'. In *Judah and the Judeans in the Neo-Babylonian Period*, pp. 55–74. Edited by O. Lipschits and J. Blenkinsopp. Winona Lake, IN: Eisenbrauns, 2003.

Parry, Robin. 'Lamentations and the Poetic Politics of Prayer'. *TynBul* 62, no. 1 (2011): pp. 65–88.

Pham, Xuan Huong Thi. *Mourning in The Ancient Near East and the Hebrew Bible.* JSOTSup 302. Sheffield: Sheffield Academic Press, 1999.

Provan, Iain. 'Reading Texts Against an Historical Background: The Case of Lamentations 1'. *SJSOT* 1 (1990): pp. 130–143.

———. 'Past, Present and Future in Lamentations 3:52–66: The Case for a Precative Perfect Re-Examined'. *VT* 41, no. 2 (1991): pp. 164–175.

Pyper, Hugh S. 'Reading Lamentations'. *JSOT* 95 (2001): pp. 55–69.

Reimer, David. J. 'Good Grief? A Psychological Reading of Lamentations'. *ZAW* 114 (2002): pp. 542–559.

Renkema, J. 'Theodicy in Lamentations?'. In *Theodicy in the World of the Bible*, 410–428. Leiden: Brill, 2003.

Roberts, J. J. M. 'The Motif of the Weeping God in Jeremiah and its Background in the Lament Tradition of the Ancient Near East'. *OTE* 5 (1992): pp. 361–374.

Saebo, Magne. 'Who is 'the Man' in Lamentations 3?: A Fresh Approach to the Interpretation of the Book of Lamentations'. In

Understanding Poets and Prophets: Essays in Honour of George Wishart Anderson, pp. 294–306. JSOTSup 152. Edited by Auld A. Graeme. Sheffield: Sheffield Academic Press, 1993.

———. 'Who Is "The Man" in Lamentations 3:1?'. In *On the Way to Canon: Creative Tradition History in the Old Testament*, pp. 31–142. JSOTSup 191. Sheffield: Sheffield Academic Press, 1998.

Salters, Robert B. 'The Text of Lamentations 2:9a'. *VT* 54, no. 2 (2004): pp. 273–276.

———. 'Structure and Implication in Lamentations 1'. *SJSOT* 14, no. 2 (2000): pp. 293–300.

Seitel, Peter. *Powers of Genre: Interpreting Haya Oral Literature.* Cary, NC: Oxford University Press, 1999.

Shea, William H. 'The Qinah Structure of the Book of Lamentations'. *Biblica* 60 (1979): pp. 103–107.

Smith-Christopher, Daniel. *A Biblical Theology of Exile.* Minneapolis, MN: Fortress Press, 2002.

Sparks, Kenton L. *Ancient Texts for the Study of the Hebrew Bible: A Guide to the Background Literature.* Peabody, MA: Hendrickson, 2005.

Sweeney, Marvin A., and Zvi, Ehud Ben, eds. *The Changing Face of Form Criticism for the Twenty-first Century.* Grand Rapids, MI: Eerdmans, 2003.

Thomas, Heath A. 'Relating Prayer and Pain: Psychological Analysis and Lamentations Research'. *TynBul* 61, no. 2 (2010):pp. 183–208.

Valkama, K. 'What Do Archaeological Remains Reveal of the Settlements in Judah during the Mid-Sixth Century BCE?'. In *The Concept of Exile in Ancient Israel and Its Historical Contexts*, pp. 39–59. Edited by Ehud Ben Zvi and Christopher Levin. BZAW 404. Berlin: Walter de Gruyter, 2010.

Vanderhooft, David S. *The Neo-Babylonian Empire and Babylon in the Latter Prophets.* Harvard Semitic Monographs 59. Atlanta, GA: Scholars Press, 1999.

———. 'Babylonian Strategies of Imperial Control in the West: Royal Practice and Rhetoric'. In *Judah and the Judeans in the Neo-Babylonian Period*, pp. 235–262. Edited by O. Lipschits and J. Blenkinsopp. Winona Lake, IN: Eisenbrauns, 2003.

Villanueva, F. G. *The 'Uncertainty of a Hearing': A Study of the Sudden Change of Mood in the Psalms of Lament*, VTSup 121. Boston: Brill, 2008.

Trauma Studies

Alexander, Jeffrey C., *et al.*, eds. *Cultural Trauma and Collective Identity.* Berkeley, CA: University of California Press, 2004.

Alexander, Jeffery C. *Trauma: A Social Theory.* Malden, MA: Polity Press, 2012.

Alexander, J. C. and Elizabeth B. Breese. 'On Social Suffering and its Cultural Construction'. Introduction to *Narrating Trauma: On the Impact of Collective Suffering*, pp. xi–xxxv. Edited by Ron Eyerman, *et al.* Boulder, CO: Paradigm Publishers, 2013.

Beulens, Gert, Sam Durrant and Robert Eaglestone, eds. *The Future of Trauma Theory: Contemporary Literary and Cultural Criticism.* New York: Routeledge, 2014.

Balaev, Michelle, ed. *Contemporary Approaches in Literary Trauma Theory.* New York: Palgrave Macmillian, 2014.

Bowman, M. *Individual Differences in Posttraumatic Response: Problems with Adversity—Distress Connection.* Mahwah, NJ: Lawrence Erlbaum Associates, 1997.

Caruth, Cathy, ed. *Trauma: Explorations in Memory.* Baltimore, MD: Johns Hopkins University Press, 1995.

———. *Unclaimed Experience: Trauma, Narrative, and History.* Baltimore, MD: Johns Hopkins University Press, 1996.

Edkins, Jenny. *Trauma and the Memory of Politics.* Cambridge: Cambridge University Press, 2003.

Eyerman, Ron. *Cultural Trauma: Slavery and the Formation of African American Identity.* Cambridge: Cambridge University Press, 2001.

Eyerman, Ron, J. C. Alexander and E. B. Breese, eds. *Narrating Trauma: On the Impact of Collective Suffering.* Boulder, CO: Paradigm Publishers, 2013.

Erickson, Kai T. *Everything in Its Path: Destruction of Community in the Buffalo Creek Flood.* New York: Simon and Schuster, 1976.

———. *A New Species of Trouble: The Human Experience of Modern Disasters.* New York: W. W. Norton, 1995.

Farrell, Kirby. *Post-Traumatic Culture: Injury and Interpretation in the Nineties*. Baltimore, MD: Johns Hopkins University Press, 1998.

Felman, Shoshana, and Dori Laub. *Literature and Psychoanalysis: The Question of Reading, Otherwise*. Baltimore, MD: Johns Hopkins University Press, 1982.

———. *Testimony: Crises of Witnessing in Literature, Psychoanalysis, and History*. New York: Routledge, 1992.

Felman, Shoshana, and Martha Noel Evans. *Writing and Madness: Literature/Philosophy/Psychoanalysis*. Palo Alto, Calif.: Stanford University Press, 2003.

Franke, William. 'Poetics of Silence in the Post-Holocaust Poetry of Paul Celan'. *JLTS* 2, nos. 1–2 (Spring/Fall, 2013): pp. 137–158.

Freud, Sigmund, and James Strachey. *Beyond the Pleasure Principle*. Standard Edition. New York: Norton, 1989.

———. *Moses and Monotheism*. Translated by Katherine Jones. New York: Vintage Books, 1955.

Geller, Jay. 'Trauma'. *Handbook of Postmodern Biblical Interpretation*. Edited by A. K. M. Adam. St. Louis, MO: Chalice Press, 2000.

Granofsky, Ronald. *The Trauma Novel: Contemporary Symbolic Depictions of Collective Disaster*. American University Studies, Series 3. Comparative Literature 55. New York: Peter Lang, 1995.

Hartman, Geoffrey. *The Longest Shadow: In the Aftermath of the Holocaust*. Bloomington, IN: Indiana University Press, 1996.

———. 'Trauma within the Limits of Literature'. *European Journal of English Studies* 7, no. 3 (2003): pp. 257–274.

Herman, Judith Lewis. *Trauma and Recovery: The Aftermath of Violence—From Domestic Abuse to Political Terror*. New York: Basic Books, 1997.

Jones, Serene. *Trauma and Grace: Theology in a Ruptured World*. Louisville, KY: Westminster John Knox Press, 2009.

Kaplan, E. Ann. *Trauma Culture: The Politics of Terror and Loss in Media and Literature*. Piscataway, NJ: Rutgers University Press, 2005.

Kearney, Richard. 'Narrating Pain: The Power of Catharsis'. *Paragraph* 30, no. 1 (2007): pp. 51–66.

LaCapra, Dominick. *Representing the Holocaust: History, Theory, Trauma.* Ithaca: Cornell University Press, 1994.

———. *History and Memory after Auschwitz.* Ithaca, NY: Cornell University Press, 1998.

———. *Writing History, Writing Trauma.* Baltimore, MD: Johns Hopkins University Press, 2000.

———. *History in Transit: Experience, Identity, Critical Theory.* Ithaca, NY: Cornell University Press, 2004.

Langer, Lawrence L. *Using and Abusing the Holocaust.* Jewish Literature and Culture. Edited by Alvin H. Rosenfeld. Bloomington, IN: Indiana University Press, 2006.

Lary, Diana. 'Writing and War: Silence, Disengagement, and Ambiguity'. *JLTS* 2, nos. 1–2 (Spring/Fall, 2013): pp. 45–62.

Leys, Ruth. *Trauma: A Genealogy.* Chicago: University of Chicago Press, 2000.

———. *From Guilty to Shame: Auschwitz and After.* Princeton, NJ: Princeton University Press, 2007.

Luckhurst, Roger. *The Trauma Question.* New York: Routledge, 2008.

Marder, Elissa. 'Trauma and Literary Studies'. *Reading On* 1, no.1 (2005): pp. 1–6.

Miller, Nancy K. and Jason Tougaw, eds. *Extremities: Trauma, Testimony and Community.* Urbana, IL: University of Illinois Press, 2002.

Mollica, Richard F. *Healing Invisible Wounds: Paths to Hope and Recovery in a Violent World.* Nashville, TN: Vanderbilt University Press, 2006.

Neal, Arthur G. *National Trauma and Collective Memory.* Second Edition. Armonk, NY: M. E. Sharpe, 2005.

Radstone, Susannah. 'Trauma Theory: Contexts, Politics, Ethics'. *Paragraph* 30, no. 1 (2007): pp. 9–29.

Saul, Jack. *Collective Trauma, Collective Healing: Promoting Community Resilience in the Aftermath of Disaster.* New York: Routledge, 2014.

Tal, Kalí. *Worlds of Hurt: Reading the Literature of Trauma.* New York: Cambridge University Press, 1996.

Van der Kolk, Bessel A. and Onno van der Hart. 'The Intrusive Past: The Flexibility of Memory and the Engraving of Trauma'. In *Trauma: Explorations in Memory*, pp. 158–182. Edited by Cathy Caruth. Baltimore, MD: The Johns Hopkins University Press, 1995.

Van der Kolk, Bessel A., Alexander C. McFarlane, and Lars Weisæth. *Traumatic Stress: The Effects of Overwhelming Experience on Mind, Body, and Society*. New York: Guilford Press, 2007.

Visser, Irene. 'Trauma Theory and Postcolonial Studies'. *Journal of Postcolonial Writing* 47, no. 3 (2011): pp. 270–282.

Young, A. *The Harmony of Illusions: Inventing Post-Traumatic Stress Disorder.* Princeton, NJ: Princeton University Press, 1995.

Trauma Studies and Biblical Studies

Balentine, Samuel E. 'Traumatizing Job'. *RevExp* 105 (Spring 2008): 213–228.

Beal, Timothy K. 'Mimetic Monsters: The Genesis of Horror in the Face of the Deep'. *Postscripts* 4, no 1 (2008): pp. 85–93.

Becker, Eve-Marie, Jan Dochhorn, and Else Holt, eds. *Trauma and Traumatization in Individual and Collective Dimensions: Insights from Biblical Studies and Beyond.* SANt 2. Göttingen: Vandenhoeck & Ruprecht, 2014.

Boase, E. 'The Traumatized Body: Communal Trauma and Somatization in Lamentation'. In *Trauma and Traumatization*, pp. 193–209. Edited by Eve-Marie Becker, J. Douchhorn, and E. K. Holt. SANt 2. Edited by Eve-Marie Becker, et al. Göttingen: Vandenhoeck & Ruprecht, 2014.

Bowen, Nancy Bowen. *Ezekiel.* AOTC. Nashville, TN: Abingdon, 2010.

Darr, Katheryn P. 'The God Ezekiel Envisions'. In *The God Ezekiel Creates*, 1–23. LHB/OTS 607. Edited by P. M. Joyce and D. Rom-Shiloni. London: T & T Clark, 2015.

Dietrich, Jan. 'Cultural Traumata in the Ancient Near East'. In *Trauma and Traumatization in Individual and Collective Dimensions: Insights from Biblical Studies and Beyond*, 145–161. Edited by Eve-

Marie Becker, J. Douchhorn, and E. K. Holt. SANt 2. Edited by Eve-Marie Becker, *et al.* Göttingen: Vandenhoeck & Ruprecht, 2014.

Carr, David M. 'Reading Into the Gap: Refractions of Trauma in Israelite Prophecy'. In *Interpreting Exile: Displacement and Deportation in Biblical and Modern Contexts*, pp. 295–308. Edited by Brad E. Kelle, *et al.* SBLAIIL 10. Edited by S. L. McKenzie. Atlanta, GA: Society of Biblical Literature, 2011.

———. *Holy Resilience: The Bible's Traumatic Origins*. New Haven, CT: Yale University Press, 2014.

Frechette, Christopher G. 'The Old Testament as Controlled Substance: How Insights from Trauma Studies Reveal Healing Capacities in Potentially Harmful Texts'. *Int* 69, no. 1 (2015): pp. 20–34.

Garber, David G., Jr. 'Traumatizing Ezekiel, the Exilic Prophet', pp. 215–235. In *Psychology and the Bible 2: From Genesis to Apocalyptic Vision*. Westport, CT: Praeger, 2004.

———. 'Facing Traumatizing Texts: Reading Nahum's Nationalistic Rage'. *RevExp* 105, no. 2 (2008): pp. 285–294.

———. 'A Vocabulary of Trauma in the Exilic Writings'. In *Interpreting Exile: Displacement and Deportation in Biblical and Modern Contexts*, pp. 309–322. Edited by Brad E. Kelle, *et al.* SBLAIIL 10. Edited by S. L. McKenzie. Atlanta, GA: Society of Biblical Literature, 2011.

———. 'Trauma Studies and Biblical Studies'. *CBR* 14 (2015): pp. 24–44.

Garber, David G. Jr. 'Traumatizing Ezekiel, the Exilic prophet'. In *Psychology and the Bible, From Genesis to Apocalyptic Vision*, pp. 215–235. Vol. 2. Westport, CT: Praeger, 2004.

———. 'Facing Traumatizing Texts: Reading Nahum's Nationalistic Rage'. *RevExp* 105 (Spring, 2008): pp. 285–294.

Garber, David G. Jr., and Daniel Stallings. 'Awakening Desire Before it is Season: Reading Biblical Texts in Response to the Sexual Exploitation of Children'. *RevExp* 105, no. 3 (2008): pp. 453–469.

Holt, Else K. 'Daughter Zion: Trauma, Cultural Memory and Gender in OT Poetics'. In *Trauma and Traumatization in Individual and Collective Dimensions: Insights from Biblical Studies and Beyond*, 162—76. Edited by Eve-Marie Becker, J. Douchhorn, and E. K. Holt. SANt 2. Edited by Eve-Marie Becker, *et al.* Göttingen: Vandenhoeck & Ruprecht, 2014.

Janzen, D. *The Violent Gift: Trauma's Subversion of the Deuteronomistic History's Narrative*. LHB/OTS 561. Edited by C. V. Camp and A. Mein. New York: T & T Clark International, 2012.

Kelle, Brad E. 'Dealing with the Trauma of Defeat: The Rhetoric of the Devastation and Rejuvenation of Nature in Ezekiel'. *JBL* 128, no. 3 (2009): pp. 469–490.

———. 'Creation and Trauma: the Devastation and Rejuvenation of Nature in Ezekiel'. *Wesleyan Theological Journal* 44, no. 1 (2009): pp. 70–90.

Kelle, Brad E., F. R. Ames, and J. L. Wright, eds. *Interpreting Exile: Displacement and Deportation in Biblical and Modern Contexts*. SBLAIIL 10. Edited by S. L. McKenzie. Atlanta, GA: Society of Biblical Literature, 2011.

Matthewson, Dan. *Death and Survival in the Book of Job: Desymbolization and Traumatic Experience. New York: T & T Clark, 2006.*

———. 'Between Testimony and Interpretation: The Book of Job in Post-Holocaust, Jewish Theological Reflection'. *Studies in the Literary Imagination* 41, no. 2 (2008): pp. 17–40.

O'Connor, Kathleen M. 'A Family Comes Undone (Jeremiah 2:1—4:2)'. *RevExp* 105 (Spring 2008): pp. 201–212.

———. 'Lamenting Back to Life'. *Int* 62 (2008): pp. 34–47.

———. 'Family Comes Undone: Jeremiah 2:1 – 4:2'. *RevExp* 105 (2008): pp. 201–212.

———. 'Teaching Jeremiah'. *Perspectives in Religious Studies* 36 (2009): pp. 273–287.

———. 'Reclaiming Jeremiah's Violence'. In *Aesthetics of Violence in the Prophets*, pp. 37–49. Edited by Julia M. O'Brien and Chris Franke. New York: T & T Clarke, 2010.

———. *Jeremiah: Pain and Promise*. Minneapolis, MN: Fortress Press, 2011.

———. 'How Trauma Studies Can Contribute to Old Testament Studies'. In *Trauma and Traumatization in Individual and Collective Dimensions: Insights from Biblical Studies and Beyond*, pp. 210–222.

Edited by Eve-Marie Becker, J. Douchhorn, and E. K. Holt. SANt 2. Edited by Eve-Marie Becker, *et al.* Göttingen: Vandenhoeck & Ruprecht, 2014.

Poser, R. *Das Ezechielbuch als Trauma-Literatur.* SupVT 154. Leiden: Brill, 2012.

Smith-Christopher, Daniel L. 'Reading War and Trauma: Suggestions Toward a Social-Psychological Exegesis of Exile and War in Biblical Texts'. In *Interpreting Exile: Displacement and Deportation in Biblical and Modern Contexts*, pp. 253–274. Edited by Brad K. Kelle, *et al.* SBLAIIL 10. Atlanta, GA: Society of Biblical Literature, 2011.

———. 'Trauma and the Old Testament: Some Problems and Prospects'. In *Trauma and Traumatization in Individual and Collective Dimensions: Insights from Biblical Studies and Beyond*, pp. 223–243. Edited by Eve-Marie Becker, J. Douchhorn, and E. K. Holt. SANt 2. Edited by Eve-Marie Becker, *et al.* Göttingen: Vandenhoeck & Ruprecht, 2014.

Stullman, Louis. 'Reading the Bible Through the Lens of Trauma and Art'. In *Trauma and Traumatization in Individual and Collective Dimensions: Insights from Biblical Studies and Beyond*, pp. 177–192. Edited by Eve-Marie Becker, J. Douchhorn, and E. K. Holt. SANt 2. Edited by Eve-Marie Becker, *et al.* Göttingen: Vandenhoeck & Ruprecht, 2014.

Stulman, L., and H. C. P. Kim. *You are My People: An Introduction to Prophetic Literature.* Nashville, TN: Abingdon Press, 2010.

Miscellaneous

Anderson, Gary A. *A Time to Mourn, A Time to Dance: The Expression of Grief and Joy in Israelite Religion.* University Park, PA: The Pennsylvania State University Press, 1991.

Balentine, Samuel E. *The Hidden God: The Hiding of the Face of God in the Old Testament.* Oxford: Oxford University Press, 1983.

———. *Prayer in the Hebrew Bible: The Drama of Divine-Human Dialogue.* Overtures to Biblical Theology. Minneapolis, MN: Fortress, 1993.

Batto, Bernard F. and K. L. Roberts, eds. *David and Zion: Biblical Studies in Honor of J. J. M. Roberts.* Winona Lake, IN: Eisenbrauns, 2004.

Baumann, Gerlinde. *Love and violence: Marriage as Metaphor for the Relationship between YHWH and Israel in the Prophetic Books*. Translated by Linda M. Maloney. Collegeville, MN: Liturgical Press, 2003.

Bleiker, Roland. '"Give it the Shade": Paul Celan and the Politics of Apolitical Poetry'. *Political Studies* 47, no. 4 (September 1999): pp. 661–676.

Boda, M. J., C. J. Dempsey, and L. S. Flesher, eds. *Daughter Zion: Her Portrait, Her Response*. SBLAIL 13. Atlanta: Society of Biblical Literature, 2012.

Brown, Sally A., and Patrick D. Miller. *Lament: Reclaiming Practices in Pulpit, Pew, and Public Square*. Louisville, KY: Westminster John Knox Press, 2005.

Carrol, R. P. 'Prophecy and Dissonance: A theoretical Approach to the Prophetic Tradition'. *ZAW* 92, no. 1 (1980): pp. 108–119.

Chalcraft, David J., ed. *Social-Scientific Old Testament Criticism*. The Biblical Seminar 47. Sheffield: Sheffield Academic Press, 1997.

Charles E. Carter. 'A Discipline in Transition: The Contributions of the Social Sciences to the Study of the Hebrew Bible'. In *Community, Identity, and Ideology*, pp. 3–36. Edited by C. E. Carter and C. L. Meyers. Winona Lake, IN: Eisenbrauns, 1996.

Carter, Charles. E., and Carol L. Meyers, ed. *Community, Identity, and Ideology: Social Sciences Approaches to the Hebrew Bible*. Winona Lake, IN: Eisenbrauns, 1996.

Darr, K. P. *Isaiah's Vision and the Family of God*. LCBI. Edited by D. N. Fewell, *et al.* Louisville, KY: Westminster John Knox Press, 1994.

Dearman, J. A. 'Daughter Zion and Her Place in God's Household'. *HBT* 31 (2009): pp. 144–159.

Festinger, L. *A Theory of Cognitive Dissonance*. Stanford, CA: Stanford University Press, 1957.

Floyd, Michael H. 'The Daughter of Zion Goes Fishing in Heaven'. In *Daughter Zion: Her Portrait, Her Response*, pp. 177–200. Edited by M. J. Boda, C. J. Dempsey, and L. S. Flesher. SBLAIL 13. Atlanta: Society of Biblical Literature, 2012.

———. 'Welcome Back, Daughter of Zion'. *CBQ* 70 (2008): pp. 484–504.

Genette, G. *Figures III*. Paris: Éditions du Seuil, 1972.

Gerstenberger, Erhard S. *Psalms Part 1, With an Introduction to Cultic Poetry*. FOTL 14. Grand Rapids, MI: Eerdmans, 1988.

Gibbs, Nancy. 'If You Want to Humble an Empire'. *Time*, September 14, 2001. Accessed May 25, 2011.

http://www.time.com/time/magazine/article/0,9171,1000761-1,00.html.

Hayes, J. H. 'The Tradition of Zion's Inviolability'. *JBL* 82, vol. 4 (December, 1963): pp. 419–426.

Himes, C. *Cotton Comes to Harlem*. Chatham, NJ: The Chatham Booksellers, 1965.

Hobbs, T. R. *A Time for War: A Study of Warfare in the Old Testament*. OTS 3. Wilmington, DE: Michael Glazier, 1989.

Hogan, P. C. *Narrative Discourse: Authors and Narrators in Literature, Film, and Art*. Columbus, OH: Ohio State University Press, 2013.

Hutchison, Emma, and Roland Bleiker. 'Grief and the Transformation of Emotions after War'. In *Emotions, Politics and War*. Edited by L. Āhäll and T. Gregory, pp. 210–221. Abingdon, UK: Routledge, 2015.

———. 'Emotional Reconciliation: Reconstituting Identity and Community after Trauma'. *European Journal of Social Theory* 11, no. 3 (2008): pp. 385–403.

Kalayjian, Ani and Dominique Eugene, eds. *Mass Trauma and Emotional Healing Around the World: Rituals and Practices for Resilience and Meaning-Making*. 2 vols. Santa Barbara, CA: Praeger, 2010.

Kelle, Brad E. 'Wartime Rhetoric: Prophetic Metaphorization of Cities as Female'. In *Writing and Reading War*, pp. 95–111. Atlanta, GA: Society of Biblical Literature, 2008.

Kelle, Brad E., and Frank Ritchel, eds. *Writing and Reading War: Rhetoric, Gender, and Ethics in Biblical and Modern Contexts*. Introduction by Susan Niditch. Atlanta, GA: Society of Biblical Literature, 2008.

King, Philip J., and Lawrence E. Stager. *Life in Biblical Israel.* Library of Ancient Israel. Edited by Douglas A. Knight. Louisville: Westminster John Knox Press, 2001.

Kübler-Ross, Elizabeth. *On Death and Dying.* New York: Touchstone, 1969, 1997.

Levenson, Jon D. 'Zion Traditions'. *ABD*, vol 6, pp. 1101–1102. Edited by D.N. Freedman. New York: Doubleday, 1992.

Mettinger, T. N. D. 'The Name and the Glory: The Zion-Sabaoth Theology and Its Exilic Successors'. *JNSL* 24, vol. 1, (1998): pp. 1–24.

Ollenburger, Ben C. *Zion, The City of the Great King: A Theological Symbol of the Jerusalem Cult*, JSOTSup 41. Edited by D. J. A. Clines and P. R. Davies. Sheffield: Sheffield Academic Press, 1987.

Olyan, Saul M. *Biblical Mourning: Ritual and Social Dimensions.* Oxford: Oxford University Press, 2004.

———, ed. *Social Theory and the Study of Israelite Religion: Essays in Retrospect and Prospect.* Atlanta, GA: Society of Biblical Literature, 2012.

Parker, Simon B. 'The Beginning of the Reign of God: Psalm 82 as Myth and Liturgy'. *RB* 102 (1995): pp. 532–559.

Roberts, J. J. M. 'The Davidic Origin of the Zion Tradition'. In *The Bible and the Ancient Near East: Collected Essays*, pp. 313–330. Winona Lake, IN: Eisenbrauns, 2002.

———. 'Zion in the Theology of the Davidic-Solomonic Empire'. In *The Bible and the Ancient Near East: Collected Essays*, pp. 331–347.

Seevers, Boyd. *Warfare in the Old Testament: The Organization, Weapons, and Tactics of Ancient Near Eastern Armies.* Grand Rapids, MI: Kregel Academic, 2013.

Ska, J. L. *"Our Fathers Have Told Us": Introduction to the Analysis of Hebrew Narratives.* SubBi 13. Rome: Editrice Pontificio Instituto Biblico, 1990.

Soskice, J. M. *Metaphor and Religious Language.* London: Clarendon Press, 1985.

Stinespring, W. F. 'No Daughter of Zion: A Study of the Appositional Genitive in Hebrew Grammar'. *Encounter* 26 (1965): pp. 133–141.

Sweeney, Marvin. *Reading the Hebrew Bible after the Shoah: Engaging Holocaust Theology*. Minneapolis, MN: Fortress Press, 2008.

Van Hecke, P., ed. *Metaphors in the Hebrew Bible*. Leuven: Leuven University Press, 2005.

Villanueva, Federico G. *The 'Uncertainty of a Hearing': A Study of the Sudden Change of Mood in the Psalms of Lament*. Leiden: Brill, 2008.

Walsh, F. *Strengthening Family Resilience*. Second Edition. New York: The Guilford Press, 2006.

Wilson, Robert R. *Sociological Approaches to the Old Testament*. Philadelphia, PA: Fortress Press, 1984.

INDEX

AUTHORS

SUBJECTS

BIBLICAL REFERENCES

www.ingramcontent.com/pod-product-compliance
Lightning Source LLC
LaVergne TN
LVHW011521200926
848484LV00001B/105